THROWBACK

18
KENDALL
KENDALL
Jason Kendall

JASON KENDALL
and LEE JUDGE

THRØWBACK

A Big-League Catcher Tells How the Game Is Really Played

ST. MARTIN'S GRIFFIN NEW YORK

Printed in the United States of America. For information, address St. Martin's Press, 175 Fifth Avenue, New York, N.Y. 10010.

www.stmartins.com

Front and back photos courtesy of Jason Kendall.

The Library of Congress has cataloged the hardcover edition as follows:

Kendall, Jason, 1974–
Throwback : a big-league catcher tells how the game is really played / Jason Kendall, Lee Judge.
p. cm.
ISBN 978-1-250-03183-9 (hardcover)
ISBN 978-1-250-03182-2 (e-book)
1. Kendall, Jason, 1974– 2. Baseball players—United States—Biography.
3. Catchers (Baseball)—United States—Biography I. Judge, Lee. II. Title.
GV865.K46A3 2014
796.357092—dc23
[B]

2013045680

ISBN 978-1-250-06866-8 (trade paperback)

St. Martin's Griffin books may be purchased for educational, business, or promotional use. For information on bulk purchases, please contact the Macmillan Corporate and Premium Sales Department at 1-800-221-7945, extension 5442, or write to specialmarkets@macmillan.com.

First St. Martin's Griffin Edition: May 2015

10 9 8 7 6 5 4 3 2 1

I dedicate this book to:
My Magooski and my Princess—
Daddy loves you.

CONTENTS

throw • back *noun* \'thrō-,bak\ : a person or thing that is similar to someone or something from the past or that is suited to an earlier time

INTRODUCTION

LIKE MILLIONS of baseball fans, I thought I knew the game. I'd been watching the sport all my life and thought I had a decent grasp of how it was played. Then I met professional ballplayers who taught me how *they* see baseball.

It was a game I barely recognized.

Baseball was more complex than I'd ever imagined. There were games within the game that I'd never seen. It was always right in front of me, but someone had to teach me to recognize what was actually happening. Baseball went from being slow and sometimes boring, to a game that was unfolding so quickly and in so many ways I didn't know where to look first. Now there were dozens of things to watch and a single at bat became a fascinating duel with multiple story lines.

While I was being taught how to predict the next pitch, spot a middle infielder who's afraid of the base runner or an outfielder who has no fear of the wall, I kept asking one question: "Has anyone ever written this stuff down?"

Now someone has.

My education started back in 1990 when my wife sent me to the Kansas City Royals baseball fantasy camp as a Christmas gift; I didn't want to go. My memories of playing baseball included strike-outs, dropped fly balls, and a lot of embarrassment. Now my wife had bought me a week of humiliation in front of ex-pros—gee, *thanks,* honey.

When I told her I was reluctant, she said, "But you watch baseball all the time." I pointed out that I'd also watch a bullfight, but didn't want her to buy me a bull. For once, I'd won an argument; until I found out she'd lose a hefty deposit because of my insecurities. I decided to man up and go.

I had a great time.

My wife's Christmas gift started a two-decade journey through the world of professional baseball. I was learning how professionals play the game and—more important to a baseball fan—how professionals *see* the game. I became fascinated (my wife might say obsessed, but what does she know? She's a psychologist) with our national pastime. It was like owning a painting that had been on my wall for thirty-eight years and one day an art expert began pointing out the painting's details. I found it fascinating. How could I be a baseball fan all my life and not know this stuff?

I began playing baseball in a men's amateur league, read every instructional manual I could find, and was lucky enough to spend time with professional players. I was learning the game from the people I met along the way—people such as Pittsburgh Pirates manager Clint Hurdle, former infielder and Boston Red Sox bench coach Tim Bogar, former big leaguer Russ Morman, Colorado Rockies pitching coach and former big league pitcher Bob Apodaca, former pitcher, and the current Los Angeles Angels general manager, Jerry Dipoto, and former major league pitcher Danny Jackson. Baseball Hall of Famer George Brett even tried to teach me to hit.

I still can't hit, but I now know why.

In 2010 the *Kansas City Star* wanted someone to watch every

Royals game played that summer. They had an online project in mind and needed someone to watch the games and feed data into a computer program. After being turned down by several people with more sense, they came to me, and I said yes. But my real interest was explaining the game to other baseball fans in the same way professional ballplayers had explained it to me.

I wanted to write about the game from the participants' point of view. I tried to pay attention to the things they found important and explain why they did what they did. Why the manager brought the infield in earlier than normal, why the third-base coach waved a runner home, or why a base runner stole second base on a 3-0 count.

Paying attention to the small stuff paid off: managers, coaches, and players *want* us to understand. If they think you're serious, if they believe you really want to know, they'll take time to explain. But first you have to admit you don't know everything. Ask any player, coach, or manager if he knows baseball and you'll hear some version of "You *never* know the game." It's just too complex, there are too many variables and situations change nightly.

If you act as if you've got nothing to learn, ballplayers won't waste their time on you. If you already know everything, you can't learn anything.

In 2010 the Kansas City Royals' Brian Bannister beat the Washington Nationals' Stephen Strasburg in a 1–0 game. Strasburg was a media sensation and—to put it kindly—Bannister wasn't. Brian got some attention after his unlikely victory, but someone else caught my eye during that game: veteran catcher Jason Kendall.

During the Bannister-Strasburg game, Kendall blocked six pitches in the dirt. Two kept a double play in order (which the Royals eventually turned), one kept a runner at second base (he was subsequently thrown out at the plate), and three came with a runner on third (none of them scored). Brian Bannister deserved a lot of credit for the win and got it. Jason Kendall also deserved a lot of credit for the win and went unnoticed.

Kendall had come over to the Royals that season and I didn't know much about him—other than he'd had a horrific injury when he dislocated his ankle by hitting first base at a bad angle and he seemed to get into a lot of fights. Jason Kendall had previously played for the Pittsburgh Pirates, the Oakland A's, the Chicago Cubs, and the Milwaukee Brewers.

Jason wound up with a sixteen-year career (he played for fifteen, but insists on getting credit for sixteen—he got paid for it). He was only the fifth player in major league history to catch 2,000 games. He finished with over 2,000 hits. He was also hit by 254 pitches, fifth all-time.

Kendall had to quit playing when he had a shoulder injury so serious he was forced to lift his arm into throwing position with his glove—he couldn't lift his throwing arm on its own, but he *could* snap it down—and he still managed to throw out base runners. Jason's arm was in such bad shape he couldn't use it to play catch with his son during the day, but he used that damaged arm to play major league baseball at night.

Jason eventually admitted how bad his arm was, submitted to surgery, tried to come back, reinjured his arm, had another surgery, tried to come back *again,* and finally retired in 2012 when he felt a pain in his damaged arm during a rehab stint in the minor leagues. But while he was still playing, Kendall was quite a presence in the clubhouse. Shaved head, covered in tattoos, incredibly blunt—Jason Kendall is the walking definition of a badass. This is a guy who intimidates other players, much less the media.

So how did this guy wind up writing a book with me?

I'd been covering the Royals for a few months when I approached Jason. He's not known for being media friendly, and some reporters are reluctant to confront him. When Jason saw me headed his way, he didn't want to talk to me until I asked him this question:

"Do you know how many times you've blocked a pitch with a runner on third in a game the Royals went on to win by one run?"

"I have no [bleeping] idea."

"Seven."

"How the [bleep] do you know that?"

"I've been counting."

I then took a thorn out of his paw and we've been friends ever since.

Actually, he asked what the hell I was doing, so I told him I was trying to explain how baseball is played from the players' perspective. I told him I wanted to write about the small, often unnoticed details that affect the game's outcome. Jason said that was the coolest idea ever. Like a lot of players, coaches, and managers, he wants people to understand, but he doesn't think most people have the patience to learn.

One day Jason said that I should write a book about the game, and I said no, *we* should write a book. Despite the fact that I'd been studying and playing the game for twenty years and covering it professionally for three, I was sure that Jason Kendall knew several thousand things about baseball that I didn't.

I underestimated.

Most of what I knew came from instructional manuals—it was theory. Jason had been out on the field testing those theories—that was reality. If you went to the Pentagon and asked someone about war, they'd probably give you a slightly different version of events than if you asked someone who had been in the trenches.

Jason Kendall has been in trenches.

Every time we got together to work on the book, Jason would tell me something mindboggling, something that changed the way I saw the game. Even after twenty years of studying baseball, I still found myself saying, "I did *not* know that."

One night we were working on the book and had the Royals game on TV. There were two outs, Chris Getz was on second base, and whoever the batter was, he hit a ground ball to the left side of the infield. With two outs Getz was advancing to third base while the infielder was getting the third out at first base. The infielder overthrew first and suddenly Jason shouted, "Send him—he's left-handed!"

I had no idea what the hell Jason was talking about and said so. He looked at me with disgust and showed me the replay. The overthrown ball was in foul territory, Getz was rounding third, and the first baseman chasing the ball was left-handed. Throws from left-handers have movement toward their arm side. When the first baseman retrieved the ball and threw it to home plate, the throw pulled the catcher away from the plate, into foul territory on the first-base side. Getz was held up at third. It would have been close, but with two outs the risk would have been worth it, and Getz had a good chance of being safe.

I should point out that we hadn't been locked in on the game; it was just background noise. Jason was walking through the room and didn't appear to be watching the TV. He had just automatically registered the left-handers on the field and knew which players the Royals might want to challenge, long before the play popped up. Because I hadn't automatically registered the lefties on the field, that meant I was a step behind. Big league baseball players, especially catchers, and especially catchers with careers of fifteen—okay, sixteen—years, know an awful lot of baseball. If we'll listen, they'll teach us.

If there are any mistakes in the book, if I've used the wrong term to describe something or gotten a story wrong, the mistakes are mine. Jason's job was to provide the information; my job was to get it down on paper. As much as possible, I wanted you—the reader—to have the same experience I had: listening to a big league ballplayer talk about what it's *really* like out there. This is not a sanitized, cleaned-up version of baseball. This is not the version Major League Baseball sells to the public. This is not what a columnist, a mathematician, or a guy with a website thinks about the game. This is big league baseball as it's played in the real world, by real ballplayers.

This is *real* baseball.

When he was behind the plate, Jason Kendall rarely removed his catcher's mask. Keeping the mask on was part of his philosophy: during the game you don't call attention to yourself, you bust ass, you don't play to the crowd, you do your job. You reveal as little as possible to the media—in other words, you keep the mask on.

Now Jason Kendall is ready to reveal what he thinks about teammates, opposing players, umpires, coaches, managers, the media, and the people who come to the park at 2:00 p.m. to get yet another baseball signed. He's ready to explain how the game is being played at the big league level, and how he believes it *ought* to be played. He's willing to show us what to look for, so we have a better understanding of the game and the people who play it. This is a guy who played baseball for a long time, at a high level, being honest. This is Jason Kendall taking off the mask.

This is a big-league catcher telling us how the game is really played.

—Lee Judge

1
PREGAME

EVERY BALLPLAYER needs to do two things: hustle and be prepared.

For me, being prepared meant getting to the ballpark at least six hours before a 7:05 game. Getting there early gave me a chance to look at video, read scouting reports, go over possible late-inning matchups, and create a game plan for my starting pitcher.

Getting there early also allowed me to avoid autograph seekers. Kids are different—every ballplayer I know makes time for kids. But the people who want you to sign an autograph at twelve thirty in the afternoon usually aren't kids. They're mostly adults wanting to get items signed. And many of them resell those items. Even when it *is* a kid, the experience can leave you bitter. You try to personalize a ball for a kid—put his name on it—and his dad tells you, "No thanks, just sign it"?

The dad wants to resell the ball.

You see the same guy every day, and every day he asks you to sign something. How many autographed baseballs does one guy need? Honestly, what can you get for a signed Jason Kendall card? One cent? Two cents? Ten? When the same guy asks you to sign something every day, players know he's reselling those items and don't feel bad about blowing the guy off. After a game you come out and sign twenty autographs, the twenty-first guy doesn't get one and he calls you an asshole in front of your son. *Really?* Here's the deal: I'm done signing because I'm trying to get my son to bed so he can go to school tomorrow.

That kind of thing ruins the experience for everyone.

I'm grumpy—everybody *knows* I'm grumpy. If I've got work to do at 12:30 to get ready for that night's game and if it's 12:25, I ain't signing shit.

Early work

I got to the ballpark earlier than most, but all ballplayers are at the park early in the afternoon, getting ready for that night's game. Fans don't see everything we have to do to get ready for that 7:05 game. Players have work they do on their own, but teams also schedule early work for individuals or groups.

Early work means anything done before the team stretch and batting practice. We usually don't do early work before a day game, but for a night game, there's almost always something happening on the field by two or three in the afternoon.

Early work can be anything done on the field: extra batting practice, working on bunting, a middle infielder wants to clean up his double-play footwork, or the base stealers are listening to a coach go over the other team's starting pitcher and his pickoff move. Early work can be scheduled by a coach, or a player might ask to work on something.

And some early work is eyewash.

Eyewash is anything done just because it looks good. The owner's in town today? Let's run the bases: let's work on our secondary leads and going first to third. A coach who's trying to protect his job might want everyone to see how hard he's working and schedule early work for the players. That can actually be a negative: you're twenty games out of first place, it's August, and the players are dragging—do they really need extra time in the sun? If you don't know how to run the bases by August, you're already screwed.

If you're a big league ballplayer, you should know what you have to do to get ready for a game. But whether it's needed or not, somebody is doing early work almost every day. Players don't just show up an hour before game time, throw on a uniform, and go.

It's one thing to get to the big leagues—it's another thing to stay. Someone is always trying to take your job. If you want to stick around, you better be prepared to play.

The ballpark

Part of being prepared to play is knowing the ballpark. Every ballpark has quirks, and players need to know what they are. In Boston, the Green Monster—the thirty-seven-foot-high left-field wall—changes the way you run the bases. The Monster is so close to the infield, taking the extra base on a ball off the wall may not be possible.

When you played the Twins in the Metrodome, you had to know you couldn't take your eye off a fly ball: the roof was white. Take your eye off a pop fly and you may never see it again.

In Toronto, the warning track is a different color, but it's made of the same stuff as the rest of the outfield: turf. In most parks, outfielders know they're getting near a wall when they step off the grass and feel themselves running on dirt. An outfielder going back on a ball in Rogers Centre needs to know he won't get the usual warning before he hits the wall.

If a bad throw gets past the first baseman in Oakland, there's so much foul territory, a runner going down the first-base line can automatically turn for second base and *should* be thinking about getting all the way to third. In Kansas City, the same ball might hit a screen protecting a camera bay and come right back to the first baseman—the runner can't advance at all.

In *every* park, players need to check the area behind home plate. How close is the backstop? Is it padded or brick? Can a runner on third automatically score on a wild pitch? Base runners need to know this stuff before they take off for home plate and then realize the ball is bouncing right back to the catcher.

Every ballpark is different, and ballplayers need to know how each park can change the game. If a player is unfamiliar with a park, before the game a coach will hit baseballs off all the surfaces that might come into play. That way the player can see how he needs to play each ball. You need to know all this stuff before the game starts. You don't want to play a ball off the wall in front of forty thousand people and then realize you're standing in the wrong place.

Conditions

Players also need to check the flags: Is the wind blowing in? That might mean a low-scoring game. A smart pitcher can use the conditions by letting a batter crush a ball—straight into the wind. Here it is, dude, hit it as hard as you want; with this wind howling, it ain't going anywhere. If the wind's blowing out, it might mean a high-scoring game. Then the pitcher *really* needs to keep the ball down. He doesn't want a routine fly ball getting pushed out of the park by a strong breeze.

The inning can also make a difference. If it's a night game—depending on where you are—the ball might fly better in the early innings. Once it gets cool, the ball won't carry as well. A pitch that left the park at 6:15 might be a long out at 9:15. If it's a day game, it might be the opposite; the ball might jump better in the later innings when it's smoking hot.

Ballplayers also pay attention to the shadows. Vision is everything in this game, and if you can't see the ball, it changes the way the game is played. If it's a 1:10 start, the shadows will come into play late in the ball game. When there's a shadow halfway between home and the mound, it's hard to pick up the ball. Some people think you should throw more fastballs when visibility is tough, some people think you should throw more breaking stuff. But the main thing is to work quick. Once a pitcher has the shadows working in his favor, he needs to use them to get as many outs as possible.

If it's a night game, especially a 6:05 start on a Saturday, the setting sun can be a problem in the early innings. In some parks, the first baseman can't see a pickoff throw until the sun goes down. Colorado's the worst. Early in the game, the pitcher needs to keep any pickoff attempt low; that way his first baseman won't be blinded by the sun. If the sun is in the right fielder's eyes for the first two innings, he's not likely to come up with a great catch and throw on a sacrifice fly—the third-base coach and a runner on third need to know that. The runner might be able to score on a fly ball hit to right in the second inning and have to hold on the same fly ball an inning later.

Players need to know this stuff before the game starts.

Batting practice

Batting practice is a war zone. If the people on the field don't pay attention, they can take a line drive to the head. These are grown men at the plate, and the ball is coming off the bat *hot*. When you're standing at third base and the ball is traveling one hundred miles an hour, it doesn't take long to get on you.

That's why BP has to be planned out. A coach throws a pitch and the hitter swings. Another coach—standing off to the side of the batting cage—uses a fungo bat to hit a ball to an infielder. The coach hitting fungoes has to time it so that two balls aren't heading toward the same infielder. Make a mistake and you can jack up a multimillion-dollar player. Sometimes another coach is on the other side of the batting cage hitting *another* fungo to a *different* infielder. Three or four balls can be in play at the same time, all headed to different parts of the field. It's a rhythm. Break the rhythm—look in the wrong direction at the wrong time—and it's easy to get drilled. If you watch BP, everyone on the field is paying attention.

If fans want to know what's going on, they should, too.

Pay attention during batting practice: Take your eye off the hitter and watch the fielders. See who gets his work in and who's goofing around. Does the second baseman flip the double-play ball to the shortstop at second base the same way he will in the game? Or is he playing around with behind-the-back flips? Is the left fielder approaching balls at game speed or is he just going through the motions?

Once a guy has his work in, he may stand around and joke with a teammate, but when it's time to do his job, he needs to go about it the right way—work ethic is just as important for ballplayers as it is for everybody else. The guys who take this work seriously are the guys who stick around the game for a while. And they're the same guys you want fielding the ball with the game on the line. The guys who goof around when they should be working may not have a long career.

Now look back at the hitter: if he's taking *his* job seriously, he's not up there playing home-run derby. Fans might like to see a guy hit ball after ball into the seats, but it's not good batting practice. Every team has a batting-practice routine. They can vary some, but here's an example:

FIRST ROUND:

The hitter lays down two bunts, one to first, one to third, then hits seven balls to the opposite field.

SECOND ROUND:

First swing: hit and run (the runner will force a middle infielder to cover second base, so right-handers hit a ground ball toward the hole at second, left-handers hit a ground ball toward the hole at short).

Second swing: move the runner over from second to third (the ball needs to be hit to the right side).

Third swing: get the runner in from third with the infield back (a fly ball to the outfield or a ground ball to short or second will do).

Fourth swing: get the runner in from third with the infield in (the ball needs to be hit in the air to the outfield).

Fifth swing: a suicide squeeze.

The last three swings: hit away.

THIRD ROUND:

Everyone in the hitting group takes five swings, then rotates through again and takes two more swings.

If a guy wants to load up and hit a long ball, it's usually in that third round. But before that, line drives, hard grounders, and balls hit the other way should be the goal. Pay attention to who takes this work seriously, and you'll have a better idea of who will come through when he faces the same situation in a game.

A good time to ask for autographs

If you want an autograph, try asking after batting practice. Ask as the team leaves the field, but like everybody else, we're on a schedule. Different players have different routines, and it's important to stick to those routines. *You* may read a newspaper and have a cup of coffee at the same time every day. It helps you function and gets you started on your day. The same thing applies to ballplayers: we've all got a routine that helps us function.

If it's me, I was coming off BP at the same time every day. I had a routine: I left the field, headed back to the clubhouse, went over the scouting reports one more time, and took one last look at my notes. That was my job. At that point in the day, I was so mentally locked in I might not have signed for you. I was so locked in I might not have even *noticed* you.

Some guys sign autographs every day. Stopping on the way in from BP and signing autographs may be part of *their* routine. Position players, outfielders, pitchers—most of the time—they'll sign; especially if a kid asks. Although when a ten-year-old asks you to sign a ball on the "sweet spot"—the narrow spot between the seams and the spot favored by autograph collectors—you figure an adult put him up to it. When that happens, we'll ask the kid's name and personalize the ball, just to make sure it can't be resold.

Ballplayers want to do what they can for the fans, but walking over to sign one autograph might turn into signing ten. Sign ten and the eleventh person who wanted an autograph will be upset. The time it took to sign those ten autographs may mean a player comes up five swings short in the batting cage. It may mean he doesn't have time to go over the scouting report one last time. I've had a routine from my first day in the big leagues all the way to my last game. I always got to the park early. If I got to the ballpark late, it was because of my kids. If I got off my routine—if I wasn't stretching in the indoor batting cages before 6:01—I felt like I was going to have a bad game.

Have enough bad games and no one's going to *want* your autograph.

The meeting at the plate

At this point in the pregame schedule, players have changed into game uniforms and are back on the field. They've had a chance to relax, take one last look at scouting reports, or watch video. They might be down in the indoor batting cages, taking a few more hacks.

The umpire and the managers—or whoever the manager sends out with the lineup card—meet at home plate and go over what's in play and what isn't. If the park had some off-season renovations, the umpire will point out those changes to the visiting team. The meeting at the plate is probably longer before the first game of each series, but before games two or three, the guys at the plate are probably making dinner plans or telling jokes.

The national anthem

Bottom line: the faster the better. I know singing the anthem is a pretty big thing for the singers—but hurry up. You want to get a big ovation? Get it done.

Put it this way: if you're gonna be slow, you better be good.

I've heard thousands and thousands of national anthems, but my favorite took place in the minor leagues. I was playing High-A ball for the Pirates, and one of the coaches was Rocky Bridges. I'm standing next to Rocky, listening to the anthem, when he says, "Hey, kid, I hate this song. You know why? Every time they played this [bleeping] song, I had a bad game." I don't know what else I should have expected; Rocky had a personalized license plate that said O FOR 4.

Okay, song's over—time to play ball.

2
THE PITCHER

FANS THINK a baseball game starts when the umpire yells, "Play ball," but for the players, it started eight pitches earlier. When the pitcher got on the mound and started warming up, we started paying attention. And umpires don't actually say, "Play ball"; they'll point at the pitcher and say something like "Let's go." The only reason umpires say anything at all is to warn the catcher and leadoff batter that it's time to quit talking about the wife and kids. It's time to get serious.

The warm-up pitches

At the beginning of an inning, or whenever a reliever comes in, the pitcher is allowed eight warm-up pitches. He doesn't have to use all of them, but eight's the limit. Starting pitchers usually throw all eight warm-up pitches, but I've worked with relievers who like to play mind games. They might use just three or four warm-ups, trying to intimidate the guy at the plate. The reliever is sending a message that he's already got his good stuff and doesn't need any more pitches to get ready. That might be true or it might mean that the pitcher is gassed from overuse, or his arm is killing him and he doesn't want to make any more throws than he has to. The batter won't know the answer until he sees a few pitches.

Neither will I.

Guys have been lights out warming up and then been hammered once the game started. I've also seen pitchers who had nothing down in the bull pen, then threw no-hit stuff. Nobody—including the pitcher—knows exactly what will happen once he starts throwing to the hitters.

The pitching mound

Those eight warm-up pitches aren't thrown just so the pitcher can loosen his arm. The warm-up is also a chance for the pitcher to get used to the field mound. If it's your home field, you're probably already familiar with the mound; if you're the visiting pitcher, you're not.

All pitching mounds are supposed to be the same, but they aren't. Even when the grounds crew is following the rules, there are differences. And apparently some crews don't try all that hard to follow the rules. You hear stories about teams that make the visitors' bullpen mound steeper or flatter or harder than the field mound, and that might throw the visiting pitcher off when he comes into the game.

Screwing around with the pitching mound is only one of the tricks a grounds crew uses to help the home team. They might water down the base paths to slow down opposing base stealers. Or keep the grass a little longer in front of a third baseman with poor range so ground balls don't get by him. Or slant the base paths so a bunted ball rolls foul.

I supplied the grounds crew with beer, and in return they prepared the area around home plate just the way I liked it. If it was too soft, I didn't feel like I could move to block a pitch in the dirt. Too hard, and I felt like I was on concrete. A good grounds crew can give the home team a slight edge, and sometimes that's enough.

The warm-up signs

Once the pitcher's done digging around on the mound and is ready to throw his warm-up pitches, he'll let the catcher know what pitch he wants to throw with a motion of his glove or bare hand:

- If the pitcher flips his glove at the catcher with the palm down, he's going to throw a *fastball.*
- If the pitcher points his glove at the catcher and then pulls the glove directly back, he's throwing a *changeup.*
- If the pitcher flips his glove at the catcher palm-up, that's a *curveball.*
- A downward motion of the glove is a *splitter* or *forkball.*
- A horizontal glove motion is a *slider.*
- A downward, diagonal motion with the bare hand while holding the ball is a *sinker.*

The pitcher isn't giving anything away to the hitters by showing these pitches. Everybody already knows what pitches he has. We've either faced him before or we get the information from video or scouting reports. We can also tell what pitch he's throwing just by watching it.

We're major leaguers—it's what we do.

Those signals with the glove are just so the catcher knows what's coming. Pitches come in so fast, a catcher has to be able to anticipate the ball's movement or he may not catch it cleanly. I tore every ligament in my thumb when I was looking for a pitch down and away and the pitcher threw a cutter that moved up and in. If I get crossed up on a pitch, I've got a good chance of taking a ball in the neck.

Now that you know the warm-up signs, pay attention to what pitches were thrown for strikes. If the only pitch that stayed in the strike zone during warm-ups was a fastball, it might mean that's what the pitcher will throw when he has to throw a strike.

But it all depends on who's standing on the mound. Some veteran pitchers will be wild during warm-ups, but throw strikes once a batter steps into the box. Some guys can throw eight pitches in the dirt and it doesn't mean a thing: game time, they'll throw strikes. With a pitcher you haven't seen before, it might be different. If a rookie is throwing everything in the dirt during warm-ups, a smart hitter might want to take a pitch and see if the kid can find the plate. No sense helping him out if you don't have to.

Why hitters watch the warm-ups

Look in the opposing dugout during those warm-up pitches and you'll see the hitters watching closely. If it's a pitcher they haven't already seen, they want to see his stuff: his movement and velocity. If it's a pitcher they're already familiar with, they want to see what his stuff looks like *tonight*.

Big league hitters have seen video on the pitchers they'll face that night and scouting reports on how pitchers like to work: What do they throw to get ahead in the count? What do they throw after they get ahead in the count? What do they throw if they fall behind?

If you do your homework, you know what a pitcher's got, but hitters still want to see what it looks like live.

After the warm-ups

After six warm-up pitches, you might see the umpire hold up two fingers, reminding the pitcher how many throws he has left. If it's at the start of an inning, before his last warm-up pitch the pitcher will make a motion back over his shoulder toward second base with his glove or bare hand. He's telling the catcher that this is his last pitch and the catcher should throw the ball down to second base. If it's a young catcher, maybe he gets something out of making the throw, but once you've been around awhile, you make the throw because it's a baseball tradition, not because you need practice throwing a ball to second base.

After the pitcher signals for the throw to second base, the catcher makes a signal by holding his mitt or bare hand out to the side. This sign tells the middle infielder taking the catcher's throw that the warm-ups are over and the ball is about to be thrown his way. The second baseman—who usually takes the throw—holds his hand or glove out to the side to let the catcher know he's aware the ball is about to be thrown to second base.

Once in a while I might bounce that throw. If the umpire isn't paying attention and keeps the ball in play, now my pitcher has a scuff on the ball—which he can use to get more movement on a pitch. I'd only do that if I had a pitcher on the mound who knew what to do with a scuffed baseball. Veteran pitchers know how to take advantage of a scuffed baseball. If I were a pitcher and got a scuffed ball, I'd be thinking it was awesome. Some of the kids pitching today get a scuffed baseball and want a new one.

The Dig-Me Tribe

When the catcher throws the ball to second, the second baseman catches it and throws it to the shortstop, the shortstop throws to third, and the third baseman throws the ball back to the pitcher. If you see the third baseman studying the ball before he gives it to the pitcher, he's not really accomplishing anything except looking cool: he's part of the Dig-Me Tribe. You can spot them by their wristbands and the batting gloves hanging out of their back pocket. These are the players who worry about looking pretty.

But if the *pitcher* looks closely at the ball, he's checking the surface for scuffs or nicks. As I said, a scuffed or nicked baseball will have extra movement if the pitcher knows what he's doing. If the pitcher suddenly has extra break on a pitch, you might see the batter ask the umpire to check the ball. He knows something's not right. Either that or the hitter's also in the Dig-Me Tribe and just wants to look cool on TV. These prima-donna players are getting more TV time for themselves: *Hey, look how cool I am. I can tell the umpire to check the ball.*

None of this worry about scuffed baseballs makes sense to me. If a pitch hits the dirt before I catch it, the umpire puts a new ball in play. But if the batter hits a sixteen-hopper to short, the ball goes right back to the pitcher—that ball is pretty [bleeping] scuffed. Nobody asks to check the ball then. We use over a hundred baseballs every night; being consistent about taking balls out of play would force us to use even more. Balls get scuffed all the time and we keep them in play. A ball gets hit off the wall, bounces on the warning track, the throw back to the infield bounces in the dirt—and the ball goes right back to the mound, we're good to go.

When the pitcher falls behind in the count

If fans want to know what's happening on a baseball field, they have to pay attention to the count. Here's why: The easiest pitch to throw for a strike is a fastball; it's got less movement and that makes it easier to control. But because it's pretty much straight, a fastball is also the easiest pitch to hit, as long as it's up in the strike zone.

If a hitter gets a fastball up when he's looking for a fastball, he's in good shape—his timing will be on, his swing will be balanced. That's why all hitters want to work their way into fastball counts. These are counts where the pitcher needs to throw a strike, and a fastball is his best bet. Depending on the pitcher and the situation, 2-0, 2-1, 3-0, 3-1, and sometimes 3-2 are usually considered fastball counts. A pitcher who finds himself in one of these counts is *behind* in the count; the hitter is *ahead* in the count.

But throwing a fastball in a fastball count is what an average pitcher does. If a pitcher wants to be better, if he wants to stay in the big leagues for a while, he needs to throw off-speed stuff in those counts—that's what a smart pitcher does. A legitimate big league pitcher should be able to throw a strike with any of his pitches in any count. If a pitcher can't throw his off-speed stuff for strikes, he's in trouble every time he has a fastball count. Hitters will look for a fastball and be ready when they get it.

When the pitcher gets ahead in the count

When a pitcher gets ahead in the count, he can throw any pitch he's got: he has more options. Counts like 0-1, 0-2, 1-2, and—depending on the pitcher and the situation—sometimes 2-2 or 3-2 can be counts where the pitcher can throw what he likes. If the pitcher can throw a breaking pitch for a strike, he can throw it when he's 3-2.

Depending on the situation, the pitcher might not care if he throws his slider for a strike in a 3-2 count; he might even throw it out of the zone intentionally. If there's a good hitter at the plate, a man in scoring position, and first base open, it might be better to walk the hitter than give him a hittable fastball when any hit can drive in a run. Put the hitter on and go after the guy on deck—as long as the guy on deck is someone you don't mind facing.

When the pitcher's ahead in the count, the hitter is at a disadvantage. Before a batter has two strikes, he can let a tough pitch go by and hope for something more hittable on the next pitch. But once he has two strikes, a batter has to get less picky. He can't afford to take a pitch that's just off the plate; the umpire might see it as strike three.

All this can change, depending on the situation, the hitter, the pitcher, and what he has that night. But if you know the count and what the pitcher is able to throw for strikes, you have a chance of predicting what is going to happen on the next pitch—and you won't go to the bathroom when Albert Pujols is about to get a 2-0 fastball from a nervous rookie.

The bastard pitch

Hitters want to know what a pitcher throws once he's ahead in the count and has two strikes on the batter. It's called an *out pitch, chase pitch,* or a *bastard pitch*. It's usually something that looks like a fastball, starts in the strike zone, then turns into a slider or splitter moving out of the zone after the hitter starts his swing. With two strikes, a hitter's got to protect the strike zone and there's not much time to decide.

A bastard pitch can make a hitter look silly, and fans might wonder why someone swung at a pitch so far out of the strike zone. If every fan in America could stand in the batter's box, they'd realize how quickly the ball gets on the hitter. And if they could see a fastball and a slider, they'd realize how similar those two pitches appear to be—until the last split second. Trust me, when you see a major league hitter chase a pitch a foot outside the strike zone, he probably just saw a bastard pitch.

On the other hand, when you see at bats go on and on—eight, nine pitches—and it's happening with more than one hitter, it's probably because the pitcher doesn't *have* a bastard pitch. The pitcher can get the hitter to two strikes, but once the hitter goes into a two-strike approach—choking up and slapping at anything close—the pitcher doesn't have a pitch nasty enough to get a swing and miss.

Identifying pitches

Here's my take on identifying pitches. I've got over 2,000 hits in the big leagues, and once or twice a season, for about ten days each time, every pitch looked like a beach ball. I could see the rotation on the ball. I'd be so dialed in I'd recognize the pitch as it came out of the pitcher's hand.

The rest of the time, every pitch looked like a golf ball.

The days when you're totally focused are unbelievable; the game seems easy. But the feeling goes away so fast. One day I'm completely locked in: I'm going 3 for 4, 4 for 4. The next day I feel like I've never stood in a batter's box before. When they're going good, hitters can see the ball spin, but fans in the stands will never be able to spot the rotation on a baseball—they're just too far away. So I'll make pitch recognition simple: check the scoreboard.

Most stadiums now show a radar-gun reading; look around and find it. If a pitch registers more than 90 miles per hour, you probably just saw some type of fastball. If you see something a lot slower—say ten miles an hour slower—you probably just saw an off-speed pitch. It's rare, unless someone's coming out of the pen, for a guy to throw two different pitches in the 90s. And if you see a reliever throw a fastball *and* a slider in the 90s, he's a badass.

If you're watching the radar-gun readings, you should know that some pitchers add or subtract a few mph from pitch to pitch. One fastball will be 92, the next, 95; that can throw the hitter's timing off. And a guy like Curt Schilling might build velocity as the game goes along. He'd throw in the low 90s during the first inning and dial it up to the upper 90s late in the game.

Also remember that radar guns are notoriously inaccurate, and some teams have been accused of juicing the readings to excite the crowd. But once you determine a pitcher's top velocity, you can begin to figure out what pitch was just thrown. Even if the gun is a few miles an hour off, just remember that something ten miles an hour slower than top velocity is usually an off-speed pitch.

And don't get too excited about velocity.

In my opinion, late movement is a lot more important than lighting up the radar gun. That usually means a sinker, a cutter, or a fastball with natural movement—something with a little giddyup at the end. That makes it hard for a hitter to get the barrel on the ball. At the big league level, hitters are capable of handling a 100 mph fastball. If they see 100 twice, they'll get it the third time. Location and movement are more important than putting up big numbers on a radar gun.

Pitch location

Home plate is seventeen inches wide. Depending on the umpire, you might get a little extra on either side of that seventeen-inch plate. A lot of pitchers try to work on the corners of whatever strike zone they're getting that night. In fact, too many pitchers *try* to hit the corners, nibble, and fall behind in the count. That's when they get in trouble.

Too many pitchers try to avoid contact: they're afraid to let the batter hit the ball. They don't trust their stuff. Forget pitching on the corners—you might be able to do that a handful of times each year if everything is working that night. Just throw the ball at the knees and there's a pretty good chance you'll get guys out.

Pitchers who keep the ball down around the knees can use the entire width of the plate. A guy who pitches up in the zone has to hit a corner or he'll get whacked. Some guys will pitch up *above* the zone—once they're ahead in the count—and try to get a hitter to chase a high pitch. But generally, pitchers try to keep the ball down around the knees or hit the corners, while most hitters look for the ball in the middle of the plate.

I'd say 90 percent of all hits at any level of baseball are on pitches in the middle of the plate. *Every* pitcher makes mistakes; I can't stress that enough. Hitters should look for the ball in the middle of the plate.

That other shit is too hard to hit.

Pitching inside

A setup pitch is a pitch you do *not* want to throw for a strike: it's a pitch thrown to set up the next one. You got a guy 0-2? Throw one up around his neck. The guy's up on the dish? Knock him off—knock him on his ass. You don't want him just *leaning* back; you want him *on* his back—or at least moving his feet. Put him on his back or at least make him back out of the box.

If you make a hitter uncomfortable, you win—*and everybody else sees it.* You're on deck and the guy at the plate gets knocked on his ass? You're not too comfortable when it's your turn to step into the box. These days, hitters dive: they stride toward the plate to cover pitches on the outer half. I ought to know, I was the biggest diver ever—I was *totally* diving. But if you want to come up and in and keep me from diving, you'll hit me and I'm on first base. I refused to move off the plate, which is why I was hit by a so many pitches.

Hitters are so comfortable at the plate now, unless you've got a badass on the mound; and there aren't many badasses left. Nolan Ryan was the best, just watch the highlights: hitters were not comfortable. You throw a ball up and in on a guy that dives these days? They're scared to death. You go up and in, put a guy on his ass, and then you throw a fastball down and away; that part of the plate has been opened up. Pitching inside is a huge part of the game. It was a huge part of the game a hundred years ago and it will be a huge part of the game a hundred years from now. So why are some pitchers reluctant to do it?

Fear.

First, fear of the home run. If an inside pitch is in the strike zone, it's easier to hit for a home run than a pitch away. The inside pitch is the pitch the hitter will pull, and pulling the pitch puts the ball in the short part of the park. A guy can hit a ball four hundred feet and make an out if the ball is hit to center field. Hit a ball four hundred feet down the line and it lands halfway up general admission.

And some pitchers are afraid to hit a batter. A ball traveling 95 miles an hour can do some damage, and some pitchers are uncomfortable throwing a pitch that might seriously injure another player.

Finally, some pitchers fear for their own safety. Hitters aren't crazy about getting drilled, and some don't mind visiting the mound to deliver that message. When that happens, it's the catcher's job to get to the hitter and drag him down from behind before he can get to the pitcher.

If a pitcher is afraid to give up a home run, hit a batter, or have someone charge the mound, he's not going to last long.

Hitting a batter

One thing I can't stand is a guy who gets hit by a pitch and stands there huffing and puffing. If a guy gets hit by a pitch—if he wears one—and then stands at the plate pointing at the pitcher and yelling, he's weak. The hitter just wants to *look* tough while he waits for his teammates to arrive. Guys who actually are tough? They don't wait around; charging the mound is a split-second decision, and they're just *gone.*

Here's the way I see it: If you get hit by a pitch and you think it was something personal, go get the pitcher. If it wasn't personal, walk your ass to first base.

I've charged the mound two times: once with Joe Kennedy pitching and another time when John Lackey was on the mound. Kennedy hit me with a hard cutter that ran in on me. I couldn't get out of the way. I was minding my own business, running to first base, when Joe yelled at me for wearing a pad on my left elbow. Pitchers don't like it when hitters come to the plate wearing protection. *I* don't like it when someone yells at me, so halfway down to first base I took a left turn and charged the mound.

The incident with Lackey was different: I was at the plate with the bases loaded when he threw a curveball. I got out of the way, but Lackey thought I was trying to get hit by the pitch. He yelled an insult that started with the word *mother,* so I went to the mound.

Kennedy and Lackey were not trying to hit me, but if a pitcher wants to hit a batter, there's a right way to do it: throw a fastball just about belt-high behind the hitter. The hitter sees an inside pitch and backs up—it moves him right into the pitch. The hitter may not be happy about getting drilled, but it was done the right way: below the shoulders, away from the head, and the only damage is a bruise.

Players usually know when a pitcher intentionally hits a batter. There's probably some kind of history there: a guy hit a home run and showed up the pitcher by standing at the plate too long, or the last time the teams played, the guy at the plate took out a middle infielder with a questionable slide.

If a team feels the need to retaliate, they'll usually try to pick a comparable victim: You hit our designated hitter, we'll hit yours. You hit our 3-hole hitter, now yours is going to wear one. If Miguel Cabrera gets hit, there's a pretty good chance Billy Butler will also get hit. Sometimes the guy with the target on his back will plead his case to the other team. The first baseman on your team sees the first baseman on the other team get drilled, figures he's now a target and starts telling opposing players, "You know, I *really* don't think your guy getting hit was intentional."

That's part of what I liked about the National League: pitchers have to hit. To hell with going after their eight-hole hitter because our eight-hole hitter got drilled—I want the guy who threw the pitch to know how getting hit by a 98 mph fastball feels. Let the players police themselves. Too many warnings are issued these days. A guy gets drilled and the umpire issues a warning. The other side can't retaliate in *that* game, so they get even the next day. Issue a warning too soon and you can start a beanball war over an entire series. And it can stretch into the next series; even the next season. Let the players take care of it—you hit our guy now we'll hit yours—and it's over in one game.

One way for fans to tell if a hit-by-pitch was intentional is the radar-gun reading on the scoreboard. If you're gonna hit somebody on purpose, it's coming in hot. Pitchers do not send a message by hitting someone with an off-speed pitch: if it's intentional, it'll be a fastball. And if the pitch is *way* off the plate, pay attention: A pitch slightly inside may be missed location. A pitch *behind* a guy is a message.

But you still don't mess with the hitter's head. We all have families. You can come up and in—under the chin—but you don't throw *at* somebody's head. Nobody likes a headhunter, not even his own teammates. A headhunter is a guy who throws at a hitter's head intentionally. If you're the batter and you think the pitcher threw at your head? You *better* go to the mound.

At least in the National League, a headhunter has to go to the plate and face retaliation. In the American League, a pitcher can throw at someone's head and then hide on the bench; which means his teammates are going to face retaliation for something they didn't do.

Neither team likes it when a pitcher decides to hit someone for no good reason. I was with the Brewers, we were playing the Pirates, and Ryan Braun hit a home run. He didn't pimp the home run as he went around the bases, but the pitcher still decided to hit Ryan the next time he came to the plate. Maybe the pitcher was embarrassed about giving up the home run or maybe he just wanted to look like a tough guy. Maybe the pitcher was just tired of the Brewers beating the Pirates.

The umpire issued a warning. We were in a pennant race and couldn't afford to lose our pitcher, so we had to wait to retaliate. Next time we saw this guy, he was a reliever and we figured we'd never get a shot at him because relievers rarely come to the plate. But his manager left him in the game to get an at bat. His manager should've known we weren't going to forget about Braun getting drilled. I went to the mound and told my rookie pitcher he needed to drill this guy—don't worry about why—just drill him. The kid said okay and got the job done. Both benches cleared and the other team's pitching coach came after *me,* not the rookie who threw the pitch. I visit the mound and the next pitch nails the hitter? The pitching coach knew who was responsible for his pitcher getting drilled.

Keep that in mind when you're watching a game: if someone visits the mound and the hitter gets smoked on the next pitch, you may have just seen someone taking care of some unfinished business.

Situations

Here are some of the most common situations a pitcher will face. Pay attention to what the hitter is trying to do and if the pitcher is able to prevent it. Then you'll know who won the game within the game.

Runner on first base, less than two outs—the pitcher needs a double play: The pitcher wants the ball hit on the ground. You'll see a lot of sinkers here. If you're watching on TV, focus on the catcher's signs. If he moves his finger in a circle while pointing straight down, he's asking for a sinker. If a pitch is moving down, it's more likely the hitter will make contact with the top half of the ball and hit a grounder.

Runner on first base, nobody out (if it's a National League game, you'll also see it with one out and a pitcher at the plate): Depending on the situation, the hitter, the runner, and so on, the sacrifice bunt may be in order. You sometimes see the pitcher attempt a pickoff to start this at bat, but keep your eye on the plate, not first base. The pitcher throws to first because the defense wants to see if the hitter will tip that he's bunting by starting to square around too soon.

Pitchers will do this even when the bunt is obvious. I got most of my bunts down because I didn't try to fool anybody; I squared around early. The whole game revolves around eyes and balance. By squaring around early I got my head in the right position and kept it there. Square around late and your head is still moving when the ball arrives. That makes bunting much harder. A bunter needs to keep his head straight and his eyes on the ball. Why hide it? It's a bunting situation. If you're a bunter, bunt. I'd square early, I'd give it away. If they gave me a microphone, I would have announced it to the crowd: *"Now bunting, Jason Kendall."* If I knew the manager on the other team, I'd hold the bat up and show *him* I was bunting.

And yet some derelict on the mound would still throw the ball over to first, *hoping* I'd give the bunt away. Pay attention, dude; I'm not hiding it.

Once the pitcher knows the hitter is going to bunt, a lot of instructional manuals tell the pitcher to throw a high fastball. The idea is to make it hard for the hitter to keep his bat above the ball, which he has to do to make the bunted ball go down. If the hitter makes contact with the bottom half of the ball, it'll go up, and the defense gets an easy infield pop-up. Personally, I thought the best pitch in a bunt situation was a changeup. Everybody practices their bunting against fastballs. Throw a changeup and *let* the hitter get the bunt down. Lower velocity on the pitch means the ball doesn't roll that far from the plate. Now I can jump out from behind home plate, grab the ball, go for the lead runner, and—if the bunter can't run—we turn two. I can't tell you how many double plays we turned throwing changeups in sac-bunt situations.

Runner on third, less than two out, a suicide or safety squeeze is in order: On this play, the hitter *can't* give the bunt away. If the batter squares around to bunt too soon and gives the play away, the pitcher will know the squeeze is on. He can then throw a pitchout with a left-handed hitter at the plate, or go up and in with a right-handed hitter at the plate.

If the pitcher does it right, the left-handed hitter won't be able to reach the pitchout and the location of the pitch will move the catcher up the third-base line, in a good position to tag the runner coming home. If it's a right-handed hitter, the up-and-in pitch will put the hitter on his ass, which gets him out of the catcher's way. Now the catcher can see the runner coming and make the tag.

Runner on third, less than two outs: If it's early in the game or his team has a big lead, a pitcher might concede the run. The pitcher doesn't worry about *how* he gets an out, he just wants an out. Now the pitcher can throw whatever pitch he likes. He doesn't care where the ball gets hit as long as he gets an out.

If the pitcher is trying to prevent the run, he needs a strikeout, an infield pop-up, or—if the infield is playing in—a ground ball at someone. The hitter wants to hit a fly ball to the outfield and is looking for a pitch up out over plate. The pitcher might go *way* up in the zone—higher than high—and see if the hitter will chase. If the pitcher gets ahead in the count, he might go for the strikeout. That might mean a bastard breaking pitch for a swing-and-miss, but, with a runner on third, the pitcher has to trust his catcher to block a pitch in the dirt.

Runner being held at first: When the first baseman holds the runner, a hole is opened on the right side of the infield. If the runner is a threat to steal or the double play is in order, the second baseman may have to play closer to second in order to cover the bag. That makes the hole on the right side even bigger. So with a left-handed hitter at the plate, the pitcher doesn't want him to pull the ball through the hole on that side of the infield. In this situation the worst pitch you can throw a lefty is a changeup. That hole on the right side is just where most left-handers will hit that pitch.

When a runner is being held on first base, some hitters—the guys with bat control—want to hit the ball through that hole on the right side. The pitcher wants to prevent that.

Runner at second base, nobody out: A lot of the time the hitter is trying to move the runner to third base by hitting the ball to the right side of the field, and the pitcher is trying to prevent that by having a ground ball hit to the left side. Most of the time if the ball is hit in front of the runner, he'll have to hold at second base. If the ball is hit *behind* the runner—to the right side of the field—he can advance ninety feet. Once he's on third with less than two outs, the runner can score on a ground ball or sacrifice fly.

If a right-hander is at the plate, you'll probably see something slower, or down and in. That's a pitch a righty will pull on the ground, freezing the runner at second base. A lefty will usually get something hard, down, and away. He'll be more likely to hit that pitch to the left side, which also freezes the runner.

All this can change, depending on the hitter and the situation. If it's one of your 3-4-5 hitters at the plate, you might want the hitter to drive the run in himself. That means he might *not* be trying to hit the ball to the right side to move the runner over; he'll be looking for a pitch he can drive to any part of the park.

Pitching around a hitter with a runner in scoring position: Say there's a runner or runners on second or third and first base is open. The hitter at the plate is hot and you've had success against the guy on deck. In this situation, the pitcher might work around the hitter at the plate. That means he'll throw pitches just off the plate and give the hitter a chance to get himself out by swinging at a pitch out of the zone. Guys get greedy for RBIs and sometimes chase pitches.

If the hot hitter stays disciplined and walks, that's okay. Sometimes you'll see a pitcher purposely throw a couple of balls out of the zone, and if the batter doesn't chase, the manager will decide to intentionally walk the guy. The manager will signal the intentional walk by holding up four fingers to the catcher.

The intentional walk: The catcher signals the pitcher that the manager has called for an intentional walk by holding his glove or bare hand, whichever is farther away from the batter, straight out to the side. The pitcher uses the glove or hand for a target. Intentional walks are often issued for the same reason a pitcher works around a hitter: you do not want to let their best guy beat you. You avoid him and take your chances with the next hitter.

There *are* other reasons you might issue an intentional walk. With a runner on second and first open, the defense might want to put a man on first base to set up a double play. If it's a National League game in the middle innings, the pitcher might be on deck and the intentional walk will force the other manager to choose between letting a poor-hitting pitcher go to the plate or pulling him for a pinch hitter. If the pitcher hits, his team might lose an offensive opportunity with a runner in scoring position. If the pinch hitter goes to the plate, the team loses its starting pitcher and gets into its bull pen early.

That's why it's important for pitchers in the National League to take their hitting seriously. If they can't hit, or at least bunt, they can find themselves out of the game early on.

Pitching with a lead

Big league pitchers should be able to throw strikes more often than they do. A lot of them try to be too fine and paint the corners of the plate. Then, when they fall behind and have to come into the heart of the zone, they get whacked.

A pitcher always needs to throw strikes, but once he gets a lead, he really needs to go after hitters. He has to force the hitters to swing the bat. The guy on the mound has to have a "here it is, try to hit it" attitude. If you've got a 3-run lead and the batter hits the ball into the parking lot, you've still got a 2-run lead. Force contact and let the defense get some outs for you. If the pitcher has a big lead and is still falling behind in the count and walking people, watch for the pitching coach to make a visit to the mound. He's probably telling the pitcher to get his head out of his ass and throw strikes. Right after one of these visits, hitters should look for a fastball. It's the most likely pitch after the pitcher gets an ass-chewing about throwing strikes.

If the mound visit doesn't work and the pitcher is still nibbling, watch the bull pen. If a reliever gets up, that might be the manager sending a message to the pitcher: start throwing strikes or I'm pulling you. Managers want to get their starters through five innings for a win, but a manager isn't going to watch a pitcher piss away the lead—the manager might get someone up in the pen for motivation.

But before he does that, a manager has to know his guys: he can't do that with a pitcher who's soft. If a guy who isn't mentally tough looks out to the bull pen and sees a reliever warming up, he might fall apart. A bulldog will get mad when he sees a guy warming up and bear down.

Staying mentally tough

After your team scores, pay attention to the next half inning; it's *incredibly* important. What you're looking for is a shutdown inning: an inning where the opposing team doesn't score. The pitcher can't relax just because he got a few runs. He needs to come back out and put a zero on the board. If he does that—gets through the next half inning without giving up a run—the other team starts to think about getting beat. And thinking about getting beat often leads to *actually* getting beat. Let the other team put up a run in their half of the inning and your opponents believe they're still in the game.

Pitchers have to stay mentally tough at all times. They can never start to feel good about the situation and ease up. The same thing applies to getting a tough hitter: a pitcher can't think he's over the hump because he got Miguel Cabrera, relax, and then let the next guy beat him.

You'll also see pitchers make the same mistake with two outs in an inning: they think they're home free, relax, and start messing around with the third hitter. With two outs, I hate to see the pitcher ease up and give the third guy a curveball. Don't fall behind in the count. Go after the hitter; make him earn his way on. Go for the kill.

The pitcher and the stolen base

Pitchers have a couple ways to control the running game. One of the simplest things they can do is to vary how long they hold the ball in the set position. Once a runner takes a lead, he has a lot of tension in his body, like a sprinter in the blocks. Holding the ball in the set position can make the runner's legs go dead and prevent a steal.

It seems simple, but I'd still have to remind pitchers to do this: slow down, take your time, mix it up. Pitchers get so locked in on the plate they forget the runner. Pitchers like to find a rhythm, and they'll hold the ball in the set position the same amount of time, *every* time. Then base runners can just count off—one thousand one, one thousand two—and break at the right time.

I wouldn't just remind pitchers to hold the ball; I'd also tell them when to attempt a pickoff. If you're watching the game on TV, pay attention to the catcher's signs: one of the signs for a pickoff is the catcher's flicking his thumb as if he were flipping a coin. He's telling the pitcher to throw the ball to first. The catcher has a better view of the runner's lead and might want the pitcher to shorten that lead. The call to go over to first base can also come from the bench. They may have information about the runner's pattern of attempting steals—he might like to run on certain counts—and they'll signal the catcher to signal the pitcher to attempt a pickoff. Multiple pickoff attempts can tire a runner's legs, but if the pitcher attempts several pickoffs in a row, pay attention to his next pitch. A pitcher can lose focus and rhythm while making a bunch of pickoff attempts and throw something hittable when he finally goes to the plate.

And if a guy throws over to first base a bunch of times, check the bull pen; he may be stalling while a reliever warms up.

I liked to call my own running game, but when you see a big league catcher look in the dugout, he's probably not getting pitches called from the side; he's getting the running game called from the side. They not only call for pickoffs, they also call for pitchouts and slide steps.

A slide step is a quicker delivery motion by the pitcher. He can shorten the time it takes to deliver the ball to home plate by not lifting his front knee as high as he usually does. The pitcher barely lifts his foot off the ground and *slides* toward home plate. Pay attention to the pitcher's front foot: if he barely lifts it, the catcher has a chance to throw out the runner. If the pitcher lifts his foot high and the runner gets a good jump, there's not much a catcher can do. If you're watching on TV, you might be able to anticipate the slide step. A lot of catchers will slide their hand down the inside of their thigh, signaling the pitcher to deliver the next pitch with a slide step. That'll get the ball on its way to home plate faster, but there can be a cost.

If the front foot gets down faster than normal, the arm doesn't always catch up and get to the right release point on time. Pitchers who use a slide step sometimes struggle with the ball being up in the strike zone, just where hitters like it. If a guy hammers a high pitch, check the replay and see if the pitcher was using a slide step. The effort to stop a base stealer may have backfired. Another way that can happen is when catchers who are worried about base stealers call more fastballs. The ball gets to home plate sooner and gives the catcher a better chance to throw out the runner, but once again, hitters like fastballs. The catchers who call fastballs so they can throw out runners care more about their stats than the team. If a catcher calls a fastball, it should be because of the hitter, not the runner.

A team can do some things to shut down a running game, but those things can also help the guy at the plate.

How a pitcher changes the pitch

The catcher calls a fastball and the pitcher wants to throw a slider. If the pitcher wants to change the call, he might use adding and subtracting. Pitchers use two kinds of adding and subtracting: one I like, one I hate. The one I like is changing the speed of a pitch by a few miles an hour, adding and subtracting velocity to keep hitters off-balance. The one I hate is the pitcher changing the signals he gets from the catcher.

Here's how that kind of adding and subtracting works: Say the catcher puts down two fingers for a curve. If the pitcher uses adding and subtracting to change calls, he can swipe a body part with his glove to change the pitch. If jersey is "add," one swipe would change a curve—two fingers—to a slider, which is three fingers. If pants are "subtract," one swipe would change that curve sign—two fingers—to a fastball, which is one finger.

I think the whole thing is too damn complicated, but pitchers get paranoid about hitters stealing signs. Pitchers come up with all kinds of weird systems to prevent sign stealing. One pitcher wanted me to use the second sign after the previous pitch. If the previous pitch was a fastball, I'd run through a series of signs and once I gave the fastball sign—one finger—the second sign after the fastball sign was the real sign.

Lost? So was I.

I told the pitcher the hitters weren't stealing signs: *I* didn't know what was coming, so how the hell would the hitters know what was coming? Pitchers who want more complicated signs are usually guys who don't trust their ability. They don't think their stuff is good enough, so they want to trick the hitter. But I need to know what's coming—I'm a catcher, not a mathematician.

Here's how I suggest we solve the problem: if I catch a hitter stealing signs, we hit him in the ribs. Next time you watch a game on TV, pay attention to the catcher's eyes as he gives the signs; he'll be looking up at the hitter. Some hitters try to peek back at the sign without moving their head.

Another way hitters will steal signs is to get a signal from a runner at second base. If the runner can figure out our sign sequence, he might have a system set up so he can signal the batter if the pitch will be a fastball or off-speed. Two tugs on his pants will be something off-speed, one tug, a fastball. Two looks over the shoulder, off-speed; one look, fastball. There are a lot of ways to do it: adjusting the cup, shuffle steps; anything that can signal the hitter what's coming.

More often than signaling which pitch is about to be thrown, the runner at second base will signal location. If the catcher sets up too soon, the runner can let the hitter know if the pitch is going to be inside or outside. If you've got location, you may also have the pitch: if both the pitcher and the hitter are right-handed and the pitch is going to be inside, it's probably going to be something hard. The same goes for lefty on lefty. The runner at second base is why you see catchers set up late: they wait until the pitcher starts his motion because, by then, the hitter will have to focus on the pitcher, not the runner.

But instead of coming up with all these complicated signals to keep the other team from stealing signs, I say simplify it: if you think the other team is stealing signs, drill somebody. And let them know what you're doing: "Here's the deal: if that runner on second base signals location, we're going to drill you."

Trust me—they won't steal signs after that.

Fortunately, you don't see pitchers adding and subtracting to change signs as much as you used to, at least at the big league level. Most pitchers don't like to think too much when they're on the mound. If we've done our job going over the hitters before the game and between innings, we should be on the same page about what pitch to throw next. But if a pitcher still doesn't like the catcher's call, you're more likely to see him keep staring in (I didn't like that call, show me another one) or make a spinning motion with his bare hand (roll through those signs again). Both these methods are now more common than adding and subtracting.

Adding and subtracting velocity

If you're smart, you can use a hitter's count *against* the hitter. One of the best pitches in baseball is a 2-0 BP fastball. If you throw 90, everybody knows it. Radar guns are everywhere now—they're for the fans, but we look at that shit, too. If a pitcher's consistent—if he's throwing 90, 89, 91—you know what you have to sit on as far as a fastball is concerned, something about 90 miles an hour. You get to a 2-0 count and the whole ballpark knows a fastball is coming? Instead of throwing 90, throw 85. Take a little off.

Adding and subtracting velocity is the key to pitching.

Hitting is balance. The pitcher and catcher want to get the hitter *off-balance*. If you see 90, 90, 90, that's what you'll be ready for. You get to 2-0 and you're thinking, *Here comes my 90*—and all of sudden you get 85? You're off-balance. You swing too soon and hit a weak grounder to third. Drop a 90-mile-an-hour fastball to 85 and you're going to get some weak grounders, but it's not that easy to do. You've got to work on it. You can't let the hitter see the pitching motion or arm speed slow down. Otherwise, he'll adjust and stay back. Everything's got to look absolutely the same. Joe Blanton did it better than anybody else I ever caught.

You've got to figure out a way to take five miles an hour off the pitch without visibly changing anything. Change the grip, hold the ball farther back in your hand—do *something*. But work on it: learn to add and subtract velocity. It's hard work, but if you don't want to work, you've got no business being in the big leagues.

Tipping pitches

If a hitter is stealing signs, we'll retaliate, but if the pitcher is *giving* the pitches away, it's his own fault. Pitchers sometimes unintentionally let hitters know what's coming by tipping their pitches. The clues can vary. They might hold their hands in a different position for different pitches, they might vary their stance. Hitters and coaches are always looking for clues.

That's why you see some pitchers take the signs while holding the ball in the most difficult grip they have. It's often a split-fingered grip that requires them to jam the ball back between the fingers. They'll start in that difficult split-finger grip every time. Then—if the call isn't a splitter—the pitcher can switch to the easier grip for a fastball or slider without visibly moving the glove. If pitchers started with an easy fastball grip, *then* went to the difficult split-finger grip, hitters would see them struggle to make the switch in their glove.

Another way to prevent tipping pitches is the trick you see Ryan Dempster use: he covers up any glove movement that would tip pitches by moving the glove all over the place on every pitch. It may look weird, but it's brilliant.

A lot of pitchers think they're tipping pitches whenever they get hit. Pitchers are a different breed: 80 percent of them are insecure people with a great arm, 20 percent of them are bulldogs. If one of the pitchers in the 80 percent starts getting hit, he'll look for an excuse: "I must be tipping my pitches." No, dude, you just suck today.

On the other hand, if you're hitting and a pitcher actually *is* tipping pitches? It's great.

I was with Milwaukee and we were playing Houston. We were losing to the Astros and Jose Valverde came in to close the game. Valverde had two pitches, a fastball and a splitter. He was throwing out of the stretch, and when he reached the set position and paused for a moment, we knew he was throwing the split-finger. When Jose reached the set position and had almost no pause, it was the fastball.

It was so obvious the entire Brewers bench was calling out the pitches before he threw them. I worked the count to 3-2, saw the pause in his delivery and knew he was going to throw me a splitter. I took the pitch and walked. Mike Cameron was also reading pitches and walked. Ryan Braun also knew what was coming and hit a double. Prince Fielder came to the plate, fouled off pitch after pitch, and finally hit a home run to win the game.

Prince knew every pitch that was coming.

Another time I was facing Ted Lilly in Chicago. It was late September and we really needed the win. It's pretty unusual, but Ted had the habit of telling his catcher what he wanted to throw by silently mouthing the word *fastball* or *curve*. He'd do it whenever the hitter was looking away—finishing his swing or getting the signs from the third-base coach.

I'd caught Ted the year before, so I knew he'd do this. I never took my eyes off him. He could've thrown the ball at my head and, while I was falling over, I would've still been staring at the mound. The bases were loaded when I came to the plate, and I saw Ted mouth *curveball.* On the next pitch, I hit a double. After the game I saw Ted and said, "Dude, what are you *doing*? I saw you say 'curveball.' Did you forget I caught you last year?"

Ted said, "Oh, shit! I got so locked in on the plate I forgot!"

That time Ted made it pretty easy, but most of the time, the windup is where pitches are tipped. Pitchers might hold their glove in a different position on a fastball than they do on a breaking ball. The pitching motion might be faster or slower. The set position might be different. Every team has someone watch video and analyze opposing pitchers. When you know what's coming, hitting's a lot easier.

Unfortunately, some guys are so good it doesn't make any difference. I faced Johan Santana when he was with the Twins and the Mets, and you could tell when he was going to throw his changeup because he'd change his position on the pitching rubber.

But it was so nasty I still couldn't hit it.

Meetings on the mound

Too many meetings on the mound mean things are out of sync. There are a bunch of reasons to have a meeting on the mound; some good, some bad. We do it every time we change a pitcher, every time the manager thinks the pitching coach can help the pitcher get back on track, and we often do it the first time a pitcher gets a runner on second base.

With a runner on second we use a more complicated sign system, and we meet to make sure we're all using the same system. If you see a catcher use multiple signs the first time a runner is on second base, then go out to the mound after one pitch, that probably means the pitcher crossed up his catcher: he threw a different pitch from what the catcher expected. They thought they were using the same sign system, but weren't.

I might also go to the mound with a pinch hitter coming to the plate to make sure we're in agreement about how we want to pitch to him. But meetings should be kept to a minimum; they destroy the flow of the game and upset the pitcher's rhythm and pace. The infielders are rolling their eyes about having another meeting and start getting back on their heels defensively. The umpires aren't crazy about mound meetings either; they want to keep the game moving.

One thing I hate in those mound meetings are the players' covering their mouths with their gloves. This is supposedly done to keep the hitter from reading their lips. So you got a bunch of guys having a discussion while holding their gloves over their mouths, and they all sound like the adults in a Charlie Brown Christmas special—*waa, waa, waa, waa.* "Dude, you're worrying about the hitter knowing what you're saying and he's sixty feet away. I'm standing right next to you and *I* don't know what you just said."

That's one of the reasons those meetings take so long; no one can hear anything.

Another thing that bugs me is the meeting on the mound that happens right after the pitcher runs to cover first base. The guy sprints ten steps, and now someone has to come to the mound and slow the game down so the pitcher can get his breath back.

Really? And they call themselves professional athletes?

Position players like to give pitchers a hard time for being nonathletes, but I will give these guys credit for the effort they put into every pitch. How many times per game does a catcher throw the ball as hard as he can? Half a dozen? How about an outfielder? Three? Two? Zero? Starting pitchers give maximum effort a hundred times a game. The next day they're so sore they might need help going to the bathroom. Nobody knows what a starting pitcher goes through.

But even though having a lot of mound meetings bothers me, there are still good reasons to visit the mound. One of them is to buy time while a reliever gets ready. The catcher goes out to the mound and stalls as long as he can. Everybody can see the guy throwing in the pen, and we all know the real reason for the meeting. Eventually the umpire will come out and say enough, let's go—and the game will continue.

The manager has a sign he gives the catcher to tell him when to go to the mound and stall. It's the same sign we all use to signal "talking" (hold a hand up and tap the fingers against the thumb), and one day Jim Leyland gave it to me with Danny Darwin on the mound.

Danny was a forty-year-old veteran and was getting the crap kicked out of him that day. I was a rookie and scared to death. Leyland needed time for a reliever to get ready, so he gave me the sign to go talk to Darwin and stall—I shook my head no. I didn't want to go out there. Darwin was in a bad mood because of the beating he was taking, and I thought he'd rip my head off. I figured if Leyland wanted someone to go the mound and stall, *he* ought to do it. Leyland kept signaling for me to talk to the pitcher, so I eventually walked out to the mound and was greeted with the usual question:

"What the [bleep] are you doing out here?"

I didn't know what else to say so I asked, "What do you want to throw?"

"I don't give a [bleep], kid. Whatever you put down, I'll [bleeping] throw. Get back behind the plate."

Darwin didn't want to think, he just wanted to execute. For the most part, you don't want pitchers thinking about what they're going to throw. The Hall of Fame types might know what they want to do, but you don't want most pitchers thinking. That's when the ball gets up and gets whacked.

For the most part, the only time a catcher should go out to the mound on his own is when he and the pitcher aren't on the same page: "Can't you see Rodriguez isn't going to hit the slider tonight?" The catcher has the best idea of what the pitcher's stuff is doing that night, and the best idea of what the hitter is trying to do at the plate.

So stay behind the plate, drop the sign, move the game along, and keep the mound visits to a minimum.

Pitch counts

First of all, I think pitch counts are bullshit. Go ask Nolan Ryan, Tom Seaver, or Bob Gibson: Were those guys on pitch counts? Ask them what they would have said if they'd been told they were getting shut down and weren't going to pitch in the play-offs because they'd thrown too much. I'm pretty sure the first word would have started with an *f* and the second word would have started with a *y*. When the game's on the line with your ace on the mound, there shouldn't be a pitch count. But despite what I think, teams still use pitch counts; there's too much money involved. Nobody wants to be blamed for ruining an arm worth millions. For better or worse, here's how pitch counts work.

Say a starting pitcher is going to throw somewhere around a hundred pitches. Some guys will throw more, some guys will throw less; but let's say that a hundred is the pitch limit on this guy tonight.

If the starting pitcher averages fifteen pitches per inning, he'll be at 105 pitches after seven innings. It's great whenever a pitcher can go even deeper—it saves the bull pen pitches—but if the starter can go seven and leaves with a lead, he gets the ball to the back end of the pen. The back end of the pen is the setup man, who throws the eighth inning, and the closer, who throws the ninth. These are usually the two best relievers in the bull pen.

The other team wants to avoid these relievers if they can. They want to grab a lead *before* they get to the eighth inning and keep those guys in the pen. Unless one of his best relievers just needs some work, a manager isn't going to burn quality relief innings when he's losing a game. If the starter's pitch count is high, he might leave the game before he gets the ball to the back end of the pen. If that happens, the game goes to the middle relievers. These are the guys who pitch between the starter and the setup man and closer.

Getting the game to middle relief is what every offense wants.

It's why you see teams like the Boston Red Sox and the New York Yankees take so many pitches. No matter what the starter does, if the Sox or Yanks can get him out of the game after five innings, they've accomplished what they set out to do. They're facing what is probably the weakest part of the other team's bull pen.

That's the downside of a lot of strikeouts: pitchers who strike out a lot of batters also tend to throw a lot of pitches. Fans might be happy because the starter has struck out eight in five innings, but his pitch count is climbing. That high pitch count may mean the starter is going to leave early and give the other team a chance to win the game against middle relief.

Fans focus on the ninth inning, but the sixth and seventh are the hardest innings in baseball—without a doubt. If the starter is tiring and it's too early to bring in the setup man or closer, the manager has no choice but to hand the ball to a middle reliever.

Keep track of high-pitch-count innings early on. Fans might blame a middle reliever who blows a lead in the seventh, but the real problem was the second baseman who made an error in the fourth. If his error made the starter throw ten more pitches, it might be the second baseman's fault that the middle reliever ever came into the game.

Pay attention: lots of games are decided between the time the starter leaves and the back end of the pen comes into play.

Of course, the better the pen, the easier it is to hold a lead. If a team has three shutdown relievers, the starter can keep the game in the hands of the best pitchers by having a lead after just *six* innings. The best pen I ever saw was in Houston when the Astros had Brad Lidge, Octavio Dotel, and Billy Wagner. If you didn't have a lead against them after six innings, the game was pretty much over.

Bottom line, the starter wants as many quick outs as he can get. Ideally, he wants to have thrown maybe fifty or sixty pitches after five innings. I had a deal with all of my pitchers: give me at least one ten-pitch-or-less inning and win the game and I'll buy you a bottle of your favorite liquor. If you *don't* do that, you owe *me* a case of Bud Light.

And they say today's athletes aren't properly motivated.

How you know when the starting pitcher is done

I'd say when you hear the ball get hit really, really loud, but being as close as I am to the hitter, it's easier for me to hear when a batter crushes one. (The sound is *amazing*.) Here are some other things you can watch for:

Pay attention to pitch counts (even though I disagree with them): Most managers use them when deciding to pull the starter. Some starters can stay strong after throwing a hundred pitches and some may tire sooner, but once a starter is in the neighborhood of a hundred pitches, the bull pen is usually warming up.

Watch the pitcher's behavior: If he starts taking a long time between pitches, that's not a good sign. When a guy gets close to ninety pitches and he starts walking around the mound, going to the rosin bag, he's tired. Pay attention to bad body language.

Pay attention to location: When a pitcher is up in the zone, it's a bad sign. When a guy is pitching well, he'll be ahead in the count and down in the zone. When he starts to labor, he'll be up in the zone and behind in the count. The most important factor in a pitcher's success is being down in the zone, throwing low strikes.

Watch for long counts and walks: They can mean the pitcher is tiring and missing his spots.

Keep track of multiple at bats: Hitters who face a pitcher for the third or fourth time in a game have a better idea of what the pitcher's doing that night. That's why starters need more pitches than a reliever: the starter may need three or four ways to get a hitter out, a reliever needs one. If a hitter had success against the starter in his previous at bats, the manager may not want him to get a third or fourth look at the starting pitcher late in the game—especially in a crucial situation.

Check the bull pen: If the starter is getting near the end of his appearance and a left-handed hitter is due up, the manager will probably have a left-handed reliever warming up. If the left-handed hitter already has a couple hits—or even made a couple of loud outs—and another hit could do damage, the starter probably won't face him. That's what situational lefties are for.

Keep track of the winning run: If the starter is in line for the win and it's getting late in the game, some managers won't let him face the winning run. They figure the starter did his job—put his team in a position to win—and they're not going to let the starter take a loss. But it depends on the pitcher.

If he's a veteran, the manager might let him face a crucial out. If the guy has busted his ass for seven or eight innings and doesn't want to turn the ball over with a win on the line, the manager might let him go. In the same situation but with a young kid on the mound, the kid's gone. If the veteran fails, he should have enough experience and confidence to absorb the loss. If the kid fails, it might crush him. The manager might be trying to build the kid's confidence. Every win the kid gets, the confidence snowballs. The kid wins one—he starts to believe he can compete in the big leagues. He wins three or four—he starts to think he's a badass: the kid develops an attitude.

Remember, managers want to get their starter a win. It makes the starter happy and all the other starters jealous: "Hey, *he* got a win, now *I* have to get one." In all honesty, it's like high school: everybody's ridiculously competitive, but it makes everyone pick his game up.

A lot of my managers would rely on me to tell them what I thought about pulling the starter. The catcher knows what the starter has left. If the pitcher was starting to get up in the zone, that's a big thing. Another warning sign was when I found myself trying to trick hitters that I shouldn't be trying to trick. Say the right pitch is a fastball inside, but I know the pitcher doesn't have enough left to get that fastball in there. Now we're going to have to fool this hitter because what the pitcher has left at this point in the game isn't good enough. He's done.

I'd go tell the manager it was time to get the pitcher out of the game.

Bottom line: there is no magic formula for when a starting pitcher needs to come out of the game. It depends on the guy, the stuff he has that night, and the situation. But if you pay attention, you can at least start to figure out when a manager might make his move.

The bull pen

Without a doubt, starting pitching is the most important thing on a baseball team. But the bull pen isn't too far behind. And I'm not just talking about the closer; *everybody* has a role. Here are some of the different bull-pen roles and their responsibilities.

The long reliever: The long reliever is a guy capable of pitching multiple innings if need be. Different pitchers have different routines. The closer may not come down to the pen until late in the game; he knows he won't be used earlier. For the first few innings the middle relievers—the mix-and-match guys—might be goofing around, talking with fans. They know they probably won't get a call until after the fifth inning.

The long reliever has to be mentally ready right away. If the starter gets lit up early, the long reliever's the first guy out of the pen. But if the bull pen only has one guy capable of long relief, the manager might be reluctant to use him. Throw your long reliever for three innings on Monday and you won't have one available on Tuesday. That's when you see guys shuttle back and forth between the big leagues and the minors.

Depending on the situation, the manager may decide the starter needs to stay out there for a while and take a beating for the good of the team. Say it's the first game of a series: if the manager pulls his starter after two innings, he's going to use a lot of relievers by asking for seven innings from his bull pen. That means his team might not only lose the first game of the series, but the next two as well, all because his pen was used up in game one. Unless it's a must-win situation, the manager might decide his starter has to give the team enough innings to protect the bull pen from overuse. Sometimes a team has to accept losing a game today to have a shot at the team's winning a game tomorrow.

Middle relief: If the starter gets through five innings, the long reliever can usually relax; he won't be needed today. Now the middle relievers start focusing up and getting mentally prepared. These are the mix-and-match guys. The closer will face *whoever* comes to the plate—he should be that dominant. The mix-and-match guys are used against certain hitters and in situations where they should have an advantage. Especially in the American League, this is the manager's main job: get favorable matchups in the late innings.

Most bull pens have at least one left-handed specialist. His job is to come in and face a left-handed hitter in a crucial situation. The same thing might hold true for a submarining righty. Guys who have an unorthodox delivery can be tough—especially if the hitter only gets one look at them. A right-handed pitcher who throws from down under might be brought in to face a tough right-handed hitter. Another reliever might be a ground-ball specialist. When the team needs a double play, they'll bring this guy in. He's usually a sinker-ball pitcher who specializes in getting ground balls.

Some relievers can throw two or three days in a row and then need a day off. Guys who face one hitter at a time might be able to throw every day.

This mix-and-match portion of the game slows everything down. You might be flying along; you've played six innings in an hour and a half, but once they start bringing in three relievers to get through one inning, the game starts to crawl. Middle relievers are like linemen in the NFL: the only time they get noticed is when they screw up. A middle reliever can get a crucial out in the seventh, and by the end of the game, everyone forgets what he did.

The back end of the pen: The best relievers are in the back end of the bullpen. These guys throw the eighth and ninth innings. If a team has a really outstanding pen, they may have a guy who throws the seventh on a regular basis. These guys are usually so dominant they face whoever is due up—lefty, righty—it doesn't matter.

Fans sometimes see a guy throwing great in the eighth inning and wonder why the manager doesn't leave him in for the ninth; it's because everyone has set roles. Say you do send the setup guy back out for the ninth; suddenly you have a bunch of people wondering what's going on. The setup guy might have been great *because* he was maxing out on effort, knowing he was only throwing one inning. Ask him for more, and the next time he goes out, he might wonder if he's throwing one inning or two and change his approach.

The closer

Closers tend to have set routines; they go out to the bull pen at the same time every night, stretch at the same time every night, and get mentally prepared in the same way every night. A guy like Trevor Hoffman would do the same things every night whether his team was winning or losing. A 6-run lead can become a 2-run lead with one swing of the bat. A closer doesn't want to be caught off guard. If he *prepares* to close every night, then he's *ready* to close every night. Tell a closer to sit back down—the setup man is going back out for the ninth—and you throw a wrench in the works.

Then, if the setup man creates a mess, a closer is thrown into an unfamiliar situation: coming into a jam he didn't create. Sometimes relievers just don't have it when they leave the bull pen. They have to find it in the warm-ups or even after facing a batter or two. If you see a reliever give up a walk and a hit and *then* he's lights out, he may have found something while throwing to the first two batters. A guy who has that pattern may need a clean inning when he comes to the mound.

Relievers are not interchangeable: a guy may be lights out in the eighth, but ask him to pitch the ninth and he looks lost. Some guys can handle the pressure of closing, some guys can't. You see some guy whose stuff is unbelievable—but ask him to close a game and it's a disaster.

Closers are a different breed: one night they're a hero, the next night they're the goat. Twenty-four hours later and they're back to being the hero. They're sick—that's why they're good at what they do. Closers have a different mind-set. If it's three runs or less in the ninth inning, they go into "screw you" mode. They believe in their stuff and come right at hitters. You may beat a closer, but the good ones don't beat themselves.

If the other team has a dominant closer—a Trevor Hoffman, a Mariano Rivera, a Joakim Soria—you better grab a lead before the ninth inning. You don't want to see these guys. History says that if they come into a game, you're screwed. Once again, fans focus on the ninth inning, but pay attention to what happens in the eighth—that may be where the game is actually decided. The eighth inning may be the last legitimate chance to take a lead before a dominant closer comes in and shuts you down.

The insurance run

Say your team is up by one run going into the eighth inning and adds a run so you're up by two going into the ninth. That insurance run is huge. The closer can go right after people. He doesn't have to worry about a long ball tying up the game. Give up a homer and he still has a 1-run lead. Closers don't care about giving up a home run as long as they get the save. They just want to open the paper the next morning and see an *S* next to their name.

The insurance run also helps your defense. It means they don't have to guard the lines to keep a ball from going down into the corners and turning into extra bases. That means the corners can play back, off the lines, and cover more ground. It means the first baseman doesn't have to hold a runner. It means the pitcher doesn't have to mess around with slide steps or change his pitch selection to get the ball in the catcher's hands more quickly. It means the defense doesn't have to worry about the bunt; the other team won't play for one run in the ninth when they need two runs to tie.

The insurance run means the defense can concentrate on the hitter—at least until the tying run comes to the plate.

There are still a thousand things about pitching we haven't touched on, but pay attention to the things we *have* talked about and you'll have a better understanding of the game.

3
THE CATCHER

IT STARTED the night before. As soon as the last out was made in *that* game, I started thinking about what I was going to do behind the plate in the next game. Who's the starting pitcher? What reliever did we burn tonight? Who's available in the pen tomorrow? If it's late in a close game, what reliever will face what hitter? If Dan Plesac faces Larry Walker, what did Walker hit in that 3-1 count to get the run in from second base six weeks ago?

I'd come home, try to get some sleep, and wake up in the middle of the night saying, "2-1 fastball!" I'd actually say it out loud at four in the morning.

I remember when I blew my arm out. I got up in the middle of the night to get some Gatorade and couldn't lift my arm to open the refrigerator. I'd jacked up my arm sliding into a base the night before, but the next day I was gonna play no matter what; my son's baseball team was coming to see me. We were playing the Oakland A's that day. I had all these kids coming to see me, and I didn't know if I could throw a ball. My career was probably over and I was *still* thinking about how we'd pitch Coco Crisp—I was still going through the whole Oakland A's lineup.

I wish I'd never been like that—so obsessive—I would have liked to get a good night's sleep once in a while. But throughout my career I couldn't stop thinking about calling the next day's game. The brain of a catcher is like a hamster running on a wheel: it's going all the time. The guys who care about what they're doing, the guys who take pride in it, their brain does not stop for six months. I can't do my son's third-grade homework, but I can tell you what I threw Todd Helton in his first game in Three Rivers.

Catching is the most difficult, most intriguing position on the field.

Preparation

On the morning of game, I'd get up, get the kids to school, and head out to the ballpark. I'd get there at about 12:30 for a 7:05 game. The day's routine might change depending on how early or late in the year we were. Had we already seen this team or was this our first series against them? That would change your preparation.

You might prepare one way with a rookie pitcher on the mound, another way if the starting pitcher was a veteran. If the starting pitcher hadn't faced that particular team, you looked for somebody similar—another pitcher who throws the same way—so you could compare them. If you had a soft-throwing lefty starting that night, you found video of another soft-throwing lefty facing the same team. What worked for him? What didn't? Now you can start putting a game plan together for *your* soft-throwing lefty.

But everybody makes adjustments; what worked for the other guy a week ago might not work for us tonight. The good hitters adjust game by game, pitch by pitch. Could we get them out the same way another guy got them out last week, or have the hitters made an adjustment since then?

Calling a game is an art; it took me five or six years in the big leagues to figure it out. When I started, we were using VHS tapes. Nowadays when a catcher gets to the big leagues, they'll tell him to get an iPad and they'll load it with all the video he needs. I don't like computers, so I never did that, but every team has a video room and I'd go in there and find what I needed.

When I was watching video, I wasn't just looking at a similar pitcher; I'd also look at certain counts. What did the other pitcher throw Justin Morneau in a 2-1 count with a runner in scoring position? What did Morneau do with the pitch? You go over all these situations and what you plan to do in them. It didn't always happen, but when one of those situations came up, you were completely prepared: you knew just what you wanted to do.

Pregame meeting with the pitcher

Before the game I'd sit down with the pitcher. We'd go over the lineup, different situations, and how we were going to pitch certain guys. We'd talk about what we might do the first time through the order, and what we might do the second or third time. Some hitters you can keep pitching the same way; with the better hitters, you have to keep making adjustments.

We'd also look at the scouting reports; we'd go over who's hot and who's not. If the Twins were flying in that night and we hadn't played them in a month, we wanted to know what Mauer did last night in Chicago. What pitch did he hit? What did he do with it? What count was it? If that same situation comes up again tonight, Mauer might be looking for the same pitch.

The star players know exactly what you threw them two months ago in a 2-0 count. If you threw Joe Mauer a 2-0 changeup two months ago and got him out, he'll be sitting on a 2-0 changeup tonight—he'll make an adjustment and be ready for another changeup. So I'm not throwing him a 2-0 changeup this time around; I'm throwing Mauer something else.

If Mauer's sitting on a changeup, he's looking off-speed; that means he can still hit a curveball. So go inside with something hard instead. If Mauer got a 2-0 changeup last time, he's going to sit on that same off-speed pitch until he sees *us* make an adjustment. He'll sit changeup until he sees us throw something else in that situation. And I *won't* throw him that changeup in that situation again until I see *him* make an adjustment to hit something hard.

These are the games within the game.

Get the hitter thinking

Okay, what if Joe Mauer got a *hit* on that 2-0 changeup two months ago? Now he's looking for something else. He showed us he could hit that pitch in that situation, and now he figures we'll make an adjustment. *Unless* he starts thinking that I'll call the changeup again *because* he got a hit.

If a catcher thinks a guy is now sitting on a different pitch, he can get the hitter out by throwing the same pitch the guy hit the last time. I can't tell you how many times I've had that conversation with hitters after a game: "How could you throw me that pitch? Are you kidding me? What are you gonna do next?" That's the fun part of catching: You're screwing around with the hitters. You get them thinking about what you might do. And if you think when you're hitting? You're screwed.

Part of my job was to get the hitters thinking.

Gut instinct

The scouts do an unbelievable job with their scouting reports, but they're not behind the plate. They can't see the adjustments the hitter is making that night, pitch by pitch. Adjustments that change what the hitter is doing since the last time the scouts saw him. The scouting report might say don't throw this guy a curveball, but if my gut tells me it's the right pitch, that instinct is *always* what you go by. If I think it's the right pitch, I'm gonna throw it. If I get burned on it, go ahead and yell at me.

If the scouting report says throw this hitter fastballs down and away, what if your pitcher doesn't have that pitch tonight? What if he can't get it there right now?

Back there behind the plate I have a feel for the game that nobody else has. You have to go with that feeling, *all* the time. It may not always be right, but it is 99.9 percent of the time. When you go against that gut instinct, you're almost always wrong. Gut instinct is your subconscious talking to you. You may not even know what it is you've picked up on, but you've got to trust it.

Being on the same page

There's nothing better than being on a roll with your pitcher: it's the seventh inning and he hasn't shaken you off once. When you have a good relationship with the pitcher, you can put a sign down and he's already in his windup. He's not thinking, he's not wondering if this is the right call; he's putting all his concentration on executing the pitch.

The hard part is dealing with all the different personalities that show up on the mound. You've got to know which pitcher to kick in the ass and which pitcher to pat on the ass. So much more is going on out on the field than people realize. One pitcher's weak, another pitcher's a hard-ass. One guy goes with whatever you call, the next guy is hardheaded. But no matter who you have on the mound, the catcher has to take control.

If you're in the stands and you look up and the game's in the seventh inning an hour and fifteen minutes after it started, there's a pretty good chance the pitcher and the catcher are on the same page. If you see a pitcher shaking off the catcher's signs over and over, the catcher's not doing his job. If you see a lot of shakes and mound meetings, things aren't going well.

Calling pitches

Take all the information available—the video, the scouting reports, the spray charts, the hitters' hot zones—and how you call a game still changes night by night, especially with the good hitters. Mark McGwire, Jeff Bagwell, Sammy Sosa—you just can't generalize about how to pitch these guys. It's pitch by pitch, at bat by at bat, game by game. There's no one formula for calling pitches.

There are things that only a catcher can see. If somebody's flustered at the plate, he'll change position pitch by pitch. It might be really small: the hitter's hands are in a different position, or he opens up his stance a little bit. As a catcher, you're right there; you can *see* the uneasiness. When a hitter is flustered, he moves around in the box. He'll sell himself out for a pitch: he thinks he's getting a fastball down and away and he'll move closer to the plate to cover that pitch.

I can *see* the hitter adjust to what he thinks is coming.

And I'm the only one in the stadium who can see that—but you have to pay attention. The catcher is the only guy who can see the entire field. Managers and pitching coaches can't see everything from the dugout. Unless they turn around, pitchers can't even see the defense behind them. I also have a better idea of what a pitcher has than he does: I'm on the receiving end. A pitcher might think his slider is awesome that night, and I have to go to the mound and tell him it ain't that good—try something else.

That's why catchers call the pitches.

Most of the time when you see a big league catcher look into the dugout, he's getting signs to control the running game. In the big leagues, the bench isn't calling pitches. The bench keeps track of a runner's tendencies: the counts or situations that might result in an attempted steal. So the bench calls pickoffs, slide steps, and pitchouts for most catchers—although in my case, I liked to control the running game myself.

If the bench calls the running game, it allows the catcher to concentrate on calling pitches. And if the catcher calls the pitches, that allows the pitcher to concentrate on execution.

A pitcher can shake off the catcher's sign—ask for a different pitch—but a pitcher standing 60 feet 6 inches away can't see that the hitter has just moved his front foot an inch closer to home plate. If a pitcher trusts his catcher, the game goes much more smoothly: the catcher drops a sign, the pitcher nods his head and concentrates on throwing the pitch. But it takes a while to get that trust. If you want the pitcher to trust you, you have to be a stand-up guy. A pitcher needs to know that his catcher will take some of the responsibility for calling a pitch that gets crushed.

It took me years to begin to notice and understand how good hitters change during an at bat. When you're watching a game on TV, pay attention to the catcher's eyes; the catcher will look at the hitter's feet. He's reading the hitter's stance and figuring out what pitch the hitter's looking for—then a smart catcher will give him the opposite.

But how you go after a hitter changes every night. If the hitter's hot, we'll pitch him one way. If he's struggling, we'll pitch him another way. Everyone has spray charts, everyone knows where the hitter tends to hit the ball, what he does in certain counts, what parts of the zone he hits well. There's so much information available now.

During a game, I don't worry about any of that stuff. It's my job to know what's going on *that night*. I'll go with whatever's working for my pitcher *right now*. You always go with the pitcher's strength as opposed to the hitter's strength. As I said before, the scouting report may say, don't throw this hitter a curveball, but if my pitcher has a great curve going that night and the situation calls for a curve, I'll go with my gut, even if it contradicts the scouting report.

The scouts

These guys bust their butts. My brother's a scout, and he's one of the hardest-working major league scouts out there. My brother's one of the best at what he does. I played for fifteen years and he can *still* tell me stuff about a player that I didn't know. The scouts work just as hard as the players do; they travel nonstop so they can see everybody and give the players the information we need.

But there are still some scouting reports that cover the asses of everybody involved. A bad scouting report will tell you that you can pitch a guy up and in or down and away. No shit—that describes how you pitch everybody.

Good scouting reports say, you get this guy out *here* with *this* pitch—they're specific. "If you get this guy in a 2-2 count, throw him a fastball down and away and eight out of ten times he'll hit a weak ground ball." Or they might tell you, "This guy's a free swinger; he doesn't see three pitches very often; 0-0, you don't necessarily have to throw him a strike." They might also tell you what to avoid: "Don't throw this guy a 2-1 fastball; he's hitting .390 off when he gets one."

Other scouts might just give you generalities: the curveball down and away is a good pitch, the slider down and away is a good pitch, the change up down and away is a good pitch, the fastball up and in is a good pitch, the fastball down and away is a good pitch. Hey, you just covered everything; of *course* those are good pitches. The scouts just covered their asses by telling you what everybody already knows.

Scouts are like anybody else: there are good ones and bad ones. As a catcher, you know who the good scouts are; they'll tell you *specifically* how to get this guy out—*if* they have that information. If the scout thinks he's got something, he'll say, "*This* is what is going to get that guy out. If it doesn't work, it's my fault. I just watched five hours of video and he could *not* hit that pitch. Blame it on me if you throw it and it backfires."

The guys who put themselves on the line? Those are the ones that you go off of, not the guys who give you a bunch of generalities.

Taking responsibility

If you stick with the scouting report, you've covered your ass. Throw the pitch they told you to throw. If it gets hit? It's the scouting report's fault. If you go away from the scouting report because of what you see that night and the pitch gets whacked? It's on you.

Stick with the scouting report and you're safe, but I don't *want* to be safe. Safe means being predictable, doing what everybody else does. How about doing something a little bit off the wall? That's what wins games—that's what wins championships.

Safe is just covering your ass.

Say you go away from the scouting report. You can throw the right pitch in the right situation, but if the pitcher hangs it—if he doesn't execute it well—the fact that it was the right pitch won't make any difference. But if you try to cover *your* ass by going around saying it was the right pitch, but the guy on the mound didn't execute it, now the pitcher won't trust you. You call a pitch and blame the results on him? The pitcher thinks, *Screw this. From now on I'm throwing the pitch* I *want to throw.* When you call a pitch and it backfires, that's when you have to earn the trust of the pitcher. Take responsibility: I called it, blame it on me.

You want a catcher who knows what's going on, knows what's in the scouting report, but still isn't afraid to go against the report when the situation calls for it. You can't be afraid to get yelled at.

The safety zone

Down and away is the safety zone. You throw a good fastball down and away? Most of the time, you're not going to get hurt. You keep banging the glove down and away, down and away, down and away—and you get a hitter leaning out to cover that pitch?

Now you go up and in.

Let your catcher learn

In pro ball when you see a catcher look into the dugout, he's looking for signs to control the running game. In high school or college ball, when a catcher looks into the dugout, a lot of the time he's also getting the pitch. College coaches are reluctant to let a nineteen-year-old catcher control the pitch calling, so a kid who played college ball might be three or four years behind where he should be in terms of calling a game once he gets to the big leagues.

Doing it yourself is how you learn.

You're going to screw up, that's part of the process: you make a mistake and tell yourself not to make that mistake again. That's when a coach needs to call you to one side between innings and talk about why you called the pitch you did, what went wrong, and what you might do differently next time. But a lot of college coaches want to win right *now* because they're worried about their jobs, so they call the game themselves. In my mind it's also an ego thing; coaches need to take the ego out of it and let these kids learn.

Calling the game from the side also makes the games so much longer. And these college coaches come up with incredibly complicated signs: one touch after the third touch times two. Meanwhile the catcher's thinking, *Dude, all we want to do right now is go down and away with a fastball and I think we got him.*

Let your catcher call his own game; let your catcher learn.

Reading the hitters

Don't worry about a hitter's stance. They all start in different stances, but it doesn't make any difference because they all move to the same good hitting position: weight balanced, head still, hands back. You read hitters by checking *where* they set up. I knew every hitter's toe hole—the hole he digs for his back foot to get some leverage. I knew where every hitter set up in the box. If he changed, I'd notice. But the change might be really small.

If the guy moves his front foot a fraction of an inch away from home plate, that means he's looking for something in; throw something down and away.

If the hitter moves his hands a bit lower, he's getting beat inside, the pitcher's throwing too hard. The hitter's moving his hands a bit closer to where they need to be to hit a fastball; throw him something off-speed.

If the hitter takes his stance and his back foot opens up a bit, he's looking to pull the ball; throw something away.

If his back foot is slightly closed, he's looking to go the other way; bust him inside.

When a hitter changes his position in the batter's box, he might not even know he's doing it. He's looking fastball in and—without thinking about it—moves slightly away from the plate. I can look down at a hitter's feet and see what he's looking for. You also need to know what a hitter's done in his last ten at bats. If someone's been getting beat inside in his last ten trips to the plate, you'll see him open up his stance a bit. You've got to pay attention because the adjustment might be small.

If a hitter did something different—up in the box, back in the box—I knew.

Looking for an advantage

Some hitters want to set up *outside* the batter's box. Fans can see it. A hitter will walk up to the plate and use his foot to wipe out the back line of the box. They do that because they plan on making the toe hole behind that line—and it's usually your star players who try to get away with that. That's when a catcher needs to say, "No, no, no—get your ass back in the box."

If the hitter doesn't move up on his own, you tell the umpire to move the hitter back into the box. But a rookie catcher probably isn't going to tell a hitter to get his ass back in the box, especially if the hitter is someone like Albert Pujols—hell, a rookie's just happy to talk to Albert. If you've been around a while, you tell Albert to get his ass back in the box.

It's not like taking steroids, but *everyone* is looking for an advantage, an edge. How far can I bend this rule and still get away with it? If a catcher lets a hitter get away with that—setting up with his back foot out of the box—the catcher also has to move back or he's going to take a backswing to the head. Now the catcher is letting the hitter take six inches off the pitcher's fastball. If the catcher doesn't speak up, he's giving the batter an advantage.

It was a good pitch

One thing I hate is when a pitcher says, "It was a good pitch, but he hit it out." Hey, he hit it *out* of the ballpark; it was *not* a good pitch. The pitcher will say the pitch was down, but it wasn't down enough: the guy just ran around the bases. They'll tell you the pitch was six inches outside; well, make it *twelve* inches outside, because he just hit the shit out of it.

I can't *stand* the pitchers and pitching coaches that tell you a guy hit a ball 400 feet on a good pitch. It must not have been *that* good of a pitch; they just went up three runs. If it went off a sixty-year-old lady's head, twelve rows up in left center, it was *not* a good pitch.

When the game plan goes out the window

You go over the lineup and decide you're going to throw a slider in a certain situation, then the game starts and the pitcher doesn't *have* that slider—this happens a lot. That's the beauty of catching. You gotta say, okay, his slider's not working; now we *really* have to mix things up. That's actually fun. It's more of a challenge, but you can actually use the fact that your guy's slider *isn't* working to your advantage.

The hitters are now looking for a pitch that the pitcher doesn't have. They keep looking for that slider in certain situations and they're not getting it; you're changing the scouting reports. Scouts are everywhere—they're at every game. They've told the hitters what to expect. Every player knows how he's going to be pitched. So you use the fact that the slider has been shit-canned *against* the hitters. They're looking for a pitch that the pitcher isn't going to throw.

And sometimes the *pitcher* doesn't know he doesn't have his slider. He thinks it's fine and you have to go to the mound and tell him it sucks. You go to the mound, tell the pitcher the slider's not working, and ask him to trust you; you'll walk him through it. You try to get the starter through five innings, then get him the hell out of the game.

It's a mind game every night.

Any pitch, any count

Getting ahead in the count is the most important thing a pitcher can do—absolutely. Getting ahead gives you options: you can throw so many more pitches in an 0-1 count than you can when you're 1-0. You've got so many more options in an 0-2 count than you have when you're 2-0.

At the same time, when you get in those 2-0, 3-1 fastball counts, a pitcher can use that—*if* he can throw all his pitches for strikes. Just like the situation where the hitters are looking for a slider the pitcher doesn't have, the hitters are now looking for a fastball that the pitcher isn't going to throw.

If you see a pitcher throw a 3-0 curveball or 3-0 changeup, the hitter is looking for a fastball in those counts. The hitter might say the pitcher's scared because he didn't throw a fastball in a fastball count: the pitcher didn't challenge the hitter. But in my mind, throwing an off-speed pitch in a fastball count actually means the pitcher *isn't* scared: he'll throw any pitch in any count.

Knock on wood

On certain counts you have to get lucky to get away with the pitch you're about to throw, so maybe on a 2-0 fastball, I'd knock on wood for luck. There was no wood handy out there behind the plate—I didn't think the hitter would lend me his bat—so I'd knock on my own head.

Ray Miller was the Pirates pitching coach my rookie year, and he asked me about it: How come you're always knocking on your head? "Because I don't like the call, but I'm not going against Danny Darwin or Zane Smith. I'm knocking on wood for luck."

"That's funny, because I'm in the dugout going like this." He stuck his fingers in his ears and screwed his eyes shut—just like a guy waiting for an explosion. So if we were in a fastball count and about to throw a fastball from a guy who didn't have shit, I'd be knocking on wood and Ray would be plugging his ears. We knew something bad might happen on the next pitch.

And if you pay attention, so will you.

Having the balls to throw a 3-2 off-speed pitch

As I've said before, if you're in the big leagues, you should be able to throw any pitch in any count—you're *supposed* to be able to do that.

If a pitcher throws a 2-2 curveball, he better be unpredictable if the count moves to 3-2, because every hitter in a 3-2 count is looking for a fastball.

But does the guy on the mound have the balls to throw something off-speed in that situation?

I couldn't tell you how many times I was signaling for a 3-2 curve—two fingers—and the pitcher shook me off. Two . . . shake. Two . . . shake. Two . . . shake. I'd keep putting two fingers down and he'd keep saying no. That's when you call time and go out to the mound and have a meeting.

If there's a runner on first and the count's 3-2, that's a *great* time to throw something off-speed. Most managers—maybe 80 percent—will put the runner in motion on a 3-2 count. With two outs, putting a runner on first base in motion is automatic; with less than two outs it helps the offense stay out of the double play. The manager counts on the hitter to make contact if the ball is a strike or take his walk if the pitch is out of the zone.

If the pitcher has got a good straight change, a 3-2 count with a runner on first and less than two down is a great time to throw it. It looks like a fastball coming out of the pitcher's hand; if you get a swing and a miss, now you're in a strike-'em-out, throw-'em-out double-play situation. Putting the runner in motion on a 3-2 count is so common that it's a good time to try a pickoff at first base. The runner at first usually gets a lousy jump because he has to wait to see if the pitcher is really going to the plate. In my opinion, the changeup is one of the better pitches you can throw 3-2.

But you've got to have the balls to throw it.

Shaking off calls

If a pitcher shook off one of my calls, I'd think, *All right, go ahead. He* had the feel of the ball in his hand, not me. But in a situation where I was thinking, *No, no, no*—you need *to throw this pitch,* I'd call time and go to the mound. "Hey, if you want to throw that pitch, you better bury it. The other pitch is the right one to throw, and all you have to do is hit my glove."

I might have the right idea, but the pitcher might not have the feel for the pitch I called for *right then.* A pitcher can lose the feel of a pitch during a game and get it back two innings later. I *know* the right pitch is a fastball down and away, but if the pitcher feels better about his slider at that point in the game? I'm not the one throwing the pitch. But once again, the pitcher can't see what I can see behind the plate. That's why I'm out at the mound.

Nowadays a lot of catchers won't do that: go out and argue for their pitch. They let the pitcher shake them off and figure, "Okay, whatever." Young catchers have to learn to take charge. But it takes time: you have to earn that respect. You don't want pitchers to think; you want them to execute. The more the pitcher trusts you, the better his execution will be. It's just like hitting: the more you think, the worse you get. If you've got a pitcher out there thinking, *I don't know if we should throw this pitch—maybe we should throw the other one,* that's when he's going to hang something: he's going to leave it up in the zone. You want a pitcher with a clear mind; he sees you drop a sign and he throws it.

But if he's *convinced* he wants something else? Okay, I'm not throwing it, he is.

Suggesting versus demanding pitches

The final call on whether or not a pitch gets thrown is up to the pitcher—*most* of the time.

But if it's a crucial situation in the game, a catcher calls the right pitch and sticks with it. It doesn't matter who's on the mound: veteran or rookie. *You're* the one behind the plate. You're the only person in the whole stadium that knows. *This is it, this is the right pitch.* If the pitcher puts the ball where I want him to, the hitter's out.

You put down a two . . . the pitcher says no. Two . . . the pitcher says no. Two . . . the pitcher says no. Okay, time to go to the mound. I put it down three times, and the third time he shakes me off? I'll go out to the mound and argue for my pitch. He could be Greg Maddux and I could be Joe Blow—I'm *still* going out there.

The rest of the time it's a suggestion: you don't have the ball in your hand—the pitcher's got the feel—but with the game on the line? You go out and argue. I'm not saying every pitch I call is the right pitch, but the catcher has a better feel than anybody else in the whole stadium about what pitch should be thrown next. I'd go out and say, "You *really* want to throw this fastball? Okay, but you know what? You better hit my glove."

At that point a lot of pitchers would agree to throw the curve: they didn't want the responsibility if *their* pitch got whacked.

Pitchers are the most important part of the game. I'd love to say that catchers are the most important part of the game, but they're not—it's the pitchers. How hard I fight for my call depends on the situation. If it's the second inning and the score's 0–0, and I call for a fastball down and away because I think it's the right pitch, but the pitcher says he wants to go inside? I'd say, all right, throw it, let's see—prove me wrong. But if it's the eighth inning and the score's 1–1 and there are runners on base? I'm going out to the mound to say, "You want to throw the slider? You *better* bury it." In the second inning the wrong pitch might not lose you the game—you've still got time to make up for anything bad that happens. In the eighth inning the wrong pitch can put you in a hole you don't have time to climb out of—that's the difference.

But I'm still not the one on the mound. *I* think the fastball down and away is the right pitch. If a pitcher wants to throw the slider, he *better* throw it with conviction; a pitcher needs to throw *every* pitch with conviction. If a pitcher tells you, "I can do it, I can do it, I can do it"—okay, show me. If the pitcher throws it and gets away with it, maybe you trust *him* a little more. If he throws it and it gets smoked, maybe he trusts *your* call the next time.

Pretending to shake off the catcher

If I'm catching and we're in a 2-0 count, I might give the sign to the pitcher while shaking my head. If you see the catcher give a sign to the pitcher and shake his head at the same time, he's telling the pitcher to shake *his* head. The catcher wants the pitcher to pretend he doesn't want to throw the pitch the catcher just called. The catcher is telling the pitcher to shake him off: to pretend to ask for a different pitch.

Everybody knows 2-0 is a fastball count. A fastball is the most common pitch in baseball, so whenever a pitcher shakes off a sign, a lot of hitters figure the pitcher wants to throw something off-speed. A hitter sees the pitcher shake—especially a young hitter, a less experienced hitter—and he thinks he might not be getting a fastball. If I ask the pitcher to shake twice, now the hitter *really* doesn't know what to think.

Once we put that thought in the hitter's head—that we might be throwing something other than a fastball in a fastball count—we've got a better chance of getting away with throwing a fastball, just like we planned all along. The hitter looks off-speed in a fastball count and we lock him up—freeze him—when we stay with the fastball. And fans will wonder why a hitter just took a fastball down the middle in an obvious fastball count.

Multiple signs with a runner on second base

Pitchers and catchers have a set of signs in place so they can communicate without a runner on second base seeing the signs and signaling the hitter what pitch we just called. For example: *last sign, shake, first.* The catcher gives a series of signs, but the only one that matters is the last sign. If the pitcher shakes that sign off—if he doesn't want to throw that pitch—the catcher gives another series of signs and the only sign that matters is the first sign of the next series. That's how *last sign, shake, first* works.

You could also use *last sign, shake, last*—same deal. Or *first sign, shake, last* or *first sign, shake, first.* If you see a pitcher shake off the catcher with a runner on second base, most of the time it's the first sign in the next series of signs because nobody wants to play a five-hour ball game.

Pitchers get paranoid. They've got all these different sequences they want to use: *outs, plus one* (if there are no outs, it's the first sign; if there's one out, it's the second sign; it there are two outs, it's the third sign) or *previous pitch, plus one* (we just threw a curve, so once the catcher flashes a two, the next sign counts). We're going through all this bullshit to communicate, and I take a glance at second base and the runner isn't even looking at the signs—and if you've got a pitcher with a peanut for a head, you better use something simple.

Getting crossed up

With all these sets of signs it's easy to get crossed up; you're looking for a curveball and get a 95 mph fastball. You take one of those off the mask and it hurts. Fastballs are coming in so hard a catcher has to know what direction a fastball will move—if it will run, sink, or cut—to have any chance of catching the ball cleanly. I'd tell pitchers, "Here's the deal, bro. That pitch is coming in at ninety-five miles an hour. I can't adjust in time. I have to know what you're throwing."

Like I said, that's what happened to my thumb: I was looking for a pitch down and away from a left-handed pitcher and he threw a cutter inside. Hey, let me *know,* dude. I've got too many other things on my mind. I just called a pitch and I got something I'm not looking for? My glove hand got caught in an awkward position and the pitch tore every ligament in my left thumb.

Any wonder I hate all these complicated sets of signs for calling pitches?

I still can't bend my thumb all the way. They took ligaments from my wrist and rebuilt my thumb. I snapped *everything* in that thumb. I've had a lot of surgeries; the one on my thumb was the worst. I used to be able to swing a bat with two hands, but after that injury, every time I connected with the ball, it was like a knife going into my hand. I started releasing my top hand and any power I had was gone.

If you've got a pitcher with good run or sink on his fastball, you've got to know what's coming. It's not as important if nobody's on, but with a runner on base, you need to know what the pitcher's about to throw. Otherwise you're going to have passed balls all over the place—and maybe a screwed-up thumb.

Know the signs in advance

To make this all more confusing, each pitcher has a different set of signs he wants to use with a runner on second base. Every starting pitcher also has a second set of signs he wants to use if we think the runner on second base has figured out the first set. When you see the catcher hold his throwing hand up and spin it in a rolling motion, he's signaling the pitcher and the infielders that he's switching up the signs: he's going to the second set of signs. Infielders change their positioning based on the pitch, so they also need to know what's coming.

I can't stand it when a reliever comes in, warms up, and the catcher has to go out to the mound and ask what signs they're using with a guy on second base—it's a waste of time. A catcher should *know* what signs each guy uses. A runner on first gets to second and you've got to waste thirty seconds going out to the mound to go over signs? What does that do to the infielders and outfielders?

They go from being on the balls of their feet to being on their heels: it hurts your defense.

If you get crossed up, if you're not on the same page, fine, go to the mound and straighten things out. But other than that, a catcher should already know the signs each pitcher likes to use before the game ever starts. If a reliever starts an inning, you should *not* see the catcher have to go out and check the signs they're going to use; but it still happens 80 percent of the time. All you're doing is getting your defense on its heels.

A catcher needs to take care of this before the game even starts. If he's got a new pitcher on the staff—a guy who just got called up from Triple A or came over in a trade—the catcher needs to get together with the pitcher and make sure he knows what signs the new pitcher likes to use with a runner on second base. But you do this at two o'clock in the afternoon, not during the game. If a catcher didn't take care of this beforehand—if he goes out to the mound, lifts up his mask, and wants to go over the signs—it's probably somebody wanting a little more TV time.

A meeting with the runner at second base

A catcher can tell when a runner at second base is trying to steal signs; the runner will be focusing just a little too hard on home plate. Sometimes I'd go to the mound to talk to the *runner,* not the pitcher. I'd leave my mask on so no one could tell what was happening, but I'd let the runner know if he kept trying to steal signs, someone was going to get hurt—and it was probably going to be him.

I've had the same thing happen to me when I was on second base. I've had pitchers tell me to quit looking at home plate, and I'd tell them to get screwed. At that point, most guys drop their heads.

Most of the time I wasn't stealing signs; I was afraid of screwing up the hitter. I had a hard time seeing that far even after I had eye surgery. It's hard to see the signs from second base when the sun's going down and the catcher's wearing white pants. Later in the game it was hard to see the signs if the catcher was wearing gray pants. Granted, at times the lighting was better, and I could see the signs, and I had them—if a catcher's on second base and he sees three or four pitches, he's got the signs.

If I could see the signs and it was obvious, I'd pass it along. But most of the time I didn't do that. You tell a hitter to expect off-speed and he gets a fastball? You talk about shittin' yourself. I just didn't want to screw anybody up.

Even though I wasn't stealing signs—most of the time—I wasn't going to let anyone tell me to quit looking in. People are afraid of confrontations. These kinds of situations are like playing poker: you're calling someone's bluff. Most people don't like confrontations or controversy—it looks bad on their résumé. Nobody wants to be in a confrontational situation, but what if you're in one anyway? If the runner at second base is looking in and stealing signs, you either say something or back down and give the other team an advantage. If I confronted a runner about looking in, most of them would back down. They'd start staring into the outfield or get real concerned about checking the shortstop—they'd twist their heads off to the side just to make sure I knew they weren't staring in to the plate.

But if I told a runner to quit staring in and he told me to shove it and get my ass back behind the plate? We're fighting right there and then. Would I think a guy who stood up to me did the right thing? Absolutely—I'd respect the guy for standing up for himself. I'd probably try to beat the shit out of him, but I'd respect him while I was doing it.

Multiple at bats

A starting pitcher does not want to show all his pitches the first time he goes through the other team's lineup. He'd like to save something for later at bats, usually an out pitch he wants to use with the game on the line. But getting through the order on just a fastball and changeup isn't always going to happen, especially if the pitcher gets in trouble in the first inning. If he has people on base right away, chances are pretty good the pitcher will throw every pitch he has just to get out of the first inning with as little damage as possible.

If a pitcher can make it through the lineup the first time with nothing but a fastball and a changeup, he's in good shape. It doesn't happen that much, but if he can do that, the team hitting against him is probably in trouble. Here is where adding and subtracting velocity comes in. If you're in a fastball count and you want to throw a fastball, take a few miles an hour off. If you've been throwing 90 all night, throw one 87. It may only be three miles an hour, but to the hitter, that's a huge difference.

Pay attention to which pitches a starting pitcher throws the first time through the order and you'll have a better idea of how he'll do the second and third times.

Starters versus relievers

Relievers don't have to worry about saving pitches and getting hitters out three different ways in one night, but they might have to get a hitter out three different ways over a series. Say left-handed reliever Dan Plesac faces someone like Ichiro Suzuki in the first game of a series; Plesac might face Ichiro tonight, tomorrow night, and the night after that. With some hitters, Dan could get them out the same way every night—with a hitter like Ichiro, Plesac better mix it up.

If you get Ichiro out one way on Wednesday, you might need another way on Thursday. If you got him out on a curve on Wednesday, he'll probably be looking for a curve on Thursday. That's where reading the hitter comes in: a catcher should watch the hitter's feet and hands; a catcher can tell if a guy's looking for a breaking ball, so you throw him a fastball.

If you get him out one way on Wednesday night and then Ichiro does something different Thursday night, *you* go with something different. If you *see* something different, that tells you to *throw* something different. That's what good hitters do, they adjust. Larry Walker, Tony Gwynn, Barry Bonds, Todd Helton—your All-Stars, the guys who hit .330 every year—they change pitch by pitch.

Relievers can't see shit from the bull pen, it's too far away; but some of them still come in and shake you off repeatedly. They don't want to throw what the catcher calls. You know what? Screw you. I've been back here for seven innings; you ain't shaking me off. Relievers might be prepared—they've read the scouting report or faced the guy in the past—but a hitter might have changed throughout the game. The relief pitcher can't see it from that far away; it's impossible. The catcher's been back behind the plate for a hundred or more pitches. He's the one that knows what's happening *that night.*

It goes back to the trust thing: relievers need to trust their catchers—and catchers need to remember that the pitcher is the one with the ball in his hand. But in the end, calling the right pitch is *always* on the catcher: that's my job—calling pitches is what I do. But if the pitcher can convince me to go with a different pitch, he better throw the shit out of it. If he doesn't and the pitch gets whacked, I'm going to air his ass out. I'll do it one-on-one—when nobody else is around—but I *will* air his ass out.

Making adjustments over the long term

Smart hitters not only adjust pitch by pitch, they also adjust over a season. If we're in August, a hitter might be a little late on the fastball at that point; he might be tired. At the end of the year, a hitter might make an adjustment to get around on a fastball. His hands might not be held as high, they might not be held as far back: he's shortening his swing. He might move back in the box a little more to buy a little more time.

Most hitters, every time they step in the box, they put their feet in the same place. If a hitter changes where he puts his feet, a catcher needs to ask himself why. When you're behind the plate, noticing this stuff should be automatic; it should be like Good Will Hunting shit.

Hitters will also go to lighter bats later in the year; they're getting worn down and feel slow at the plate. If the hitter dropped his bat by the plate, I'd pick it up and hand it to the batboy. While I was doing that, I'd also check the weight and model. It's written right there on the knob. All my bats say 33/31 (inches/ounces) or 33/32 or 34/31. If a hitter is changing models, it might let you know what kind of adjustment he's trying to make at that point in the year.

And players *have* to make adjustments.

The guys who stick around for ten or fifteen years are the ones who have made adjustments throughout the season *and* their careers. When you're twenty-one years old, you feel like you're Superman: you can do anything and everything. You feel like you don't *have* to make adjustments because you're so strong and so quick—that's how it is when you're young.

Cut to eight, nine years later: you're a little slower—it happens to every player. When it happens, you're *gone* if you don't make adjustments. That's *it*—no ifs, ands, or buts. You can't be stubborn and pretend you're the same player you were when you were twenty-one. You're not as quick, you're not as fast—you're smarter—but your physical ability isn't what it was when you were twenty-one. You were Superman when you were twenty-one, but nine years later, a little bit of Kryptonite has kicked in.

Even young players might have to adjust during a season. You get tired later in the year, especially if you've never played 162 games before. A veteran will come over and say, "Hey, dude, instead of swinging a 34/32? Try a 33/31." Taking an inch off the bat's length and two ounces off its weight can make a difference at the end of year.

You see young guys come up, play a longer schedule, and start to drag in August and September. At the end of the season, ballplayers are *tired.* You're playing every day, you're going from time zone to time zone, you go from hundred-degree weather to sixty-degree weather—by late September, you're flat-out *tired.*

The young guys have never had to deal with this before so they try to tough it out. When you've been around a while you realize you better admit you're tired and make an adjustment. If you've been swinging a 34/32 all year and you've never played 162 games? A 34/32 is going to feel like a 38/38 before the end of the year.

Whatever adjustment a hitter makes—changing his batting stance, where he sets up in the box, or the bat he uses—a smart catcher will pay attention and use that information to try to get him out.

The hot hitter

Everybody pays attention to the All-Stars, the number three or four hitters, but if the hitter at the plate is six out of the last ten—he might be the 8-hole hitter, but *he's* the hot one. *He's* the one you've got to look out for. You don't want the big boys—guys like Barry Bonds or Jeff Kent—to beat you, but you know what? If J. T. Snow is ten for his last twelve, he's hot as hell. If Bonds is one for his last ten and Kent's two for his last fifteen, pitch to Bonds and Kent.

Why?

The guy who is ten for his last twelve is more dangerous *right now.* If Bonds and Kent are scuffling and Snow is hot, that's something you have to know going into the game. If I'm making that choice, I'm pitching to Bonds and Kent. Granted, you don't want either Bonds or Kent to beat you, but you always base your decisions on what's happening *right now.* And right now, J. T. Snow is dangerous.

Frustrating the hitter

My last ten years in the big leagues, it became so much fun to call a game; to screw around with the hitters. There's nothing better than getting a guy so frustrated he's throwing his helmet in the first couple innings. If you see that, the guy is *done* for the series. He might get a couple hits here and there, but I'm in his head. If you fool a guy, get him to roll over and hit a ground ball to third because he was looking for something else, and he goes in the dugout and starts throwing stuff and cussing? As a catcher, I'm laughing: "Dude, I've got you. You're screwed!"

And I know *he's* thinking the same thing. If he gets in a big situation later in the series, he'll start thinking about what happened earlier. That one at bat will affect him for three games.

If you see frustration—especially early in the game—that guy is done for three days. Now he's trying to guess with me, and you don't want to think when you're hitting. Now you've got the hitter second-guessing himself. If you see a guy banging his helmet in the first inning, the catcher can play with the guy for the entire series. That's the game within the game for a catcher: you've got that hitter in the palm of your hand.

So watch for a guy who gets easily frustrated in the first game and see what he does over the rest of a series.

Bringing the intensity level down

You want to keep the mound visits to a minimum, but sometimes you need to go out there just to bring the pitcher's intensity level down. It depends on the pitcher and the situation. Some serious conversations occur out on the mound—conversations about mechanics or strategy—but sometimes you're just changing the pitcher's mind-set. Sometimes you just go out and say, "What's up, bro?"

Pitchers can get so amped up that they need to be brought back down. Sometimes they're getting the ball up in the zone because they're overthrowing. Instead of talking mechanics, you might tell them to check out the redhead sitting behind the dugout or ask where they want to eat that night or how their kid's baseball game went the day before.

You get their mind *off* pitching—and they calm down.

Separating offense and defense

Catchers have to split the two up, more so than any other position. Between pitches you might see outfielders practicing their swings while they're on defense; catchers can't do that. An outfielder can lose focus for a while and, if a ball isn't hit his way, nobody will ever know. If you take what you do on offense behind the plate—if you lose focus calling pitches—you're screwed.

If I had a bad offensive night, but did well behind the plate, I figured that was a good night. There's always something you can do to help your team out, even when you suck at the plate. But the game still revolves around hits; every player looks at the scoreboard. Some guys get a couple hits and start digging themselves. When a guy is getting hits, he can lose focus on his defense. He's out there on the field, but he's checking out the scoreboard and thinking about his batting average. Now a ground ball that he usually gets to is a single up the middle because he wasn't locked in mentally.

Players *dig* their offense.

But is a player the same player once he gets a couple of hits? It's a mental thing: the guys who are mentally tough stay the same no matter what's going on. The guys who aren't mentally tough tend to let their mind wander once they've got their hits. The team's batted around and you've got two hits by the second inning? You're the *shit.*

But how is it going to affect your defense?

You have to separate the two. Otherwise, it's easy for a catcher to get passive with his pitch calling when he's hitting well. If the pitcher shakes him off, he figures, "Hey, you don't want to throw that pitch? Okay, whatever." You have to separate offense from defense whether you're going good *or* bad. Going good can be just as distracting as going bad. If you're digging yourself because you have a couple of hits, you're not concentrating. If you're moping because you don't have any hits, you're not concentrating. When you're not concentrating, you might let a pitcher throw the wrong pitch, and it might be the pitch that costs you the game.

If you get excited because you got two hits, your focus isn't where it should be. Separate your offense and defense.

Going unnoticed

If a catcher goes unnoticed for a whole game—I'm not talking about offense, I'm talking about defense—the catcher did a good job. On defense, the less a catcher gets noticed, the better a catcher he is. That's why I never took my mask off.

I can't *stand* catchers who take their mask off. That's a "Hey, look at me" move. You go to the mound and take your mask off? You get noticed. Watch how many catchers constantly take their mask off these days. If you're thinking about TV time or how awesome you look standing on the mound, you're probably not thinking about the right stuff.

Defense is rewarding, but it's totally different from offense: defense generally goes unnoticed. Everybody wants to get three knocks, but what a catcher does *behind* the plate matters more than what he does *at* the plate—without a doubt. You gotta hit, too, but—bottom line—you get a catcher who hits .230, .240, and can call a game? Nowadays a lot of teams will take that.

Catching the ball

Anyone who talks about "framing" a pitch is full of shit. You *catch* the ball, that's it. You just *catch* the ball. If a broadcaster says that's a great job of framing? No, the catcher just *caught* the ball. If you make an exaggerated show of catching a borderline pitch, it's fifty-fifty if the umpire is going to call it a strike. All that dramatic framing—snatching the ball back into the zone—makes the umpire feel that maybe it wasn't such a good pitch. After all, if it was a strike, why did you have to change the way you caught the ball?

Exaggerate holding the ball in place and it won't help you get the call. There's no such thing as framing; anybody who says there is can go screw himself. Umpires want to see you *catch* the ball. If the pitch is on the black and the catcher makes a big deal out of catching it? That's going to be a ball. Everything is supposed to be quiet and soft: catch the ball like you were catching an egg.

If I want to get a pitch, I might subtly shift my body when I'm making the catch. Now a pitch that was going to be caught above my right knee is being caught in the center of my body. When the umpire looks down, it looks like it was going to hit me square in the chest protector. If I'm reaching out to one side or the other—outside my knees—the pitch won't look like a strike. Everything happens so quickly. You can get away with a subtle shift of the body to keep the pitch centered—but only a *subtle* shift. Do it too much and you won't get away with it. The umpire will see it and figure you wouldn't have to do that if the ball were a strike.

But the main thing is still soft hands: you catch the ball, you *don't* frame it. There's no such thing.

Lobbying the umpire

To make things even more complicated, the strike zone changes nightly depending on the umpire behind home plate. I've had beers with 80 percent of the umpires, and I talk to them nonstop during a game. They're all good people; they're busting their butts just like we are.

After a while, you develop a relationship with an umpire and you can get away with complaining a bit: "Hey, you just gave the *other* guy that pitch." I might get the umpire to take another look at it and start giving us the same pitch. When I'm behind the plate, I'm always lobbying for my pitcher—you have to. There's no doubt veteran pitchers get calls rookie pitchers don't. When that happens, it's my job to argue for my pitcher, no matter how young he is.

All this negotiating goes on every inning, right in front of the fans, but as long as we all keep staring straight ahead, the crowd won't know what's happening.

Say my pitcher doesn't get a call on the outside corner. I might say, "Are you kidding me? That ball is *not* outside. I'm going right back out there; he's going to be there all night." I'm putting in the umpire's head the idea that this pitch might be a strike—but the hitter also hears. Now the idea that a pitch in that location might be called a strike is in the *hitter's* head. He might decide he better swing at it next time. If the hitter starts swinging at that pitch because he thinks the umpire might give it to me, I've changed the strike zone.

Sometimes the arguing includes the batter. Say I'm hitting, Ivan Rodriguez is catching, and the late Wally Bell is umpiring. Wally calls a pitch on the outside corner a ball and Ivan complains. I'm not letting that go by, so I say, "Don't listen to Ivan, Wally. That's a good call. I catch, too, and that pitch was off the plate." Ivan and I are both catchers, and now he's trying to do the same thing to me that I do to everybody else—and I'm not letting him get away with it. The three of us can argue all we want, and as long as we follow the unwritten rule—as long as we keep staring straight ahead—nobody knows we're arguing.

But say an umpire gets fed up with the complaining and decides to confront the catcher face-to-face; the umpire can hide the confrontation by cleaning the plate. Fans won't know it, but he might be telling the catcher it's time to knock it off. Catchers and umpires can hide disagreements as long as the catcher doesn't look back at the umpire or the umpire doesn't come out in front of the catcher without cleaning the plate as a cover-up. If either of those things happens, it means we don't care who knows that we're bitching at each other and we'll go at it.

Most of the time, it's all forgotten the next day.

We were playing the first game of a series and I was scuffling offensively. I hit a little jam shot off Julian Tavarez to short and beat it out. The first-base umpire, Jim Wolf, called me out. I got in his face because I *really* needed that hit. If you're hitting .330, a blown call doesn't kill you—you might let it go. If you're scuffling and a call is blown, you might go ballistic.

I was going bad, so I really went off on Jim. In the middle of the argument, I started to gag on my chew. I had my fingers down my throat, trying to dig the tobacco out to keep from choking to death, but everybody thought I was planning to throw the chew at the Jim. I got tossed out of the game because of what I said to him about costing me a hit. The next day Jim was behind the plate. I walked up and said, "What's up, dude? Sorry about yesterday, you caught me on a bad day."

That stuff happens, now we're friends.

Umpire-catcher relationships

Because we keep staring straight ahead—because we follow that unwritten rule—most people don't realize that throughout a game the catcher and the umpire are talking nonstop:

"Where was that pitch? That's a good pitch right there, Bob, whad'ya think?"

"I got it a little out."

"It's not out, Bob. He's gonna be there all night. If he was wild, I could see it."

All this talking goes on, but the catcher never turns his head around. If a fan pays attention, he might see our heads bobbing up and down; then he knows things are getting animated. But you never want to show up anybody on a baseball field. If you do turn around—if you let the crowd know you're disagreeing with the umpire—somebody's getting ejected.

In some ways, the umpires have it harder than players: they're in a city for three days—boom—gone to the *next* city for three days. They live out of a suitcase for six months; they've got no home games. Granted, they get some time off, but they're out there busting their asses, just like we are—and they don't get to sit down every half inning.

The better a catcher's relationship is with an umpire, the better it is for your pitcher. If the pitcher is consistent, you can talk to the umpire and get your pitcher that borderline pitch; if he's all over the place, you won't. But if the pitcher keeps banging the same spot, I can say, "C'mon, Bob, he's pretty close. He's going to be there all night." If a guy is consistently hitting a spot, I can eventually get that call for him. The pitcher's demonstrating control. He's on the black—the border of the plate—because he *wants* to be on the black, he's *that* good. If a pitcher is hitting the black one out of five times, he ain't gettin' shit.

Bottom line, if you throw strikes, you're gonna get calls. If you don't throw strikes, you won't. Umpires *want* to call strikes, but if you're all over the place, you're not going to get that borderline pitch. If a pitcher who's wild throws a borderline pitch, doesn't get the call, and gets upset, you know what? Your previous four were all over the place—one out of five don't cut it.

Sometimes the umpire has a bad relationship with the pitcher on the mound; maybe they had a previous disagreement. In that case, it's the catcher's job to mediate. You go to the umpire and say, "Here's the deal, man, I know you guys had a run-in, but it's about tonight. I'll calm his ass down, but you give him his shit—don't squeeze him." That kind of thing goes on for nine innings.

As a catcher, I'm not only thinking about the pitcher and the hitters he'll face, I'm also thinking about the umpire. What can we get from the guy behind the plate tonight? If the umpire's got a wide zone, I can tell the pitcher that. I'll set up off the plate, tell the pitcher to keep banging the glove, and I'll get that pitch for him. But to do that, I've got to know the umpire's zone and I've got to know the umpire. I tell young catchers to establish a relationship with the umpires. The first thing I always did when I walked out there was ask, "How you doing, Jim? How's the family doing? Kids all right? How old are they now?"

It took my having kids to figure it out: there are other things in life. Before that it was baseball, baseball, baseball. Umpires have families, too, so they talk back: "The kids are good, how are yours?" That goes a long way; it helps build a relationship. Once you have a relationship, you can talk. You can talk about the strike zone, about where they're going to dinner that night, or how their family back home is doing.

Baseball's not everything.

Borderline pitches

If you *do* get a pitch on the black, you might move a little farther off the plate, just to see what the umpire will give you: How far will he go? Strike zones have changed a lot because of the technology involved. Umpires are now getting monitored on balls and strikes. They've got umpire supervisors at the games. But as a catcher, you go as far as you can: you gave me *that* pitch, I'm going to move a little farther out and see if I can get *this* one. The hitter won't like it. He'll talk to the umpire, too: "Where was that pitch? Are you kidding me, Bob? That ball's out."

After that, I'm going *farther* out because Bob is now starting to get pissed at the hitter. I can be off the plate, but if the pitcher hits the glove? It's a strike. If the hitter and the umpire start bitching at each other, I set up farther outside the zone. If the ball hits my glove, whether it's in the zone or off the plate, I'm getting that call.

It doesn't matter if the umpire is calling strikes off the plate as long as he's being fair to both teams: if he calls it both ways—then it is what it is. But if the hitter talks shit, you keep moving out farther and farther. A lot of the older players will start complaining: "Are kidding me? What the hell is going on?"

If I'm behind the plate, I'll just say, "Hey, keep calling that shit, Bob, it's perfect."

Showing up the umpire

A hitter thinks a pitch is ball four, flips his bat, and starts jogging to first. If the hitter did not wait for the umpire's call—if he *assumed* it was ball four—he can get embarrassed. If the umpire called the pitch a strike, the hitter now has to come back to home plate, pick up his bat, and get back in the box.

The hitter has just shown up the umpire.

The hitter has let everyone know that *he* thought the pitch was ball four, and that pisses off umpires. Unless the hitter comes back and says, "My bad"—unless he takes responsibility for showing up the umpire—the umpire's got a bad taste in his mouth.

The pitcher can take advantage of that. He needs to get right back up on the mound, throw the ball, and quick-pitch the hitter. The hitter, got to go back, get his bat, and get comfortable again. If I'm behind the plate, I'm motioning the pitcher to get right back on the mound and go. If I can get the pitcher's attention, I'm giving the sign for the next pitch before the hitter's back in the box. I'll tell pitchers before the game, if something like that happens, be ready to take advantage of the situation.

You think the umpire's in the mood to give the hitter time?

You don't even have to throw a strike. If the hitter flips his bat, starts down to first, and has to turn around because the ball was called a strike, you talk to the umpire as the hitter walks back to the plate: "You kidding me right there, Larry? You gonna let him do that to you? Watch where I set up: if he hits it, you better call it."

You'll get a borderline pitch—absolutely. That's what will happen unless it's a veteran hitter who comes back to the plate and makes it right, says it was my bad and apologizes. Otherwise, the umpire *wants* to call a strike; and the hitter better know that. He better not let a borderline pitch go by.

Testing the rookies

Here's another situation a catcher can use to his advantage: umpires like to test the young guys. If you're a rookie and you get rung up on a ball a foot outside, you shut up and get your ass back in the dugout. If you say anything, the umpire's going to come right back at you: "What did you say?"

All rookies get tested; they need to pay their dues and earn their stripes. If a borderline call does not go a rookie's way, everybody watches to see how the rookie reacts: Does he keep his mouth shut or act like a jackass? If a rookie shoots his mouth off, it gets around the league real quick—this dude's act is tired, he thinks he's bigger than the game—and everybody will be a little harder on him.

Catchers can use that: if they know the umpires don't like this kid, a catcher can make it worse. Set up off the plate and see if you get the call. If the kid says anything or shoots the umpire a dirty look, ask the umpire if he's going to let the kid get away with that: "Bob, did you see what he just did? You gonna let him do that to you?" I'd egg the umpire on. I'd even do it if a rookie asked where a pitch was: "Bob, he's got thirty days in the big leagues—you think he's got enough time in to ask you where that pitch is?"

After that, we'll go off the plate even more. Trust me: Albert Pujols gets a different strike zone than Bryce Harper.

All rookies get tested, but a phenom may have it even worse. With so many prima donnas in this game now, with so much money involved, these young guys think they're the shit. A rookie who gets tested will get more respect if he just wears it: if he just keeps quiet and goes back to the dugout. If a rookie reacts in the right way, that's where a veteran can step in. It's the veteran's job to go to the umpire and say this rookie is a good kid—cut him a break. That's what a veteran is supposed to do. Then the veteran goes to the kid and tells him how he needs to handle things.

This is what teams mean when they say they want a veteran presence: the guys who have been around a while help the younger guys along.

Paying your dues

The pitcher is just starting his windup and the umpire calls time—pitchers hate that. When that happens, if the umpire points at the catcher, he's letting the pitcher know it wasn't the hitter's fault: the catcher was the one who called time. You don't want the pitcher retaliating—the hitter wasn't responsible.

You see a veteran hitter call late time? Veteran players will get more leeway. They can call time late and get it. Rookies might not get the same courtesy; it's part of paying your dues. You see a guy get late time called, ask yourself, how long has he been in the big leagues?

The game is based on relationships.

My rookie year I was leading off an inning and was in the on-deck circle, putting pine tar on my bat. The guy pitching for the other team was quick with his warm-ups, so the umpire behind the plate was yelling, "Hurry up, hurry up." He wanted to keep the game moving, so he told the pitcher to go ahead and throw a pitch. I took strike one while I was still in the on-deck circle. I was a twenty-one-year-old rookie and wasn't going to say anything. My manager argued, but I was 0 and 1 before I ever stepped in the box.

Ten years later, a different manager signaled me to go talk to the pitcher. Everybody knew what was happening: I was going out to stall while the reliever got ready. Umpires don't like that; they want the game to move along. The same umpire that called strike one on me a decade earlier was behind the plate. He saw the manager give me the signal to go out and talk, so he started saying, "Hey, hey, hey," and grabbed my sleeve to keep me from going out to the mound.

I'm not sure I could give you an exact quote, but it was something along these lines: "I'll tell you what, you fat [bleep]. You punked me ten years ago—it ain't going to happen again. [Bleep] you. Get your hand off me."

He backed off, said he was sorry, and that he didn't mean it.

You've got to *earn* your respect in this game.

Stalling for time

A good catcher-umpire relationship can also buy your pitchers some extra time. You go to the mound and stall so the reliever can get warmed up, and the umpire walks out to tell you to hurry it up. You say, "Hey, I'm *tired,* bro. We all know I'm waiting for the reliever to get ready." That just bought us an extra fifteen seconds—the reliever might get in five more throws.

There are other ways to stall for time: The catcher takes a long, slow walk out to the mound and talks to the pitcher as long as the umpire will let him. The umpire walks out, breaks things up, and then the umpire and the catcher walk back to home plate. The batter steps in, and now the pitching coach comes out of the dugout. Now *he* makes a long, slow trip to the mound. The umpire has to go to the mound and break up *that* meeting. Trust me, nobody on the field or in the stands likes it when we stall, but you know what?

There's a reason. There's a reason for everything that's done on a baseball field.

Everybody knows what's going on: we're stalling so our reliever can get warmed up.

Working together

Umpires liked getting behind me because I wasn't a big catcher; I set up low and they could see. Even when runners were on, I sat kind of low. Catchers have two stances: one with nobody on and another when they have runners on base. When they have runners on, catchers have to get their ass up off the ground so they can move to block a pitch or make a throw. You get Jason Varitek–type catchers and they're big—umpires have to work around that. I was lower and umpires had an easier time seeing the plate. The catcher has to let an umpire see, for obvious reasons. If a guy sets up higher, the umpire is calling pitches he can't see; anything low in the zone will be a tough call.

Bottom line, some umpires suck, some umpires are good. Some guys set up too far back and they can't see the pitch from back there. I've also had umpires lean on me. I almost lost a game because a guy leaned on me. He was getting older and he was leaning on me, using me for support. I don't like that because you lose your balance. Some umpires put a hand on you to keep track of where you are while they watch the pitcher. I don't care too much if its light, but sometimes it's too hard.

This game was in Milwaukee. We were up by one in the ninth with a runner on third base. The pitcher threw a slider in the dirt and this umpire *pushed* me while the pitch was in the air. The ball goes off my knee—I couldn't block it. The ball went off my shin guard and the guy on third comes in to score. I asked the umpire if he was feeling all right, and he said he was feeling a little light-headed, he didn't mean to push me.

The guy was sixty something years old, he'd been umpiring forever. I told him *he* was the reason I couldn't block that pitch; he said he was sorry. "Sorry? You go tell the Milwaukee Brewers and all these fans that you're sorry. I couldn't block that ball 'cause you pushed me before the ball even got to me." I love the guy, he's a great dude, but we went from winning that game in nine innings to playing an extra four or five innings to get the win.

That umpire cost me two hours of drinking Bud Light.

Now that I think about it, I'd rather umpires didn't put a hand on you. It bothers you, but it's a comfort zone for them: they want to know where you are. If you set up late, they want to feel you move. Catchers set up late especially if there's a runner at second base. Umpires will tell you that you've got to set up sooner. "Okay, how about I go out to second base and tell the guy what's coming? I can't set up sooner or the runner at second will signal location to the hitter."

Teams are good at that. If you get a younger catcher who sets up too early? Then he's giving away location. The runner may not know the pitch, but he can signal inner or outer half to the hitter. You sometimes see catchers move inside, pop their glove with their fist, then move outside. The idea is to make the hitter think the pitch is going to be on the inner half, and then the pitcher throws the ball to the outer half. But that move is for catchers who are trying to get noticed: *Look at me! Look how tricky I am!*

I never did that shit.

Foul tips

Like I said, catchers have two basic stances: with runners on, get your ass up so you can move; with no runners on, you get comfortable. With nobody on, you sometimes see catchers get into these exposed stances: ass flat on the ground, one leg out to the side. You know what? When you do that, all you're doing is waiting for your nuts to get blown up: you're just *begging* for a cup shot. If you have your knees closer together, you have some chance of keeping the ball off your nuts.

And nuts are a big thing.

You get a foul tip off the nuts? I had my left nut blow up the size of a grapefruit from a foul tip in Double A—it was awful. All you're doing with those exaggerated stances is opening yourself up to injury. Same thing with the catchers who stand upright when they want a pitch above the strike zone: they're exposing themselves to injury.

If you're wide-open, you're asking for it. All foul tips hurt, but you get used to it. You take a ball off a thigh or an arm? You get it and throw the ball back—but you keep your mask on. But you get hit in the nuts? You feel like they're in your throat; it hurts for a while. The only time I've ever gone down is when I've been hit in the nuts. I'll ask the umpire to give me a second. He'll stall by cleaning the plate or delivering a new ball to the pitcher. Otherwise, foul tips are part of the game; it's part of catching. We could have picked any spot we wanted to and we picked catching. You see a catcher who gets hit with a foul tip and it's not in the nuts, but he *still* has to walk around and shake it off?

He's soft; all that whining is an act.

You see a catcher walk around because the ball hit off his shoulder? It's an act: *Look at me; I'm so tough I'm going to fight through this.* You know what? Screw you. Get the ball, throw it back to the pitcher, and get on with it—I'd even say that to the umpires.

Foul tips are also part of umpiring. A ball off the shoulder? Give me a new ball, I'll throw it back—let's go. When umpires get hit by a foul tip, they might ask the catcher to give *them* time. They want you to go to the mound and stall while they shake it off. If I was catching, I'd ask if they were all right. If they said they needed some time, I'd call them soft; I'd let them know what I thought.

Stopping the game because someone gets hit with a foul tip screws around with your pitcher's rhythm.

That never happened with one guy—umpire Ted Barrett's an awesome dude. The guy was an amateur boxer. If either one of us got hit by a foul tip, neither of us would ever ask for time: I'd never ask him and he'd never ask me. If he got a foul tip, I'd stare straight ahead and tell him he better not ask for time. I'd also let him know what I thought of umpires who did that.

He'd say, "Screw you, Kendall."

Ted would never ask, but if another umpire *did* ask for time, I'd let him know what I thought of him and go out to the mound. I'd give him maybe five seconds to recover. If it was a shot to the head—something serious—I'd go out and give the umpire the time he needed, but a foul tip off the arm? Toughen up.

I hated the fact that after I took a foul tip, umpires would ask if I was all right. I'm fine, get your ass back behind me, and let's go. After being in the league so long, if I took a foul tip off the shoulder, umpires wouldn't even ask me if I needed time—they knew I'd yell at them. And they knew if *they* got hit, they better give me a ball and get on with it. Umpires are only behind the plate once or twice a week; they have time to heal up.

Catchers are right back out there the next day.

Catchers tipping pitches

Everybody knows pitchers sometimes tip pitches, so people watch for differences in their set position or delivery. But a catcher can also tip pitches by the way he sets up to receive the ball. If a catcher sets up different ways on different pitches—one way for a fastball, one way for a breaking pitch—someone will spot it.

It might be the stance; it might be the free hand. If the hand is behind the back for a fastball, but the hand is out in front for a breaking pitch, someone will notice. Pay attention and if you see a catcher change the way he sets up or receives a pitch, look for a pattern that relates to what pitch was thrown.

You might catch a catcher tipping pitches.

Plays at the plate

When there's a play at the plate, watch the catcher's left foot. If it's on the line or in fair territory, the catcher is showing the runner a piece of the plate: the runner can see a clear path to home plate. As long as the runner has somewhere to go, he'll probably slide. The catcher receives the ball in front of home plate and then turns to make the tag as the runner slides to the back half of the plate.

But if the catcher's left foot is in foul territory, he's blocking the plate. The runner has nowhere to go and you're about to see a collision. The runner can't see a clear path to home plate, and his only chance of scoring is to run over the catcher.

I blocked the plate all the time—until Gary Sheffield knocked the crap out of me. I got *crushed.* I went back to the dugout in a daze. Someone said, "Kid, you're up." I had no idea I was supposed to be hitting. I went to the plate and swung at three breaking balls in a row and struck out. I went back out to catch and the first guy got on. I had no idea what the fundamental signs were—the signs for throwing over, pickoffs, and slide steps—so I walked out to the mound to ask. The pitcher knew something was wrong and I was pulled from the game. I went to the hospital and found out I had a serious concussion.

After that, I kept my foot on the line and showed the runners a piece of the plate—unless it was late and the game was on the line; then I went right back to blocking the plate. If it's a 1-1 game, a bang-bang play at the plate, and the winning run is trying to score? Then you block the plate: you don't show the plate and you wear it—whatever happens with the runner happens.

Whether the catcher shows the plate or blocks it, he needs to keep his left foot pointed at third base. That foot has to be locked into position. If the foot's pointed toward third, the ankle and knee are protected. If a runner hits your leg, the shin guard will protect you and the leg will be shoved straight back: no twisting or turning. If you get your left foot pointed toward the mound, the ankle and knee are exposed. Now when a runner hits you, the leg can get bent or twisted. You're still going to be on the losing end whenever there's a collision, but if the foot is in the right position, you won't injure your ankle or knee.

Bottom line: half the guys coming down the line are scared of a collision—they want to avoid physical contact. You show those guys *any* of the plate?

They're going to slide.

The catcher's mask

If the runner decides to run you over on a play at the plate, it doesn't matter if the runner's six feet five or five feet five—he's running full speed and you're standing still. You're going to take a shot. So you keep the catcher's mask on for protection during a collision. One of the few times you might see me take my mask off was when a runner on third was trying to score and I thought he was going to slide.

Why?

Because I'd throw my catcher's mask in the baseline, right in front of home plate. You want to slide? You're going to hit my mask or you've got to go around it. Nobody wants to slide on a mask, so now the runner has to waste a couple steps to avoid it. That might make the difference between being out and safe. I'd also remove my mask on bases-loaded double play when the first throw was coming home. The catcher, being the pivot man on a double play, has to catch the ball from an infielder, tag the plate, then turn toward first and make the throw. When you make that turn to throw to first base, the mask might spin out of position and block your vision.

If you're going to take your mask off, why not put it in the baseline, right in front of home plate?

The hardest throw in baseball

I don't care what anyone else says, the hardest throw in all of baseball is throwing out a runner stealing second base. You see the guy get a good jump out of your peripheral vision. Then it's rush, rush, rush. You see the good jump and your throwing mechanics go out the window. All you want to do is go; and that's when you rush your throw. Your footwork's not right, your body's not right, your legs aren't underneath you, your arm isn't up in the right slot.

I can launch a ball into center field with the best of them. A runner on first takes off, you look at second base, and *go*. Just get the ball to second base in the air and your job's done. Some guys want it *above* the bag because if they try to throw the ball *on* the bag, but come up short, they'll bounce it. Hopefully, you have a second baseman or shortstop who isn't going to just wave at the ball if it's in the dirt.

You have to be quick. Ideally, you want your fingers across the four seams when you throw a ball, but you can't always find the seams. Nine times out of ten you don't have the right grip on the ball. You just let it go and count on middle infielders to save you. Your arm angle can depend on the runner's jump and the pitch location. If the runner gets a big jump and you're handling a down and away pitch, you won't get your arm up where you want it—there's no time.

You don't *want* to change your arm angle at all. You want to have your feet underneath you, and you want to make a solid throw to second base. I had a great arm when I was younger. The ball never got more than a few feet off the ground all the way to second base, but as you get older, you learn to catch the ball, get your feet set, and make a solid throw.

The times you get that perfect four-seam grip? *Maybe* it's one out of ten—that's when the ball flies true. Mainly you catch it and you've got to go with whatever grip you've got. If I could bottle up the shit I threw to second base—balls running, cutting, and sinking—I'd be the nastiest closer in the world. Balls did that because I rarely got the right grip. I'd throw the ball over *here* and it would end up over *there*.

A catcher can also look bad throwing when the pitcher is slow to the plate. The pitcher lets the runner get a huge jump, and the catcher's got to rush to make up for that. He doesn't get a good grip on the ball, has to throw from a low arm angle, and the ball sails into center field. You just do the best you can. If you want to stop stolen bases, get the ball to home plate in 1.3 seconds or less.

Then the catcher has a chance.

Pickoffs

Catchers who like to pick guys off? They're usually good-arm guys and they like to show it. It's great when you catch a runner, but half the time you throw the ball into the outfield. Unless I *knew* I could pick a guy off, I didn't throw.

Now, on a missed bunt attempt, that's when I tried a pickoff. On a bunt, the runner's trying to get an extra step toward the next base—he's trying to get a good secondary lead. At that point the runner is probably leaning the wrong way and you've got a shot at him. My arm was hanging by a blood vessel my last two years; I wasn't looking for extra throws. I was saving my bullets—I only had so many left.

Blocking pitches

At this level, you don't expect a fastball in the dirt. You expect off-speed pitches in the dirt—a curveball, a slider—but you do not expect a major league pitcher to spike a fastball. It's hard to block a fastball at 95 miles an hour—there's no time. You won't block a fastball in the dirt unless it just happens to hit you because you were in the way. If you're a big league pitcher and you're throwing fastballs in the dirt? You're not going to be a big league pitcher for long.

When I blocked a pitch, I never wanted it to go off me and bounce beyond the front edge of home plate. If the ball was farther away from me than that, runners were going to be able to advance. Blocking well is all about being soft: you can't tighten up when the ball is about to hit you. Once again, do it as if an egg were coming at you and you don't want it to break.

You can't block every ball; some are impossible. That's why you see catchers grooming the ground in front of them—you see infielders doing the same thing—they're getting dirt clods out of the way. Little dirt clods develop throughout a game. A dirt clod the size of a bottle cap will send the ball off in a new direction, and then you've got no chance of keeping it in front of you.

Hitters would get in the batter's box and dig holes. They'd spray dirt clods into my area; they'd screw up my smooth dirt. I'd pick up the dirt they sprayed into my area and throw it at their knees. I'd be a dick about it: I'd take every dirt clod I could find and throw it at the hitter's knees until my area was cleaned off again. The last five years of my career, hitters never dug in because they knew I'd throw the dirt back at them. I could have been a rookie with a big star hitting, but I'd still clear my area. I'd do it because you bounce a curveball and I'm in the right position to block it, but it hits a dirt clod and bounces in another direction? I'm pissed.

It's amazing what a tiny dirt clod will do to a baseball. If it hits even a *little* dirt clod, the ball changes direction. If you see infielders and catchers constantly smoothing the dirt with their feet, it's not that we're trying to look cool, were trying to prevent bad hops.

Blocking pitches with a runner on third

If a catcher is bad at blocking pitches, the pitcher is limited in what he can do with a runner on third base. It'll be uncomfortable for the pitcher to throw that *out* pitch—that slider in the dirt—with a runner on third. He'll be hesitant to bounce it. He won't throw his nastiest shit. He'll just spin it, and it gets whacked.

If you see a catcher touch his glove on the ground, he's asking the pitcher to bounce the ball in the dirt. Generally, you're going to see this with two strikes; they're trying to finish the hitter off. It takes some balls to ask the pitcher to bounce a pitch in the dirt with a runner on third, but that's your job. Some catchers won't do it—they don't want to look bad. Those are the same catchers who know they should call a slider, but are worried about a runner's stealing and call for a fastball. It's always easier to throw a runner out with a fastball. Some catchers are big stars because of their offense, but pitchers still hate to throw to them. That's because they're selfish players. They won't do the right thing because they don't want the spotlight to be on them if they lose the game.

If a catcher doesn't block well, he can take away the pitcher's out pitch just when the pitcher needs it most.

Protecting the umpire

There's not much reason to block pitches without a runner on; that shit *hurts*. But if you can pick a pitch—and I had *sweet* hands—if you can protect the umpire from a wild pitch by catching it, you'll get more calls. I could pick 90 percent of everything thrown up to the plate. If the ball wasn't going to hit anything—me or the umpire—with nobody on, I'd let it go. Let the batboy pick it up by the backstop and give it somebody in the stands.

Let *him* try to impress a girl.

The catcher's signs with more than one runner

If the defense has more than one base runner to deal with, the catcher will step out in front of home plate and give a series of signs. He's letting everybody know what he's going to do with the ball if one—or both—runners take off.

With runners at first and third, the catcher will signal what he plans to do if the runner on first base takes off. The catcher might signal he's throwing to second base, he might signal he's throwing to third base to try to pick off that runner, or he might signal that he plans to pump-fake—pretend he's throwing to second base—to see what the runner on third does, or he might signal that he's just going to hold the ball. The catcher's signals let the infielders know who needs to cover a base and who can stay put.

As always, what the catcher does depends on the situation in the game. A catcher should know if the runner on third is a guy who might try to steal home if the throw goes to second—if not, the catcher's free to go after the runner trying to steal second base. Or the catcher might decide to ignore both runners and concentrate on getting the hitter. Sometimes—with runners on first and second—the trail runner is the best one to try to throw out. The trail runner, fast or slow, has to wait to see if the lead runner really goes. The trail runner gets a lousy jump. Even if he's fast, the runner at first gets a *terrible* jump.

If Kenny Lofton is on second and Jim Thome is on first—we're going to second. You ain't getting Kenny Lofton. If the defense goes for the lead runner, it can be an easy bag for the trailer—the runner behind the lead runner. You see a guy with one steal after four months of baseball, and it was probably the back end of a double steal.

Signs to the pitcher

Catchers don't just call pitches; they also help the pitcher adjust to whatever situation he's dealing with. The catcher needs to be able to communicate with the pitcher without making a trip to the mound every time he wants to say something. Each catcher develops individual signs he likes to use; here are some of the signs I used and what those signs meant to the pitcher:

Tapping the front shoulder: your front shoulder is flying open. When a pitcher's front shoulder opens too soon, the ball goes all over the place. When this happens to a right-hander, the ball will tend to move to his arm side. A pitch that was supposed to be on the inside half to a right-handed hitter will now be up and in; a pitch that was supposed to be down and away will be in the middle of the plate.

Making a throwing motion from down underneath: drop your arm angle. I wanted the pitcher to drop down and throw the next pitch from a lower arm slot.

Making an upward motion with the hand: throw the next pitch above the strike zone. It doesn't matter how good you are, you get a pitch that's elevated? It looks great coming out of the pitcher's hand, but you can't catch up to it. You can't physically catch up to a ball higher than high.

Two hands, palms down: slow down, calm down. I was telling the pitcher to relax.

Spinning motion with the finger: speed up, you're working too slowly. This can also mean *let's go to the next set off signs;* I think the runner on second base has figured out the first set. We'd agree to an alternate set of signs before we went out for the game, and I was saying it was time to use them. In that case I'd point at the runner on second and then make the *mix it up* sign.

Pointing to eyes, then the runner, then a chopping motion: stop him, don't let him go, I think he's reading you. If the pitcher's been taking 1.4 seconds to get the ball to the plate over and over, you can see it—the runner's timing the pitcher, he's getting ready to go. The sign reminded the pitcher to mix it up, to vary how many times he looked at the runner or how long he held the ball in the set position.

Using the hand to make a twisting motion: use an inside move. I wanted the pitcher to pick up his front foot and spin back toward the runner on second base. Some catchers make the same signal complicated; I'd just hold up my hand and twist it. I wanted to make the signs as simple as possible for the pitcher. If you're going to make the signs that simple, you have to flash them when nobody's looking. Do it while the runner is getting his sign from the third-base coach or looking into the outfield to check defensive positioning.

Pointing at first and then third: use the first-and-third pickoff move. I'd make this sign between my knees; there was no runner on second, and the runners on the corners would have their view blocked by my stance. Same thing as the *inside move* sign: flash it when the runners aren't looking.

Pointing at the pitcher with the glove. That's done after a pitcher doesn't get a call. You're telling him that he just made a good pitch—stay right there—I'll get that pitch for you. It's another way to reassure the pitcher that he's doing fine: don't adjust, stay right there.

Making a fist: c'mon, let's go. It's rah-rah bullshit. It's another *hey, check me out* move. It's a way to show everybody how much *you're* into the game. I never did that shit.

Slow the game down

Lots of errors are made when guys try to play the game too fast. Some of the best advice I ever got from my dad was to slow the game down. I didn't know what it meant when he told me that. I was a couple of years into my career and wondered, *What the hell does* that *mean?*

If you slow the game down, if you step out of the batter's box when you're being rushed by the pitcher, what's the worst that's going to happen? The pitcher is going to get mad? That's what you want: he gets mad, he makes mistakes. Now he's out of *his* game.

Slowing the game down means catch the ball . . . do your footwork . . . make the throw. You feel as if you're going so slow, but you're not. You go back, look at film of the throw, and think, "Oh my God, I was as quick as I've ever been." It's all in your mind. The mind is such a powerful thing in baseball, it's amazing. When guys let the game speed up on them, they rush: they try to do the next thing before they do the first thing. They're thinking about the throw before they catch the ball. You've got to be quick, but be *too* quick and you'll throw the ball away and the runner's got an extra base.

Things go so fast in a major league baseball game. You have to—every once in a while—take a step back. Slow the game down.

Being a catcher

Becoming a catcher is the quickest way to get to the big leagues, but you've got to have the balls to do it—you can't be afraid.

To handle being a catcher takes a certain mind-set. You have to be willing to spend hours in the video room, argue with umpires, confront hitters, stand at the plate and get run over by base runners, go to the mound and play psychologist, take the blame when a pitch is hit out of the park, fight if you have to, take 95-mile-an-hour foul tips off your body, be a leader, get the crap beat out of you *every* night, crawl out of bed the next morning even though you're sore as hell and then go out and do the whole thing again—and you're going to do that for at least six months.

I loved every minute of it.

4
THE INFIELD

EVERYBODY HAS some idea of where the infielders are supposed to stand, but in the big leagues, a step or two one way or another can make a difference; and where an infielder needs to stand changes all the time. Some hitters might try to pull the ball when they're in a 2-0 count and hit the ball the other way when they're behind 0-2. If that's the case, you can't stand in the same place for both counts.

Like everything else in baseball, defensive positioning depends on what's happening *that night*. The pitcher on the mound, the pitch, the situation, the hitter, the hitter's foot speed, the range of the teammate next to you—all of this stuff matters. And not all infields are the same: Kansas City has a fast infield, Chicago's is slow. You better know the difference before you position yourself.

Fans love the diving stop, but the better you are at positioning, the fewer great plays you'll make. Once a defender knows the hitters, the pitchers, and the speed of the infields, he'll do a better job of putting himself in the right position to begin with.

Infield positioning

The infield coach usually stands somewhere near the top step off the dugout and helps infielders position themselves as each hitter comes to the plate. The infield coach has a spray chart—a record of where each hitter has put balls in play—and the coach uses that to help position the infielders.

But if a player constantly needs a coach to tell him where to stand, he's not going to last long. If you want to stay in the big leagues, you better pay attention. Infielders who let the coach do all their positioning are missing the opportunity to get better: to learn *why* they move two steps to their right on *this* hitter in *this* count. A player who lets his coach do all the work will lose his crutch if he gets traded to another organization.

And a player on the field can see things the infield coach can't. What if the plan is to throw a right-handed hitter a down-and-away fastball and play him to hit the ball to the opposite field, but the second baseman sees that the pitcher is consistently missing that down-and-away spot? If the pitcher is leaving that pitch in the middle of the plate, the second baseman needs to be playing more up the middle.

Sometimes a ball gets hit past an infielder and the infielder looks bad when it was really a case of the pitcher missing his location.

The infielder is in a better position to see pitch location than the infield coach. Maybe the pitcher normally hits his spots, but is struggling to get the ball down and away *today.* The infielder will know that before the pitching coach does. But if an infielder starts freelancing, standing where *he* thinks he should stand, he's taking a risk. Stand where the spray charts tell you to and if the pitcher misses his spot, it's on him—it's *his* fault. Move to where *you* think you should be and the ball goes where the spray charts told you to stand? Now it's *your* ass.

The basics

Fans may not notice when an infielder shifts a step or two, but here's some basic infield positioning, easily seen from the stands. If you pay attention to infield positioning, you'll know what the defense is trying to accomplish.

Infield back: This is the most common infield positioning. The players stand on or near the outfield grass. This positioning means the defense considers the man at the plate the most important out and plans to get that out at first base.

If there's a runner on third, less than two down, and the infield is still back, the defense doesn't care if the run scores; they're going to take the easy out at first. Either the run doesn't matter or it's early enough in the game that the defense thinks they have time to get the run back in the later innings.

Double-play depth: The double play is in order. The middle infielders will position themselves closer to second base so they can turn two. The pitcher needs a ground ball to make that happen.

Infield in: The players are positioned near or on the infield grass. Managers position their infield in when there's a runner on third base, less than two outs, and they want to prevent a run from scoring on a ground ball to an infielder. If the manager brings his infield in early in the game, the other team probably has an ace on the mound. A top-of-the-rotation pitcher doesn't need that many runs to win, and the manager is trying to prevent one of them from scoring. If Greg Maddux is throwing for the other team, try not to give up *anything*—he won't need much to beat you.

Corners in/middle back: This positioning means there's an important run on third base and the double play is also in order. If the ball is hit to the first or third baseman and the runner on third breaks for home—that's probably where the play is. But if the ball is hit up the middle, the defense will try to turn a double play.

Halfway: This defense means there are less than two outs, there's a runner on third base, and the infield is now halfway between *back* (near or on the outfield grass) and *in* (near or on the infield grass). The halfway position means the infielders have to make a decision. Based on the speed of the runner at third and how hard the ball is hit, the infielders have to decide whether a play at the plate is possible *if* the runner on third breaks for home. If they don't think they can get the runner trying to score, the throw goes to first base.

Guarding the lines/no doubles: The first and third baseman are positioned close enough to foul territory to prevent a ground ball from getting between them and the foul line. If a ball goes down one of the lines and makes it into an outfield corner, it's at least a double. Guarding the lines is usually done late in a game with an important run at the plate. Even if the man at the plate gets a hit, the defense wants to keep the hitter to a single, two hits away from scoring. If the batter hits the ball down the line and moves into second base, he's now only *one* hit away from crossing the plate.

Playing behind the runner: If you see the first baseman getting the pitcher's attention and showing crossed wrists, that's the sign for playing behind the runner. The first baseman won't be holding the runner on first base; he'll be backed up, playing behind him. The pitcher can't attempt a pickoff because the first baseman won't be at the bag. Teams play the first baseman behind the runner when they have a multi-run lead late in the game. They don't care if the runner takes off, steals second, and later scores. They're trying to win, not keep the pitcher's ERA down. Playing the first baseman behind the runner gives the first baseman more range and puts him in the best defensive position to get outs.

Shifts: It's become more common to use dramatic shifts against left-handed pull hitters, the big guys—guys like Jim Thome, Adam Dunn, and Prince Fielder. The manager overloads his defense to the right side: the third baseman is now at short, the shortstop is somewhere around second base, and the second baseman is usually pretty far back on the outfield grass.

The point of the shift is to have the left-handed hitter pull the ball to the right side of the field—where most of the defenders are standing—*or* to get him to hit the ball to the opposite field. If the left-handed hitter takes what the defense is giving him and hits the ball through the left side for a single, did the shift work?

Hey, if Adam Dunn wants a single, fine, give it to him. If Dunn hits a single, who cares? He *was* trying to hit it out of the park. If the shift got a power hitter to accept a single with nobody on, the shift was worth it. If a runner was in scoring position and a single hurt? Maybe not.

When we had a shift on against him, I'd tell Dunn all the time to bunt. I'd be behind home plate, telling him to lay one down against the shift: "You could get twenty bunt hits a year. Your average could go from .240 to .260!" Granted, I knew Adam couldn't bunt. He'd try, try, try—but he'd always end up with two strikes and then he was done. But one time Adam came to the plate and I said, "You ought to Ichiro that shit, man!" Off the field, me and Adam were buddies, and we'd talk about Ichiro Suzuki while we were having beers, how Ichiro would run out of the box while slapping the ball to the opposite field.

Adam did it—he Ichiroed the pitch.

But instead of slapping a single toward third base—which was what he was trying to do—he caught the ball out in front and pulled it. Adam's so strong he hit it out of the park, pretty much one-handed. Dunn ran around the bases, crossed home plate, and said,

"How about that Ichiro shit?" I had my mask on and I was keeping my head down so people wouldn't see how hard I was laughing.

Later, I was with the Royals and Dunn was with the White Sox when he came to the plate and said, "Watch my Ichiro shit *now,* mother——r!" I was hurt and on the bench, but I still yelled back at him. I told him he wouldn't have the balls to do it again—but he did. Adam just missed it and hit a sky-high pop fly.

Playing third base in: Anytime a batter with some speed comes to the plate, check the third baseman. If the third baseman's in on the grass, the defense thinks the batter might bunt. If the batter gets one strike on him, the third baseman might back up some; now the bunt's a little less likely. With two strikes, the third baseman might back up even more and play behind the bag; the defense now thinks the batter won't attempt a two-strike bunt.

Because of my ankle injury, people thought I bunted more than I did. Everybody saw the replay of me snapping my ankle when I was playing for the Pirates and hit first base at a bad angle. Because I was bunting on that play, people got the impression that I bunted for a hit more often than I actually did. They'd play me in at third all the time after that. I got a lot of hits between third and short because of that injury. The guys who played with me knew I didn't bunt for a hit all that often. If the third baseman was a former teammate, I could show bunt and he *still* wouldn't move in. He knew I wasn't going to do it; I just wanted him to play in so I could hit the ball past him.

If a hitter never shows bunt, the defense will never play in. Anytime you see a third baseman playing in and the hitter slaps a ball past him for a hit, give some credit to past bunt attempts.

Nobody out, runner on second

With nobody out and a runner on second base, where should the third baseman stand? It depends on what the defense thinks the hitter at the plate will try to do. And that depends on the score, the situation, and the hitter.

The third-base coach will remind the hitter what he should be doing in that particular situation, although a player who's been around a while should already know his job. Sometimes you want the hitter moving the runner over from second base to third base with a bunt, sometimes you want the hitter moving the runner over any way he can—by hitting the ball to the right side *or* bunting—and sometimes you want the hitter to forget moving the runner over: the hitter should try to drive the runner all the way in.

Scouting reports come in handy here: the defense needs to know what the other team likes to do with *this* particular hitter, in *this* particular situation. Pay attention: If the defense thinks the man at the plate is going to swing away, the third baseman will play back. If the defense thinks the man at the plate is going to bunt, the third baseman will play in. And if it's Miguel Cabrera at the plate, he *ain't* bunting.

Controlling the runner on second base

If a middle infielder thinks the runner at second is getting too good a lead, he might signal the pitcher to try a pickoff at second base. The most common signal for this is an infielder showing an open glove to the pitcher. If you watch for it, you can see it from the stands. Lots of guys use open glove, but for other guys it might be a wink or grabbing their cup—anything that can alert the pitcher to try a pickoff.

Middle infielders control a runner's lead at second by faking moves toward the bag. They're trying to get the runner to shorten his lead or at least stop him from moving his feet toward third. If the pitcher sees the signal for the pickoff at second, that means the infielder is going all the way to the bag this time; no fake.

It takes experience, but good middle infielders just *know* when something's going on. It's a feel: sometimes they see a lead that's too big and sometimes it's something less obvious. But experienced middle infielders can just look at a base runner and know that something is up. Something tells them. The runner's getting a bigger lead, his movements get a little jerkier—he's just too *giddy*. Runners will do something different when they're getting ready to take off for the next base. When you're at a game, watch a runner on second base—especially a base stealer. Look at his mannerisms: they'll be totally different when he's getting ready to go. I can see it from home plate, but the middle infielders are *right* there. They can see it better than I can.

Just like the catcher, middle infielders can see stuff nobody else can see.

Anticipating the pitch

The middle infielders can see the catcher's signs, so they know if the pitch is going to be a fastball or something off-speed. If the hitter puts an off-speed pitch in play, he's more likely to pull the ball, so—depending on the situation and who is involved—the infielders might start moving that way *before* the hitter makes contact with the ball.

But the infielders can't move too soon; otherwise the hitter might see them move and know what type of pitch is coming. If the infielders move to the pull side of the field, that probably means an off-speed pitch is on its way. As a hitter, you're locked in on the mound, so an infielder's movement has to be pretty blatant to be spotted. Knowing that, the infielders *creep* over: they'll be subtle. Watch them smooth out the infield dirt with their feet and—if you're not paying attention—you'll miss that they moved two steps to their right while they did it. They'll use manicuring the field to conceal their movement.

Knowing what pitch is about to be delivered is a big advantage, and the corner infielders—who can't see the catcher's signs—would also like to be clued in. So, before each pitch, the middle infielders pass the catcher's signs along to the corner infielders. Everybody has his own signs. It might be a low hissing sound for an off-speed pitch; no hissing sound means a fastball is about to be delivered. Whatever signaling system they use, the middle infielders can't pass the information along to the corner infielders too soon. If the first- or third-base coach picks up the signal and has the time, he can then signal the hitter what to expect. So the middle infielders wait to signal the corner infielders until it's too late for the sign to be passed along to the man at the plate.

An example

Say a left-handed pitcher is about to throw a hard cutter in on a right-handed hitter's hands. The shortstop sees the sign, and as the pitcher goes into his windup, the shortstop signals the third baseman that something might be coming his way: it's a little heads-up. Now the third baseman knows that if the pitcher hits his spot and the ball is put in play, it's probably coming to him.

The same thing applies to a first baseman holding a runner. If the first baseman knows if the pitch is a fastball or something off-speed, he can adjust how far he comes off the bag. If a left-handed batter is getting a breaking pitch, the first baseman might stay closer to the bag; that pitch is more likely to be pulled down the line. If the left-handed hitter is getting a fastball, the first baseman can come farther off the bag; that pitch is more likely to be put in play toward the middle of the field.

All this depends on everyone paying attention and remembering what certain hitters do with certain pitches in certain counts. That's why the guys who have been around a while are so valuable.

Outfield signs

Along with signaling the corner infielders, the middle infielders also let the outfielders know what's coming. The infielders usually have some sign they make behind their heads or backs that lets the guys in the outfield know if the pitch is a fastball or something off-speed. Knowing what type of pitch the hitter is getting can also help the outfielders get a jump in the right direction.

When I was in Milwaukee, outfielder Mike Cameron wanted to know what was coming, but he wanted to know from *me*. He didn't want any mix-ups with an infielder. We developed a sign system, and I'd signal him from home plate when a slider was on its way.

The veteran players know where to go on every pitch. They've studied the scouting reports but are now looking to pick up an extra step by moving in the right direction *before* the ball is put in play. In my opinion, guys like Mike Cameron made playing the outfield a work of art. He'd have two steps in the right direction before the ball was even hit. Same thing with Brian Giles or Mark Kotsay: they'd make catches that were only possible because of the jumps they got on the ball. And I was the only guy in the whole stadium who could see it and knew how they made those catches.

If this all seems pretty complicated, good—you're starting to understand.

There's a lot going on out here: pitchers aren't just throwing the ball to the plate, hoping it gets hit to one of the players randomly wandering around the field. Everybody's working as a team to control how and where the ball gets hit. If you pay attention, you'll see that the fielders are constantly adjusting their position based on the pitch, the count, the hitter—anything that will give them an edge.

Me-you

With a runner on first base, which middle infielder covers second base if the runner tries to steal? It depends on the pitch and the hitter at the plate.

You can't have both middle infielders going to the bag; that would open up the entire infield. If a right-handed hitter is at the plate, 90 percent of the time the second baseman will cover the bag because when a right-handed hitter grounds out, most of the time he'll ground out to short. If a left-handed hitter is at the plate, most of the time the shortstop will cover the bag because left-handed hitters tend to ground out to second. But if I'm hitting, they might switch it up because I tend to hit the ball the other way. By the end of my career, the shortstop was almost always covering the bag.

The pitch, the situation, and the hitter might change who is going to cover second base. Once they decide who's covering, the middle infielders signal each other. Keep an eye out for it and you can see them do this from the stands: they'll turn their heads toward each other and shield their mouths from the batter with their gloves. The signals middle infielders use in this situation are universal: "me-you." A closed mouth (the shape your mouth makes when saying the word *me*) means "I'm covering the bag." An open mouth (the shape your mouth makes when saying the word *you*) means "You cover the bag." Who covers second can change depending on the hitter, the pitcher, and the situation: it all depends on the guy at the plate and what he does with certain pitches. Is the guy a contact hitter or a power hitter? What's the pitch and where is it likely to be put in play?

In my experience, infielders do all this supersecret signaling and then most of them give it away by their positioning. As a hitter, I figured whoever was standing closer to second base was going to cover the bag—and most of the time I was right.

When I was hitting, at times a runner would take off and I'd wait to see who was covering second base and then hit the ball to that side of the field—through the open hole. Not everyone can do that, but if you have that skill, it comes in handy. If the runner on first base breaks for second and I see the second baseman is covering the bag, all I have to do is a hit an eighteen-hopper to the right side. The ball will go through the hole created by the second baseman moving to cover second base, and now we've got runners at first and third and I've got an easy hit.

Covering the bag

When a runner is sliding into a base and an infielder moves to cover the bag, watch the infielder's feet. Is he straddling the bag or standing in front of the bag? Straddling the bag while receiving the throw is the right way to do it; the infielder can block off two sides of the base with his feet. The runner is then forced to tag the front of the base, and that's where the glove will be.

But some infielders still like to position themselves with both feet in front of the bag, make the catch, and then reach back to tag the runner. As a runner, if I see a guy in front of the bag, I'll slide to the back side. That makes it a long reach for the infielder and the time it takes to apply the tag might mean I'm safe. So if straddling is better, why do some infielders still come out in front of the bag?

There are two reasons, one good and one bad.

Here's the good reason: Some catchers tend to get movement on their throws, and when that happens, those throws usually run to the right-field side of second base. If a catcher does not get his fingers on top of the ball—and sometimes he has to rush his throw and doesn't have time to get his arm all the way up to the correct arm slot—the ball will move toward the arm side. If an infielder knows his catcher tends to do this, he might come out in front of the bag to be able to move sideways with the throw. Being out in front allows the infielder to move to his left to make the catch without stepping into the base path. If the infielder were straddling second base and the throw sailed toward the right-field side of second base, the infielder would be drawn directly into a collision with the runner. In that case, the catch might not be made at all.

Catchers appreciate an infielder who does whatever he can to knock the ball down when the catcher makes a bad throw. Some infielders refuse to mix it up with a base runner and will let an off-line throw or a short hop go into the outfield. They play the ball off to the side, stay out of the way, and wave at it while it goes past. Other guys blocked everything for me: guys like Bobby Crosby and Mark Ellis. Those guys would do whatever they could to keep the ball on the infield.

Early in my career, I made a throw down to second—I thought it was a good throw—but it still went off the infielder's wrist and he got an error. We were back in the dugout and I was sitting behind a big watercooler, out of sight of most of the people on the bench. A phone was above the watercooler, and the infielder who had the ball go off his wrist didn't see me, picked up the phone, and called up to the press box. He wanted the official scorekeeper to change the call and give the error to me.

I respected this guy, but I still came out from behind the watercooler, grabbed a fistful of his jersey, and confronted him. I had something like eighteen errors at the time, so I told him to go ahead and tell them to give me the error: "What's one more going to do?" It was late in the year, I was tired, and I just snapped. In the end, they didn't change the call and I didn't get the error.

Even if all an infielder does is knock the ball down, a guy who is willing to get in front of a throw saves the catcher an error by keeping the ball on the infield—and he also saves his team a base. Knocking the throw down keeps the runner at second base; let the ball go through and the runner's on third. Now the runner can score on sacrifice fly or a routine grounder, and who knows what that run might mean?

If they know what to look for, fans can spot a middle infielder who's afraid of getting hit by a baseball or a base runner—and that's the bad reason for coming out in front of the bag: avoiding contact.

Some players are afraid to get hit by anything: a baseball, a wall, or another player. Lots of guys are afraid of contact. That's why some of these guys come out in front of the bag when receiving a throw: they want to avoid getting hit by a runner. If the middle infielder is doing it because the catcher is sailing his throws off-line, that's okay. But if the middle infielder is coming out in front of the bag because he's afraid of contact, that bothers me. When a guy avoids contact—when he pulls up short of the outfield wall, when he gets out of the runner's way on a double play, or comes out in front of the bag to avoid colliding with a runner—fans might not notice, but ballplayers will.

Reputations

If you want to know which ballplayers have a good reputation within the game, pay attention to which players are willing to run into a wall, go into a dugout to make a catch, or mix it up with a base runner. A second baseman who gets flipped by the runner while completing a double play gets more respect than a second baseman who gives up on the play and gets out of the way. A shortstop who dives to keep the ball on the infield to keep a runner from scoring from second base gets more credit than a shortstop who won't lay out for a ground ball.

Fans can see this stuff from the top row. It's easy to spot the guys who play the game the right way, and the guys who are afraid they might get injured. All you really gotta look for at the end of the day is a dirty uniform. You can tell the prima-donna players from the guys who play all out.

This kind of thing jumps out at ballplayers, but often goes unnoticed by the public. If you ever wonder why a team keeps a guy with stats that you don't find impressive, maybe it's because the organization has seen something you missed.

Tags

Pay attention to how an infielder tags a runner; it can tell you if the infielder thinks the runner is out or safe. If the infielder tags the runner and brings the glove right back up to show the umpire, the infielder probably thinks the runner is out: the tag was made and now he's showing the umpire that he still controls the ball.

If the play could go either way—a bang-bang play—the infielder will do the same thing because he wants to sell the call. He'll drop the tag, bring the glove right back up, and show it to the umpire. It helps sell the call because that's what infielders do when the runner is out.

If the infielder is *really* slick—a Gold Glover, an Omar Vizquel type—he might sell the call on a bang-bang play by blocking the umpire's view. On a play like that, the infielder has to know where the umpire is. Then the infielder will catch the ball with his body between the umpire and the bag. The infielder then spins back to the bag to apply the tag, which the umpire never sees. The infielder completes the spin, rotates out the other side, brings the glove back up, and shows the umpire the ball, selling the call.

But when the infielder thinks the runner is safe, when he *knows* he's not getting the call, he'll make the tag and leave it on the runner. The infielder believes the runner beat the throw and is now hoping the runner will overslide the bag, which is more likely on a headfirst slide. If an overslide happens, chances are the runner's a small, fast guy.

I was never going fast enough to overslide a bag.

If the infielder leaves the tag on the runner and the runner comes off the base, the runner is out. If the runner doesn't come off the bag on his own, the infielder might use the tag to *help* him off. He'll be subtle about it, but a smart infielder can use a firm tag to push the runner off the base and get the defense an out.

Infield pop-ups

People have no idea how hard it is to catch a major league pop fly. The sun, the wind, the stadium—any of those things can make it tough. The ball doesn't come straight down: it's spinning like crazy and drifts back toward the middle of the infield. That's why the catcher comes out in front of home plate and turns around to face the backstop on a pop fly behind the plate; when you're in that position, the ball curves back toward you.

The catcher takes every pop fly behind home plate and a little bit past the on-deck circles. The catcher takes responsibility for making the catch until someone calls him off. But if the ball is well out on the infield grass or up by the dugouts and a corner infielder can get there, he should call for the ball and get the catcher out of the way. The corner infielders coming in on a pop fly have a better angle on the ball than the catcher. The shortstop and second baseman are too far away, so it's up to either first or third to call the catcher off.

If you're playing third base in the big leagues, you're pretty good with a glove, but some first basemen are in the big leagues because of what they can do with a bat—they might not be the slickest of fielders. Some of these first basemen are reluctant to catch a difficult pop fly. You can spot a bad first baseman right away: he'll hang back and force the catcher to make a catch that's actually in the first baseman's territory.

Good corner infielders never hang the catcher out to dry on this play. The athletic first basemen—guys like Jeff Bagwell—have no trouble with this play. To me, Kevin Young was the best. He took pride in making that play and calling me off, even though I could've made most of those catches. Kevin took responsibility whenever he could get to the ball.

Even on a routine pop fly, the first thing a catcher has to do is locate the ball: when it's popped up, we lose sight of it.

One night we were in Philly—or maybe it was Washington—anyway, *some* place with water nearby. A pop fly goes up and I couldn't find the ball. I'm thinking, *Where is it? Where is it?* I look up, spot a white blur against the night sky, and hustle to get underneath it.

I'm chasing a seagull.

The ball lands behind me because I'm chasing a damn bird. Just one more reason a corner infielder needs to call off the catcher on pop flies whenever possible. And if one of the *middle* infielders can get to the ball, he should call off the corner infielders. Once again, he has a better angle on the ball. If the shortstop wants the ball, he has priority over the second baseman.

The pitcher's job is to get the hell out of the way and direct traffic. If you've got two infielders trying to make the same catch, the pitcher needs to do his job: call out the name of the infielder with the best angle and, if necessary, physically restrain the other infielder to prevent two guys from colliding.

The double play

The pivot man on the double play—whether it's the shortstop or the second baseman—is the guy who receives the throw, tags second base, and then throws the ball to first. Some of these middle infielders are amazing: watch how little time it takes them to catch a ball and then get it on its way to first base. But middle infielders *have* to be quick: good base runners want to get to the pivot man, take him out with a hard slide, and prevent him from completing the double play. Good middle infielders hang in there and do everything they can to complete the play.

A middle infielder better know the reputation of the man on first base before he tries to turn a double play. If I'm the runner, watch out. I'll do everything I can to take you out. I'll try to knock you all the way to the outfield grass. I won't do anything illegal, but when I'm coming into second base, I'm trying to kill you.

When it comes to breaking up the double play, it's not just speed that matters. Plenty of fast runners peel out of the base path right away and only make a half-assed effort to get to the pivot man. If one of those guys is running, the pivot man's got nothing to worry about. But if a guy with a reputation for breaking up double plays is running, some middle infielders are so scared of contact they'll fake bobbling the throw; it gives them an excuse to bail out on the play.

One of my top five favorite things as a ballplayer was to be on first base and see the batter hit a slow roller to an infielder. That meant the double play would take a long time to develop and I'd get a shot at the pivot man. You *know* that the pivot man is scared to death: if he hangs in there, I'm crushing him. I'd actually get a Christmas Day feeling: getting a chance to break up a double play was like getting a gift. For a catcher, it's the best feeling in the world to take somebody out at second base. We get beat up all the time—taking out a middle infielder is our revenge.

One guy I could never get to was Barry Larkin. I know him, we got along well, I respected the hell out of him—but I still wanted to take him out. But I could never get to him; he was just too quick. Maybe that's why he's in the Hall of Fame.

To be fair, sometimes middle infielders *do* need to bail out on a double play; the play is just taking too long. If they try to turn two, they're going to get hurt. But if the double play is started with a one-hop shot, now the *runner* is the one that has to watch out.

When the pivot man gets the ball quickly, he can drop his arm down and throw from underneath when he delivers the ball to first base. A throw from a low arm angle means the ball is coming right at the runner's head. That's why you see some runners get down early: they'll slide when they're nowhere near second base to avoid getting hit in the face. Forcing the runner down early protects the middle infielder.

So in a double-play situation, pay attention to how long it takes to start the play. A slow-developing double play means the runner gets a shot at the middle infielder; I'll take him out. A quick-developing double play means the middle infielder gets a shot at the runner; I'll peel off or get down early. At times the middle infielder needs to bail out, and at times the runner should peel off or slide early, but plenty of guys get out of the way when they don't have to.

Dirty slides

If a runner comes in hard, slides at the usual time, and takes out the pivot man, it's no big deal; that's baseball. But if a runner slides late, he won't be down on the ground when he arrives at the base. He's either sliding *on* the bag—which is dangerous for him—or *after* the bag; those are considered dirty slides. It's almost as if the runner's tumbling into the infielder, and that can blow out an infielder's knee or ankle. It can end a guy's career.

Another thing you can look for is how far the runner goes out of the base path to get to the infielder. If the pivot man moves sideways—away from the base path to complete the throw—and the runner chases him, the runner should still be able to reach out and touch the base. You might even see a base runner go after the pivot man but still reach out and touch the bag—even after he's out—just to show the umpire it's a legal slide.

Check the runner's spikes; are they pointing up or down? The metal spikes on a ballplayer's shoes can cut you up. If a runner comes in spikes-down, it's safer for the infielder. Spikes-up, and the infielder might get cut. I'd come in spikes-up on guys I didn't like—guys I had history with, guys who had done something to me or one of my teammates—but if you come in spikes-up, you better be ready for retaliation.

What goes around comes around, especially in this game.

Dropping a knee

The headfirst slide is more common these days—it's easier and faster—but a base runner going in headfirst allows an infielder to drop a knee. That's just what it sounds like: while receiving a throw, an infielder goes to one knee, but he makes sure the knee is in the base path and uses it to block the runner off the base. Dropping a knee can hurt a runner going in headfirst: the knee can come down on the runner's fingers, hands, or wrists. It can even dislocate a shoulder.

We had an incident like that: a shortstop dropped a knee on one of our players and hurt him. When that happens, the pitcher and the catcher have to take care of things. The next time this shortstop came to the plate, we did. I pointed out that we'd seen him drop a knee on our left fielder—and then we drilled him. By hitting him we sent everybody a message: we're going to protect our teammates.

If someone drops a knee on a rookie and he doesn't do anything about it, someone in the dugout will be barking at somebody else. Look at the situation: you've got twenty-one-year-old kids playing with thirty-eight-year-old men. When a rookie comes in, he's supposed to keep his mouth shut and play; he's intimidated. If someone on another team does something out of line to a younger player and the younger player doesn't respond, a veteran player will take care of it. Eventually, a rookie will have to stand up for himself or he's going to get pushed around forever; but when a rookie first comes up, veterans will do what they can to protect a younger player. Of course, these days a guy who spends five years with the same team is considered a veteran player; I always thought you were a veteran once you had ten years in the big leagues. But however long you've been there, if you're one of the veteran guys on *that* team, you have to take care of your younger guys. You may not like a guy, but if he's a teammate, you protect him.

If you drop a knee on me, I'll come up swinging. Another way for a runner to retaliate is to come in spikes-up the next chance he gets. An infielder gets spiked and he won't drop a knee on you anymore—word will get around and it will stop. If you don't retaliate, infielders will just keep doing it: they know you can be intimidated. Don't drop a knee on me unless you want a fight. If you drop a knee, you better know who you're dropping it on.

Errors

The guys at this level can make the game look easy, but it's not. The players are still human and they still make mistakes. There aren't any good errors, but some errors are at least more understandable than others.

Infielders need to know who's hitting, how well he runs, and what it will take to have a shot at throwing him out at first base. If you see a shortstop rush and throw the ball away on a guy who can't run, that's an unnecessary error—it's a dumb error. But if the runner can fly and you see a shortstop make a bad throw from a low arm angle because he knows there's no time to straighten up, that error is at least understandable: the shortstop felt he had to take a shortcut to make the play, and the shortcut didn't work.

Here's another example: it's better to *body up* a ground ball. That means getting your body in front of a grounder just in case it takes a bad hop. If that happens the ball will hit your body, fall to the ground, and there might still be a play. But if the runner can really move down the line, the infielder might decide to make the play backhand. Catching the ball backhand puts the infielder's feet in the right throwing position right away. He doesn't have to catch the ball and then adjust his feet; the footwork's already done. The backhand play is riskier: if a ball takes a bad hop on a backhand play, it will continue on into the outfield, your body is not in the way.

If you make an error because you went to your backhand on a fast runner, the people who know the game will understand. But if you make the same error on a guy who *can't* run because you got lazy or didn't want to step in front of a laser beam, the people who know the game won't like it.

And sometimes *not* risking an error can be a bad play.

Some guys intentionally avoid getting in front of hard ground balls because if the ball gets through, the scorekeeper might not give him an error. Step in front of the ball and it goes off your body, getting an error is more likely: the play looks worse, even though the infielder did the right thing.

If a guy is more concerned with his own stats than his team, he might also decide to eat the ball on a bang-bang play. Holding on to the ball on a tough play might be the wrong decision. It may save the infielder an error, but depending on the situation, the team might need him to try anyway. Sometimes there's no time: the infielder just has to grab the ball and gun it. Forget fundamentals: count on your athleticism or the athleticism of the guy catching the ball. Sometimes the game requires you to take a chance.

That's why a good first baseman can make such a difference.

First basemen

Look at who's playing first—you can tell a lot about the entire infield by who's over there.

Is it a DH type who got stuck at first base because they couldn't figure out where else to put him? Or is it a guy who can actually play the position? Pay attention and you'll know if the other infielders trust the first baseman. You'll find out quickly when a bang-

bang play happens: Do they attempt a tough throw and count on the first baseman to save them? Or do they put the ball in their pocket because they have no confidence that the first baseman will at least be able to knock a bad throw down?

The first baseman makes the entire infield better or worse. If a guy can pick it—handle short hops and bad throws—he allows his teammates to attempt more plays. And those plays will be amazing: diving stops followed by a one-hop throw. The infielders will make those throws and count on the first baseman to handle a bad one. Good first basemen *work* at handling bad throws: they practice them all the time. Bad first basemen don't care; they're ditching their responsibilities. All they care about is their hitting.

The number one thing a first baseman does on defense is handle bad throws and short hops. Pay attention and you'll see which first basemen are saving errors and making their teammates better, and which first basemen are just going through the motions and making everybody worse.

The pitcher's defensive responsibilities

Don't forget that once a pitcher lets go of the ball, he becomes another infielder. Some guys take this seriously, some don't, but the pitchers who don't work at defense are only hurting themselves—and their team. Here are a few of the plays a pitcher has to handle:

In a double-play situation, you'll see the pitcher point at himself with a thumb and a middle infielder with his pinkie. Then he'll waggle his hand back and forth. It looks like the "hang loose" sign surfers use. The pitcher's alerting the middle infielder that if the ball is hit back to the mound, he'll be looking for that infielder to cover second base.

Certain pitchers have a problem throwing to bases—it's something in their heads. That might explain why you see a pitcher run the ball over to first base and then flip it underhand once he gets close enough: he's afraid he's going to throw the ball away. When a guy gets the yips throwing a baseball, we call it *the thing.*

We won't even say it out loud—we don't want to put it in our heads. I had the thing for about two months one season and couldn't throw the ball to third base after a strikeout: I'd launch balls into left field. I could throw the ball back to the pitcher, down to second, first base—no problem. It was that one little thing: throwing the ball to third base after a strikeout. Walk up and ask a player if he has the thing, and he may never speak to you again. You just don't bring it up. You say that around the clubhouse and it's the worst thing you can possibly do. The thing shows you just how mental this game can be: with the wrong mind-set, a big league player can't make a simple throw to third base.

Whether he has problems throwing to the bases or not, some plays a pitcher *has* to make, like bunts and balls hit back at him—but if the ball is popped up on the infield, the pitcher's job is to point at it and get out of the way. The defense doesn't want a player who might be out there once every five days trying to catch a pop-up; and they sure don't want him tripping over the mound while he tries to do it.

When a ball is popped up behind home plate, the catcher can sneak a quick peek at the pitcher while removing his mask. The pitcher should be pointing at the pop-up, which lets the catcher know which direction to turn while looking for the ball. It doesn't always work: I've seen pitchers point at what they thought was an infield pop-up, but the ball was a home run that landed twenty rows deep. I try to keep the pitchers out of it whenever I can; for the most part, they're nonathletes—and I'm not the only one who thinks that.

The pitcher also has responsibility for covering first base on every ball hit to the right side of the infield. If the pitcher waits to see if he's needed, he'll be late covering the bag. The catcher yells, "Get over!" to remind the pitcher to quit daydreaming and cover first. CC Sabathia asked me to remind him to get over. CC's the greatest guy in the world—one of the best pitchers ever—but I've got too much on my plate to have to remind him to get over to first base. Most catchers do it, but here's my theory: You're in the big leagues—you need someone to tell you to do your job?

Pitchers also have to back up bases, field bunts, and cover home plate if a ball goes to the backstop with a runner in scoring position. Pitchers sometimes forget their defensive assignments because they become spectators after delivering the ball to home plate. They're so involved in making the pitch, they forget these other things they have to do. After they deliver the ball to home plate, pitchers have to get moving or they'll be late for their defensive assignments. That's what makes a guy like Greg Maddux so special: even after giving a 100 percent effort on throwing a pitch, he didn't forget his defensive responsibilities.

An infielder's best friend: the slow runner

Slow runners make for great plays. If a guy can fly down the line, any momentary bobble of the ball means the runner will be safe. Whenever you see a highlight-reel play—the ones where the infielder goes a long way to get the ball and makes a great throw—remember, that takes time. When a guy dives, gets up, and makes a throw, check the runner; there's a pretty good chance he's slow. He's probably a corner guy, a catcher, or a DH who can't run. If you have to dive to catch a ground ball off a fast guy's bat, put it in your pocket—you ain't getting him.

Both sides of the ball

Both sides of the ball: that means the offensive and defensive side of the game. Keeping a run *off* the board is just as important as putting one *on*. Fans tend to focus on offense because it's easier to measure. Defense does not get the attention it should.

What a player prevents is just as important as what a player produces. Pay attention to what a guy with mediocre offensive numbers does on the defensive side of the ball and you might understand why he stays in the big leagues.

Big league infielders

The game moves so fast, but unless you're playing—or at least sit at field level—you'll never see how fast the game really is. The batted balls, the pitches, the throws: if you're on the field, it's a different, different world. Some people think the game is long, slow, and boring—it looks so easy on TV. But what these big league infielders do is mind-boggling; it's insane. The great infielders have incredible instincts: they'll read a pitch and the hitter's swing and be moving before the ball is ever put in play.

If you get a chance, go to Triple A and watch batting practice. Pay attention to the coach hitting fungoes and see what the Triple A infielders can do. Then watch major leaguers during BP: the big leaguers will make the same plays look effortless in comparison to the minor leaguers. Big league infielders make the plays so smoothly; they'll show skills the minor leaguers don't have. That's why these guys are in the big leagues and the Triple A guys aren't.

Once you look for it, you can see it: big leaguers are *that* good.

Watch a major league second baseman—a Chris Getz—field ground balls; it's a thing of beauty. But you have to know the game and pay attention to see what makes him special. In 2012 I hit fungoes to the Royals' second basemen and tried to short-hop Getz all season. He missed one ball in about five months, and he was *pissed*. Other guys would come up from the minors, take grounders, and miss five balls a day. The athletic ability big league infielders have is *incredible*. These guys are so good they make the nearly impossible look routine. If you're a starting infielder in the major leagues, you're one of the thirty best players in the whole world at your position. It's amazing to watch big league infielders like Alcides Escobar, Kevin Elster, Jay Bell, Bobby Crosby, or Mark Ellis. What these guys can do with a glove? It's crazy. They're making these incredible stops and throws, and they're so smooth: it looks as if they were playing catch with their kids. Big league infielders make it look *so* easy that people don't realize how special they are. It's *unbelievable* and people take it for granted. What big league infielders do on a daily basis? It's a work of art.

Getting to watch these guys from behind home plate was like watching Pablo Picasso paint a masterpiece—162 times a year.

5
THE OUTFIELD

PLAYING THE outfield is harder than it looks.

After I hurt the thumb on my glove hand, I played twenty-eight games out there. The Pirates wanted to give my catching hand some rest, but still keep my bat in the lineup. At first, I thought the outfield was easy. Right away, I made a highlight-reel play: a sliding, backhand catch of a sinking line drive. I was the number one Web Gem that night.

After that, it was all downhill.

A guy in the upper deck wears a nice white shirt to the game, stands up to buy a bag of popcorn, and you lose sight of a line drive because he's in the background. On the days they give away T-shirts, if the shirts are white? It's a nightmare—you just can't see the ball. The grounds crew mows patterns in the grass so the field looks nice for the fans, but every time a bouncing ball hits one of those patterns, it slightly changes direction: the ball "snakes" back and forth as it comes at you. If it's early in the evening, the lights haven't taken full effect yet, and a fly ball is exactly the same color as the sky—it goes up and you wonder where the hell it is.

I also had a problem paying attention. When you're behind the plate, you're in on every pitch. In the outfield, you might get two fly balls a game—hell, you might get none. If you've got an 0 for 4 going and you're not getting any balls hit to you, there's nothing to distract you from thinking about your hitting. And if you're thinking about your last at bat instead of the next pitch, you'll get burned. When an outfielder misplays a fly ball or throws to the wrong base, check his stats. Odds are, he's just had a bad at bat or hasn't had a hit in a while. Some outfield coaches will reposition a guy just to wake him up.

My mind was wandering all over the place whenever I was out there. It got so bad I asked Keith Osik—the other catcher on Pirates—if he'd let me call pitches from left field. We worked out a sign system, and I called a game for Keith from the outfield. Even though the catcher has a better view of what's going on at the plate, Keith didn't catch all that often and I knew the hitters. Calling pitches kept me in the game.

But when I wasn't calling a game, my mind would wander. I'd lose my train of thought. I wasn't just standing in the outfield; I was also out in la-la land—I wasn't paying attention. I was talking with hot-dog vendors. I got in arguments with hecklers in the stands: "Screw me? Screw you! I'll kick your ass!"

I'll be honest with you: dicking around with the fans was fun.

"Hey, Kendall, you suck!"

"I know—but guess what? I got two houses and they're paid for."

But if you start arguing with fans or checking out hot women—bang—the ball's hit past you. Then it's panic time, especially on those hard line drives. Put it this way: when I started playing the outfield, the people behind home plate knew what number I wore because they got a good view of my back while I was running to the warning track chasing all the balls I missed.

I never got much better in the outfield because I never got the chance to practice; anytime I wasn't in the outfield, I was behind the plate. In fact, I was so bad in the outfield, I got Kelly Leaked. Kelly Leak was the character in the *Bad News Bears* who was so much better than his teammates he kept running in front of them to catch the ball. I was camped—not moving—right under a pop fly. Gary Matthews Jr. comes over, steps in front of me, and makes the catch. It was an *easy* catch and Gary took it away.

"Bro, I know I suck, but Jesus Christ, dude."

"Hey, I'm sorry—I didn't mean it."

"The [bleep] you didn't. That's bullshit: the only balls I *can* catch are the ones right at me. Where the hell are you when I've got a tough one?"

Playing the outfield is not as easy as everyone thinks it is, and I learned that firsthand.

The outfield coach

If you want to know what's happening in the outfield, you might start by looking in the dugout. Somewhere on the top step is the outfield coach. As each hitter comes to the plate, the outfield coach will help position the outfielders. In my case—since I wasn't familiar with outfield positioning—I relied on our center fielder, Brian Giles. But if a guy's been playing outfield for a while, he should already know how to position himself. If he doesn't—if he needs a little help—he can always look at the outfield coach. This coach uses the information on a hitter's spray chart to remind each outfielder where to stand.

But if you're a major league outfielder, you should know where to stand on every pitch. Just like the infielders, the guys who aren't doing their homework are not going to last long. With all the MLB scouts and the reports each player is given every day, the outfield coach should not have to move the outfielders to the right spot. But if you're a fan, and you see a coach on the top step waving his hands, now you know he's positioning the outfielders.

Bottom line: the guys who win Gold Gloves are not looking at the outfield coach—they've already done their homework.

Outfield positioning

The outfield coach has a sign to tell the outfielders when he wants them to stand in their normal positions, which is called playing the hitter *straight up*. Straight up is the way everyone who has ever played the game plays outfield. It's the way you teach your kids to play when they're five years old. It's where you see the bare spots in the grass. Some coaches use an up-and-down motion with one hand directly in front of their body to signal straight up. If the outfield coach wants a player to move out of the straight-up position, the coach will signal the move left, right, in, or back.

If you see the coach put a hand behind his head, he's telling the outfielders to play *no doubles*. That sign's universal: everybody uses it. No doubles means the outfielders should back up far enough so that any ball hit over their head will be a home run. Outfielders play no doubles when the man at the plate represents an important run late in a ball game. You play no doubles so even if the batter gets a hit, you still hold him to a single. Most of the time a runner on first base is still two hits away from scoring. If a ball gets behind an outfielder, it's going to be an extra-base hit, and then the guy who hit the ball will be *one* hit away from scoring. That's why the outfielders play deep; they'll be close to the warning track.

If you see the coach put a hand on top of his head, that means the outfielders should keep the hitter at first base if he gets a hit—the outfielders are supposed to *hit the cutoff man*. Say you're up by two in the bottom of the ninth, runner on second, and the man at the plate singles. A long throw home to prevent a meaningless run can allow the tying run to move into scoring position. If outfielders get the sign to hit the cutoff man and keep the runner at first base, they will ignore the lead runner and get the ball in to second base.

Just like the infield, the positioning of the outfield can change with the count. If the hitter gets ahead, the outfield might play him to pull the ball. If the batter is behind in the count, the outfield might play him to hit the ball the other way—assuming that's what the man at the plate tries to do once he has two strikes. With a two-strike count, a lot of hitters try to wait as long as possible before pulling the trigger; they'll hit the ball to the opposite field. But with a dead-pull power hitter at the plate, he isn't likely to try hitting the ball the other way once he has two strikes. If his job is hitting home runs, he's still hoping the pitcher makes a mistake that can be yanked out of the park. When a dead-pull hitter—a guy who pulls the ball all the time—is at the plate, the outfield might shift the opposite-field outfielder into the opposite-field gap, because a dead-pull hitter isn't likely to hit the ball right down the opposite-field foul line.

The guy on the mound can also change outfield positioning. If you've got a sinker-ball pitcher on the mound, the outfield might move in because it's hard for a hitter to elevate the ball. If the sinker baller doesn't have it that night and he's up in the strike zone, the outfield might move back.

But whatever the scouting reports and the spray charts say, it's less important than what's happening *right now*. The guy at the plate might have a reputation for being a dead-pull hitter, but if his bat's a little slower *tonight,* the outfield will still play him to be late on a good fastball. And if we find out a guy's hungover or tired because his plane got in at four o'clock in the morning, we might change where we play him. Just like the infielders, when it comes to outfield positioning, the spray charts and the scouting reports are less important than what's happening that night.

How they played me

Teams adjust if something unusual is going on a particular night, but most of the time, they played me with left field straight up or moved toward the left-field line, and center field and right field would bunch the right-center gap.

But it varied by team and pitcher. If a guy was throwing a little more firm that night—throwing really hard—center field might move even more toward right-center and the right fielder might stay closer to the right-field line. But right fielders were almost always playing in because I made a living by dumping the ball over the second baseman's head. If I hit a fastball, I'd usually hit the ball the other way: toward the center fielder in the right-center gap or toward the right fielder. So it was common sense: put someone in that right-center gap, give me a pitch I'd hit that way, and force me to hit the ball toward the defense. If the pitcher hung an off-speed pitch, I'd pull that ball down the left-field line, and that's where they had the left fielder.

So what about the open part of the field, the left-center gap?

After I screwed up my left thumb—with my swing and the way they pitched me—if I tried to pull the ball toward the open gap in left-center, most of the time I'd ground out to short. I'd walk up to the plate, see that big left-center gap, and it was tempting to try to force the ball that way, but it took me a while to realize I couldn't let that big gap play a part in the at bat. No matter what was happening out there, I had to stick to my game plan. The other team *wants* you to go away from your strength.

This stuff is not a secret: everybody knows where you get your hits. Fans can look up spray charts on the Internet, figure out where the defense is going to set up and what part of the field the defense will leave open. If you've been around long enough, everybody knows what everybody else is trying to do. I knew how everyone intended to pitch me. I *didn't* know how good the pitcher's stuff would be that night and whether the pitcher would hit his spots, but if a hitter's been in the big leagues for a while, he knows what the pitcher is trying to do, and if the pitcher's been around a while he knows what the *hitter* is trying to do. The only question is which one of us will execute his game plan more effectively.

Pay attention to outfield positioning and you'll have a good idea of who won the battle that goes on during each at bat.

Outfield throws

Outfielders need to keep their throw low so they don't overthrow the cutoff man. Say there's a runner on first base and the batter hits a single to right field. If the runner on first base tries to take an extra base and go to third, the right fielder can't launch a high throw because the batter—now the trail runner—can then move into second base. The trail runner has to keep his eye on the ball, and if it's too high, he should be moving into scoring position. The high throw means the ball can't be cut off and redirected; it's a free base for the opposing team.

On a play with multiple base runners, take your eye off the ball once in a while and look for the cutoff man. If he gets in position and the throw is low, the cutoff man might catch and redirect the ball. That means the trail runner has to stay put. If the defense decides to let the throw go through in an attempt to get the lead runner, the cutoff man can *fake* cutting off the ball and try to freeze the trail runner.

Two guys have to do their job to keep the trail runner from advancing: the outfielder has to keep his throw low, and the cutoff man needs to get into position to redirect the ball, if necessary. If either guy screws up, a smart trail runner will advance. If you see a high throw and the trail runner didn't move up, you probably just saw some bad baserunning.

You'll also see some outfielders one-hop their throws; that can help keep the throw low. But if the outfielder is going to one-hop the throw, he needs to give the guy on the other end a good, clean hop. The hop needs to be long. Short hops—too near the fielder receiving the throw—are hard to handle.

The throw might beat the runner, but the guy catching the ball is so busy trying to catch the short hop, he can't get the tag down in time. And if an outfielder is going to one-hop a throw to home plate, it's better if the hop is on the infield grass. That gives the catcher a nice, long hop to handle. Short-hop the throw on the dirt, right in front of home plate, and the catcher might get blown up by the runner before he has a chance to catch the ball and brace for a collision.

Outfield assists

An outfielder throwing out a base runner is one of the most exciting plays in baseball, but sometimes the guys with the best arms don't get a chance to make that play. Players should know who they can run on before the game even starts; that's why they have scouts. Even if the outfielder is just up from Triple A, you should know if he has an outstanding arm.

Outfielders with a reputation for having a great arm can save runs without ever making a throw. Base runners are afraid to take the extra base or to tag on a fly ball that's too shallow. So the guy with the best arm may not be the guy with the most assists.

And it's not just the arm that matters.

An outfielder who is fast and goes back on a ball well might position himself closer to the infield. That positioning can turn into an assist when the outfielder gets a ball hit in front of him: he's got a shorter throw to the bases. The same thing applies to guys who charge the ball well or get rid of it quickly: they can throw out a runner without a great arm.

Throwing from the outfield is a completely different arm motion: you let your arm drop all the way down, then throw over the top.

Infielders don't have time to let their arm extend all the way down before throwing the ball. That's what makes Alex Gordon's arm so impressive: he's throwing with an infielder's motion, but still shows a strong arm. You've got to be really strong to do that. That short, infield throwing motion also gives Gordon a quick release and is one of the reasons he has so many assists.

Jeff Francoeur does not have the strongest outfield arm I've ever seen, but he's accurate—and he gets rid of the ball so quickly. His footwork is amazing. It's almost like having a second baseman in the outfield. The fact that Francoeur has not won a Gold Glove is ridiculous.

But the best throw I ever saw was made by Jose Guillen in Colorado. A guy hit the ball off the wall, Guillen went up to catch it, came up short, picked the ball up off the warning track, and threw the ball on the fly—no bounce—to third base to nail the runner.

Throwing a baseball is just like hitting a baseball: sometimes you get all of it, sometimes you don't. When it all comes together, the footwork is there, you get the grip you want, and you make that perfect throw. The rest of the time, you do the best you can.

Playing behind the ball

Anytime an outfielder can get to a spot *behind* the ball and field it while moving forward, he'll make a better throw. The throw will have more on it if the outfielder is moving toward the infield. If the outfielder catches the ball going sideways or back, the throw won't be as strong. Base runners look to see which way the outfielder is moving and might take an extra base when the outfielder catches the ball while going *away* from the infield, but shut it down when the outfielder catches the ball while moving *toward* the infield.

When you hear people say an outfielder ran a good route, they usually mean the outfielder got behind the ball and made the play while moving forward, toward the infield.

Playing the wall

Watch how an outfielder plays the wall; the best outfielders know where they are at all times. They sprint back and, once they hit the warning track, hold out their glove or throwing hand so they can feel the wall. They do everything they can to beat the ball to the wall, figure out where they are, and then make the catch.

They're fearless.

The guys who are afraid of the wall are easy to spot: they start to slow down as soon as they hit the warning track. They feel themselves go from grass to dirt and put on the brakes. The guys who pull up too soon are worried about other things besides making the catch. They're afraid of running into the wall, and they're not exactly sure where the wall is.

Pay attention to how the outfielders play the wall and you'll see which ones are playing the game the way it's supposed to be played, and which ones are afraid of hitting the wall.

Catching the ball in the sun

Fans have no idea how hard it is to catch a fly ball in the sun. In every park there's an inning—usually early in the game—when one of the outfielders can't see anything because of the sun. Later in the game the ball can get lost in the lights. That's why infielders point at a fly ball headed to the outfield. If an outfielder loses the ball, he can look at an infielder, see what direction he's pointing, and at least start looking in the right part of the sky.

Losing the ball in the sun happens more often than fans will ever know. I didn't play out there a lot, but it happened to me when I was in the outfield. When you're fighting the sun, your biggest weapon is your glove. You'll see the fielder hold his glove up to block the sun and wait for the ball to appear above it. If the ball *doesn't* appear above your glove, you're screwed—the ball's flight is keeping it in the sun. The longer a player holds his glove up, the worse it is.

He's trying to stay with it: he's waiting for the ball to come out of the sun—and it just ain't happening. At that point you might see a guy turn sideways. He's trying to change the background behind the ball—that and to keep the ball from hitting him in the head. If you see a guy battling a ball in the sun and he makes the catch, appreciate the effort; it's harder than it looks.

If you have any doubt about how difficult catching a fly ball in the sun is, look at the sun for five seconds and see what happens to your eyes. Then imagine a baseball coming at you while thirty thousand people watch. And remember, they'll boo you if you don't make the catch.

Pop-fly priority

The ball goes up and it's between two players; who should catch it? It depends on which one has priority. Guys coming in have priority over guys going back, so any outfielder can call off any infielder. It's easier to catch a ball coming forward than going back. And a throw from a player moving forward will have more on it than a throw from a player moving back.

The guys in the middle have priority over the guys on the corners: they have a better angle on the ball. So center field can call off the left or right fielder. Pop-fly responsibility can switch up if the right fielder tells the center fielder he's looking directly into the sun and needs help on a fly ball.

Take your eye off the ball

People tend to track the ball wherever it goes, but once in a while—once a ball is put in play and you know it's not going into the stands—take your eye off the ball. Players can't do this, but fans can. When a fly ball goes up, watch the outfielder—not the ball. The outfielder will tell you everything you need to know. In the stands, every fly ball looks like a home run. But watch the outfielder: if he's standing there like nothing's happening, it's a routine play. If he's racing for the wall, you're about to see something interesting.

The same thing applies to watching a fielder not directly involved in a play: fans should look away from the ball once in a while. On a single to right, the throw is coming in to second base. Did the left fielder move into position to back up the throw? If the left fielder turned into a spectator and the ball gets away, runners will be moving up. When a runner on first tries to steal second, did the center fielder move in to back up the catcher's throw? If the throw gets away at second base, the center fielder better be there. Otherwise, the runner can advance to third. If the center fielder does his job, he can save his team ninety feet; he can prevent that runner from going to third.

If you're behind a screen or sitting up high—someplace you won't get smoked by a foul ball—take your eye off the ball and watch the shortstop on every pitch for just one hitter. Now do the same for the left fielder. Watch what they do; it's fascinating. You'll be able to tell whether the pitch was a fastball or off-speed by their first step. Watch how they move by the count. Watch how they communicate with hand signals and gestures.

Take your eye off the ball and you'll be surprised at how much you'll see.

6
THE HITTER

WATCH A hitter come to the plate for the first time in a game and you might see him reach out with his bat and tap the catcher's shin guard; it's how ballplayers say hello. It's baseball's version of "What's up? How you doing?" It's a friendly greeting.

I can't stand it.

Albert Pujols did that to me his rookie year, and I told him not to hit me in the [bleeping] shin guards. I knew him a little bit—we had the same agent—but it was still a big deal with me. We're in the heat of battle; screw you. I get that people have friends, guys that they might have played with professionally or in college. Just watch the first basemen; most of them talk to *everybody*. They'll give the runner a tap on the ass with their glove and have a friendly conversation between pitches.

I hate it.

I might let a buddy tap me on the shin guard, but a rookie? Telling them to back off set a tone. Players start that "Hey, how you doing?" stuff and they're losing their edge. You've got your boys—guys like Brian Giles or Willie Bloomquist—and you let them get away with a little more. In fact my buddies, the guys who knew I didn't like that stuff, would screw around with me: "Hey, Jason, how you doin'? How are the kids? What's goin' on?" They'd keep tapping me on the shin guards all the time they were talking just to piss me off.

But guys I don't know? If they tapped my shin guard, I'd tell them to back off. I'd be a dick. I didn't want to lose that competitive edge. Willie Bloomquist is one of my best friends, but I still told him to get out of the way on a double play. If he's playing shortstop and I'm the base runner, I'm gonna get him: it's my job. Afterward, we'll go have a beer.

But for those three hours—while the game is being played—I'm coming after him, even if he *is* a friend.

Power versus contact

You have to figure out what kind of hitter you are. Everybody loves the home run, but not everyone can hit them. Power hitters are *strong*. They're in the big leagues for a reason: they're the best. If you don't have that kind of power, you've got to take another approach.

I've seen Barry Bonds take a pitch in on his hands and hit it out of the park to the opposite field, but—most of the time—power hitters are hitting the ball out in front of the plate and pulling it. That means they swing sooner, and that means power hitters tend to have holes in their swing. They don't wait as long to pull the trigger on a pitch, so they're easier to fool. Most contact hitters let the ball travel deeper in the zone, so they tend to hit the ball up the middle or the other way; that makes them harder to fool. Some guys try to combine approaches: they look to hit the ball out in front in certain situations, but let the ball travel deeper in others.

A lot of power hitters pull the ball almost all the time. Adam Dunn has a lot of holes in his swing—that's why he strikes out 180 times a year—but he's making $50 million for a reason. Make a mistake and he'll crush it. Adam's not a contact guy; he's paid to hit the ball out of the park. When a guy like Adam Dunn hits a home run, 90 percent of the time it's a mistake by the pitcher. Some hitters can drop the bat head and golf a low pitch out of the park, but most home runs are hit on a ball that a pitcher leaves up in the zone. Leaving a pitch up can happen because the guy at the plate is a threat to hit the ball out of the park and the pitcher wants to make his slider just *that* much nastier. The pitcher's slider is already nasty enough, but the power hitter's reputation makes the pitcher think he needs to throw a better one—then the pitcher overthrows it.

Pitchers try to make a slider better than the one they threw to the 8-hole hitter. When that happens, the slider just spins and it hangs in the zone—and power hitters know what to do with a hanging slider. That's why these power hitters continue to hit 30 home runs every year.

Contact hitters tend to go the other way, and you'll often see them hitting second in the lineup. There's nothing wrong with contact hitters who don't hit home runs, they can still make a pretty good living—just ask my ex-wife.

The 2-hole hitter's first job is to get on base for the 3- 4- and 5-hole hitters. But he's also expected to be able to move the leadoff guy ninety feet, if that's what needs to be done. Number two hitters should be able to handle the bat: get a bunt down, hit the ball to the right side to move a runner over to third, or conduct a hit-and-run. These guys let the ball get deeper and usually have an inside-out swing. (A right-handed pull hitter tends to hit the outside half of the ball and pull it to left field; a right-handed hitter with an inside-out swing tends to hit the inside half of the ball and send it to right field.)

Guys with inside-out swings—guys like Derek Jeter—are going to get a lot of base hits. Taking an inside-out approach cuts down on their power, but they have better bat control, they let the ball travel deeper in the zone, and they don't get fooled as often.

I was that type of hitter.

I could wait and see the pitch a long time before pulling the trigger. Power hitters have to guess: they roll the dice in order to hit the ball out in front of the plate; but it's worth it because they can hit the ball out of park at any time. Pitchers knew I was looking to hit the ball the other way, so they'd come inside on me. But they couldn't come *too* far inside or they'd hit me—and I wouldn't move. If you want to hit me, go ahead. That didn't give pitchers much margin for error.

The last couple years in my career I started to guess a little more. I'd been around a while and had a better idea of what pitchers were going to throw me; but I *still* couldn't hit the ball out of the park.

Knowing who you are

At the end of the day you have to know what kind of hitter you are. You have to know what you're capable of doing. If you're a bottom-of-the-order type, your job is to get on base or make sure the guys who already *are* on base move ninety feet. The problems start when table setters think they're going to hit the ball out of the park. As long as runners are moving up, good things can happen.

Runner on second, nobody out, and you're a 2-hole contact hitter? You better be thinking about hitting the ball to the right side and moving the runner over: a thirty-seven-hopper will move the runner to third base. If you're a 3- 4- or 5-hole guy; forget moving the runner with a weak grounder; look for a pitch and drive the run in yourself.

The designated hitter

If you can do it, being a DH is the greatest gig in baseball. You walk into spring training holding a pine-tar rag and a couple bats? How great is that? But being a designated hitter is so difficult to do. It's basically pinch-hitting four or five times a game—and pinch-hitting is one of the hardest things to do in baseball.

I DHed a few times in my career; it was tough. You gotta stay warm, ride an exercise bike—okay, to be honest, I never rode an exercise bike—but I'd sit on the bench, pay attention to the game, and keep swinging the bat. Now they have indoor batting cages right next to the dugout. You can go down there and whack a baseball; you get ready and stay loose. They also have two-wheel pitching machines in those indoor cages that can duplicate sliders or curves. You set the wheels at two different speeds, drop a ball in and you've got a breaking pitch. You can set the machine and duplicate a guy's slider right before you face it for real.

Good designated hitters are pretty damn special. Being a designated hitter is the best gig in all of baseball, if you can do it—most people can't.

Pitch selection

Even in the big leagues, you're going to get a pitch to hit, but you've *got* to hit it. If you don't, if you get your pitch and miss it—against certain pitchers you're done. You won't get another mistake. Fans might watch a guy strike out swinging and think the at bat failed on the last pitch: the swing and miss. Ballplayers might think the at bat was screwed up four pitches earlier, when the hitter fouled a 2-0 fastball straight back; he was on it, but he didn't get it. Hitters know they're not going to get a pitch like that again. That's why you sometimes see hitters get mad in the middle of an at bat: they know they got their pitch and missed it.

You'll also see guys load up in certain counts and try to catch the ball out in front. But before a hitter does this, he better know a pitcher's history: Does this guy generally throw a fastball in a 2-0 fastball count? If not, the hitter can look silly.

But a big swing and a miss in a hitter's count isn't necessarily a bad thing: if the count was 2-0, the count's now 2-1 and the hitter's still ahead in the count—the pitcher still has to make a pitch. The hitter took a shot, but the pitcher made a good pitch. If the hitter is gearing up for the fastball and gets the slider, it can look bad. Fans might wonder how the hitter could swing at a pitch that far out of the zone. But the hitter was loading up to do damage, started his swing a little early, and the pitcher beat him with a good pitch. The hitter rolled the dice and lost.

That's why hitters need to know the situation: Is the pitcher coming after me or will he work around me? Who's on deck? What's the score? Who's on base? Is there a base open? What's the guy on the mound got? What's he done in the past? Will I get a fastball in a fastball count?

That's also why pitchers need to be able to throw something *other* than a fastball in a fastball count. That can prevent a hitter from loading up and hitting one out of the park. If a pitcher keeps the hitters guessing, a lot of hitters will cut back on their approach. They learn they can't count on getting a fastball in a fastball count. On the other hand, power hitters might continue swinging for the fences and hope for a mistake.

A guy might look bad chasing a pitch that's out of the zone, but you can also see the opposite: the hitter is in that same 2-0 hitter's count and takes a cock shot down the middle. The hitter never takes the bat off his shoulder, and now fans are wondering why the hitter didn't swing at a fastball in a fastball count.

That happens when a guy gets a good pitch to hit, but isn't looking for it. That's why we pretend to *shake*—like I talked about in the catching chapter—we want to put some doubt in the hitter's mind. We make the guy think he's getting something other than a fastball in a fastball count. Then the guy freezes on a hittable fastball and fans don't understand why.

Anytime you see a hitter take what looks like a hittable pitch, chances are good the hitter was looking for something else.

Two-strike hitting

You have better bat control if you choke up with two strikes, but you don't see it much these days. Guys will stay down on the end of the bat; some even leave their pinkie finger off the end. If you do that, you're going to have less bat control. Check a hitter's hands once he has two strikes: Is he choking up or is he down at the end of the bat?

So if a hitter has better bat control, why don't guys choke up with two strikes? Good question.

You can see why a guy like Adam Dunn does not take a two-strike approach. His job is to hit the ball out of the park, and he's going to keep doing his job even with two strikes. Adam's going to keep his same approach: wait for a mistake and hope he can do some two-strike damage. This approach makes sense for Adam: he's a home-run hitter—but the little guys? The guys who don't have that kind of power? They should take a two-strike approach. They should choke up, but nobody tells them to. People with no power are hanging their pinkie off the knob of the bat with two strikes; it's ridiculous.

If you're not choking up in certain situations—hitting with two strikes, moving a runner over—and you're still getting the job done, okay. But if you're *not* getting the job done, you better change something up, you need to choke up. And the guys who choke up have a better chance of fouling off a tough pitch and getting another one.

Choking up and hitting with two strikes is a lost art. Why? I don't know—well, actually I do: coaches are afraid to tell players to do it. It's unbelievable. Coaches are intimidated because they're trying to keep their jobs, and getting sideways with a star player isn't the best way to do that.

Power hitters are a different deal: even with two strikes, the power hitters will just keep gambling. Power hitters will continue to guess about what pitch they'll get and hope they guess right. They're still looking for a mistake they can hit out of the park. If a hitter leaves his pinkie finger off the end of the bat, he's still loading up and trying to do damage. You can't control the bat as well when you do that; there's no way you can stop your swing if the pitcher makes a bastard pitch—you don't have that kind of bat control. You also have little chance of fouling off a bastard pitch. If you see some guy's pinkie hanging off the end of the bat in a two-strike count, he's not just trying to make contact, he's still trying to do something big.

If a hitter chokes up with two strikes, he's shortening his swing and just trying to get the ball in play. If I was choking up and got a borderline pitch—and I knew the umpire's strike zone from being behind the plate—I could intentionally foul the ball off. You just have more bat control if you choke up. Good two-strike hitters also let the ball get deeper in the zone; it's harder to fool a hitter when he does that. If a hitter is still trying to pull the ball with two strikes, he'll be easier to fool. But if you let the ball travel and then hit it to the opposite field, you'll have an easier time making contact.

Some hitters panic with two strikes, some hitters panic with one. If a guy's a free swinger, he'll treat 0-1 like 0-2, he doesn't want to *get* to two strikes. Because he knows he's not a good two-strike hitter, he's trying to avoid the situation. You'll see these guys expand the zone once they have one strike and try to get a ball in play, just to avoid the embarrassment of striking out: they're afraid to hit with two strikes. A hitter might have a low strikeout total just because he avoids the situation by making an out earlier than he has to.

It's ridiculous, but it happens.

The out pitch

As I mentioned in the pitching chapter, once a pitcher gets two strikes on the hitter, he can go to his *out pitch*, the one he uses to put hitters away. We've all seen the video and read the scouting report, but nothing replaces seeing it live. How does he use it? How much sink does it have? How does it move? Will the pitcher bounce it?

An out pitch is usually something like a nasty slider or a split-finger. The best out pitches—also called bastard pitches or chase pitches—move downward. For the hitter, lateral movement is easier to pick up: the hitter can see the ball moving out of the zone and try to lay off. Downward movement is more deceiving: you swing and the ball drops off the table.

Hitters would rather hit against 100 mph straight than a pitch with nasty, late movement—absolutely, without a doubt, 100 percent. Late movement is what makes a pitch hard to hit. As a hitter, you want to recognize an out pitch as soon as you can, because you ain't gonna hit it. All you can do is hope to lay off the pitch or foul it off and get something more hittable on the next pitch.

Good hand-eye coordination

Ballplayers *have* to have good hand-eye coordination. The best thing I ever did as a kid was play Ping-Pong. Me, my brother, my dad—we played all the time. If you want to work on hand-eye coordination, Ping-Pong is the best thing ever. My hand-eye coordination was good enough that I could foul off nasty pitches once I had two strikes—and that's a rare gift. 2-hole hitters, contact hitters—guys like Placido Polanco, David Eckstein, Wade Boggs—can foul off a two-strike pitch on purpose.

Not many hitters can do that.

But when I was playing in Oakland, I could foul a two-strike pitch off on purpose and still make an out. With so much foul ground there, if the ball was fouled off in the air, someone could still catch it.

Clutch hitters

Some hitters won't change their approach no matter what the situation is or who is on the mound. They don't *try* to rise to the occasion, they're under control. Ego's a big thing: if you *know* you're good, you know you don't have to try harder. Albert Pujols, Matt Holliday, Todd Helton, Josh Hamilton, Barry Bonds—these guys are stars for a reason. Everybody in the big leagues is good, but these guys take it to another level.

Hitters need to stay relaxed and take every at bat the same way; most guys can't do that. That's why the guys who *can* stay under control are stars. *These* are the guys you want up in a key situation. They'll treat a World Series at bat the way they treated a Wiffle-ball at bat in their backyard when they were seven years old. The stars know it's still the same game. The clutch guys can eliminate everything else that goes with playing in the big leagues—the money, the media, the crowds—and focus on the game they've always played. The pressure won't get to them.

Being clutch is the complete opposite of what's in all those sports movies: you *don't* try harder. Early in the game with nobody on, nobody out, and the score 0-0, hitters are relaxed. Give that same hitter an at bat in the ninth inning with the bases loaded and the game on the line; now he's a completely different hitter. If you can take the same approach that you had early in the game and use that approach in the ninth inning with the bases loaded, you have a chance.

If a hitter is trying too hard, a catcher can see that. You can see the veins standing out on the hitter's arm; he's grinding sawdust out of his bat. If you see those veins, the guy's swinging. The hitter's in swing mode, and it doesn't matter where the pitch is; hit the black or go just off the plate and he'll swing—if it's anywhere near the plate, he's swinging.

What hitters don't realize is that the guy on the mound is probably doing the same thing. For pitchers like Trevor Hoffman or Mariano Rivera, it's just another day at the office; that's why *those* guys are stars—but the pitchers without a big name are feeling the same pressure as the hitter.

Some guys put up good numbers when it doesn't mean anything, but fold with the game on the line. Other guys don't have overwhelming overall numbers, but keep the same approach no matter what. It's entirely possible that you'd rather have a .275 hitter at the plate than a .300 hitter up there when it's nut-cuttin' time; it just depends on their makeup.

When it's a key situation, the guys who can control themselves usually win the confrontation.

Protection

Anytime a guy has a great year, look at the hitter behind him; give him some credit. I watched Ryan Braun put up numbers for two years—but remember he had Prince Fielder hitting behind him. Having Prince behind him in the order got Ryan pitches to hit. Granted, Ryan still had to hit them, but without Fielder, maybe they pitch around Braun. You get pitches to hit if the guy behind you is just as scary.

Now Prince is hitting behind Miguel Cabrera, and Cabrera's tearing it up. You've always got to give credit to the guy doing it, but Ryan Braun wins an MVP and Miguel Cabrera wins an MVP and hits for the Triple Crown?

When you mention those two guys' names and what they did, somewhere in there you should mention Prince Fielder.

The quick inning

A guy comes to the plate and makes an out on the first pitch. Depending on the situation, the next hitter should probably take a pitch. If the second hitter also swings at the first pitch or two, the pitcher has a chance to get out of the inning using less than ten pitches. If the first two guys make two outs on three or four pitches, whoever is up third better make the pitcher work. The third guy pretty much *has* to take pitches until he has two strikes—*then* he can start to battle.

A guy who takes pitches to let his pitcher rest or make the other pitcher work is being unselfish. He's giving away an at bat for the good of the team. The guy may take an 0-fer that day; it'll look bad in the box score, but his teammates will know what he did. If the hitter takes two strikes, then starts to battle and sees seven, eight pitches, that's a hell of an at bat, no matter how it turns out.

If the catcher and the pitcher on the other team have been paying attention, they'll go right after that third hitter. They'll pound the strike zone, knowing the third hitter is taking pitches until he has two strikes. When the hitter has to take pitches, the pitcher can throw a couple fastballs down the middle and jump out in front. He can have the hitter 0-2 just like that. But you still see guys get two quick outs and then flip a curveball up there to the third guy.

What are they thinking?

They've got a chance to get out of the inning in six pitches, and they just *give* that chance away. They miss with the curve and fall behind 1-0—it's ridiculous. If you're that third guy hitting and the pitcher goes 1-0 on a curveball, you *know* a fastball is coming next because the dumbass should have thrown it on the first pitch. Throw a curve for ball one in this situation and you pretty much have to come after the hitter with a fastball. The hitter now has a free pitch and he can pick a zone and swing for the fences. The hitter sets his sights on a zone and starts his swing to that spot; if it's not there, he shuts it down. If the pitch *is* there, he can catch it out in front of the plate and do some damage—all because the pitcher threw a curve on the first pitch. The pitcher went from being in complete control of the situation to giving the hitter a chance to hurt him with one swing.

When a pitcher gets two quick outs, he needs to bear down. If he wants to throw a curve, you call time, go to the mound, and explain the situation: "You just got two outs on four pitches and you want to throw a *curveball* right here? You have a chance to throw a seven- or eight-pitch inning and you want to start this guy with a curve? Why would you even consider an off-speed pitch? The hitter's *taking:* he's not going to swing the bat. You have a chance to get the other pitcher back on the mound in less than ten pitches and you're passing that up?" When a pitcher gets two quick outs, he should *not* start the third hitter with an off-speed pitch. It should never happen, but you see it all the time.

It's amazing how often you'll see a pitcher get two quick outs and then walk the next guy. It's *unbelievable.* Pitchers will do it even when they throw all fastballs: they'll get two quick outs and mentally ease up. The next thing you know, they've got the bases loaded and the other team has a two-out rally going. You see this way too much in the big leagues.

Big moments in a ball game aren't always in the ninth with the bases loaded.

The long at bat

When a hitter has a ten- or fifteen-pitch at bat, he's wearing out the pitcher. When pitchers get tired, there's a mistake coming. The hitter's teammates are in the dugout saying, "Keep going, keep going—make this guy work."

That fifteen-pitch at bat that the 9-hole hitter had—the one where he ended up rolling over and grounding out to short—is going to pay off later in the game. The 3-hole hitter may get a hung slider an inning later because the 9-hole hitter wore the pitcher out. If the pitcher leaves a ball up, it might have been because of that fifteen-pitch at bat an inning earlier.

When I was in Kansas City, I remember Chris Getz having a long at bat while I was on deck. I got to see every pitch the guy had. I saw the movement on his fastball, I saw his slider; I saw everything and so did everyone else in the dugout. Getz eventually made an out. I walked to the plate and almost killed the guy with a line drive up the middle. After all those pitches to Getz, I *knew* I was getting a first-pitch fastball. Getzie got zero credit, but I got the reward.

When a hitter has a long at bat, pay attention to what happens next.

Taking pitches

Everybody's into on-base percentage now, but you can't just tell hitters to stand there and take pitches—it's not that simple. You've got to know the situation: Are you facing a pitcher that walks people? If so, maybe you can take a pitch and see if he gets himself into trouble. But if the guy pounds the strike zone, taking pitches will just put you in a hole. Other times you might be doing the pitcher a favor by swinging right away, but what if the bases are loaded and he throws a lot of first-pitch fastballs? You need to be ready to swing at that 0-0 pitch.

You need to know this stuff before you ever walk to the plate. Your game plan depends on the pitcher, the score, and the situation. If the Yankees are up 3–0 in the ninth and the bases are empty, you *better* be taking a pitch: you can't hit a 3-run home run with nobody on. But if it's a 2–1 game, the best pitch you see might be the first one. In my mind, if you can't tie the game and you're up in the ninth inning, you better not be swinging. But if you *do* have a chance to tie the game and you get your pitch, take a hack.

It all comes down to knowing the situation in the game. The thing that baffles me about today's game is that so many people don't seem to understand the situation they're in.

Sometimes—especially when a team isn't familiar with a starting pitcher—hitters might take pitches early in the game. If you've never faced a guy and you swing at a first-pitch fastball, you go up the second time and you *still* haven't seen a breaking pitch—and you don't even know what he can do with his fastball; you saw something straight, but the next one might have a little run to it.

As a hitter, you never want to make an out, but you might be willing to have a tough at bat early in the game—to take a hittable fastball and then battle—just so you can see what a guy has. A hitter leads off the game, takes a couple strikes, then starts to battle and eventually forces the pitcher to use all his pitches to strike him out? That's a great plate appearance: the leadoff hitter struck out, but the rest of the team got to see all the guy's pitches.

As a catcher, you don't want to show all your guy's pitches the first time through the lineup. You want to save some stuff for later in the game: you're trying to get through the batting order with just a fastball and a changeup. If the pitcher has to use his breaking stuff right away, you don't think the hitter goes back to dugout and talks to everybody? The other guys want to know what the pitch did, how much movement it had. You show one guy your splitter and he tells everyone else what to look for: hitters are constantly communicating. They go down to the video room and watch previous at bats to get ready for the one coming up. The more a pitcher is forced to reveal, the more the hitters learn about what to expect in their next at bat.

Your first two hitters in the batting order will take pitches so the big boys don't have to. You want *those* guys—the heart of the order—to have the ability to swing at the first pitch if it's in their zone. You want your 3, 4, and 5 hitters to have good at bats, and if the first two hitters have to sacrifice an at bat by taking pitches to make that happen, it's worth it—absolutely.

If the first two hitters only let you see four pitches, they're taking the 3-hole hitter out of his game. And it doesn't just happen in the first inning: it can happen in the seventh with a new reliever. If the 2-hole hitter leads off the seventh, swings at the first pitch, and grounds out, the 3-hole hitter hasn't learned much. You want your 3, 4, and 5 hitters to do whatever they want to in the box; that's why they get the big money. They're the ones that should be doing some damage. There *are* situations where those 3, 4, and 5 guys have to take pitches, but—as much as possible—you want to allow them to swing right away, *if* they get a pitch they can handle. They're the best hitters in your lineup.

Knowing when to take a pitch depends on knowing the situation, but—like I said at the beginning—you can't just tell hitters to stand there and take pitches. It's just not that simple.

Stay focused

One way a hitter can learn something about a pitcher without giving away an at bat is to watch a similar hitter. How does the pitcher work *him*? If Nick Swisher is batting left-handed and the pitcher throws him a 2-1 changeup, left-handed hitter Eric Chávez should look for the same pitch if he gets into a 2-1 count. Corey Hart should pay attention to what the pitcher throws Ryan Braun. Fans can do the same thing: watch how a guy is pitched and see if a similar hitter is pitched the same way.

Everybody is a creature of habit. Pitchers will tell you what they're throwing and how they're going to work you, but you've got to watch: you've got to stay focused. As a player, you never take your eye off the ball. You might miss a couple pitches here and there, but if you do, you ask someone what happened. What was that? What did he throw?

You see guys screwing around in the dugout? They're missing a lot.

Change the scouting report

Everybody knows what everybody else has done. You can get on the Internet right now and see where Alex Gordon hit every ball in 2012; *anybody* can do that. So if you like to take the first pitch, every once in a while go up and swing at one of those first-pitch fastballs. Pick and choose your spots, but if you do that, you can change the scouting report.

Advance scouts are everywhere and they see everything. So I'd do it right at the end of a series: I'd tell myself that tonight I was going to go to the plate and swing at two first-pitch fastballs—at *least*. The scouting report says Jason Kendall does not swing at the first pitch—at *all*. Scouts see you go after the first pitch and go back to their team and say, "Well, he's swinging at the first pitch *now*." Some pitcher would listen to that and—in the next series—start me off with first-pitch curveballs. I wouldn't swing at them and the pitcher would fall behind in the count to start my at bats.

Remember: someone is always watching—and you can use that.

Walks

If you don't have power, big league pitchers usually throw strikes. They know you can't beat them with one swing of the bat. Pitchers knew I wasn't going to hit the ball out of the park, so I didn't walk much. They'd come right after me. Adam Dunn strikes out a lot, but he still walks. Pitchers are afraid to get too aggressive with him. They'll nibble at the corners; if they walk him, they walk him. It's better than having him hit one into general admission.

As a hitter, you don't want to get *overly* picky, but you *do* look for a pitch in a zone. As long as you don't have a take sign, you swing when you get that pitch, whether the count is 0-0 or 3-0. That's what you should do: pick a zone. If it's there, you're hacking. If you don't get your pitch and you walk, it goes to the next guy. A walk's a walk: it gives you another base runner.

Late in a game, you might need to be more aggressive. At times a veteran needs to expand his zone: a runner in scoring position, first open, and a weaker hitter on deck. Some pitches out of the strike zone you can handle; you need to know what they are. If a veteran gets a borderline pitch he can handle, it might be better than taking a walk and turning things over to a rookie on deck.

I know I keep saying it, but it's true: you've got to know the situation.

Just because they walk the guy in front of you on four pitches, you don't automatically take a pitch. If the pitcher was working around the hitter in front of you, but normally throws strikes, you might be getting a hittable fastball right now, 0-0. It might be the best pitch of the at bat.

Throwing strikes

Big league pitchers should be able to throw strikes pretty much all the time. They sure as hell ought to be able to throw strikes more than they do.

I went down to the minors to catch a guy and we went out to the bull pen. After ten pitches I called time-out, walked up to him, and said, "Are you kidding me? You've been to the major leagues. You just threw two strikes out of ten pitches. I don't think you're scared, but I don't know you that well. You ain't going to last in the big leagues if you keep doing that. Hasn't anybody told you? You should be able to throw strikes nine out of ten times; you just threw two. I could get up on the mound with a blown-out arm and throw seven."

Too many pitchers want to work out of the strike zone. At the lower levels, hitters chase that stuff. They'll swing at a slider out of the zone in Triple A, but they won't swing at that same pitch up here—it's a different game. Guys have to learn how to get people out *in* the zone at the big league level. Guys who nibble? It's one of two things: they're either scared of contact—they don't want the hitter to put the ball in play—or they *can't* throw strikes. And if you're in the big leagues, you *can* throw strikes; you're just scared of contact.

A pitcher might have bad days—it happens—days when he struggles to throw a strike. If that's the case, the catcher needs to recognize that and work the pitcher through it. Now you have to be creative and find a way to get the pitcher through five innings. But when a pitcher isn't throwing strikes—not all the time, but most of the time—it's because he's scared of contact. He doesn't trust his stuff or his defense and he wants hitters to swing and miss. Then it's nibble, nibble, nibble.

Some of these pitchers walk around thinking they're a big deal because they're making $8 million. But you take them into a bar and someone bumps into them? Suddenly they're apologizing to everybody. Some of these guys just aren't that tough.

Situational hitting

Here are some of the situations a hitter can face and how he might try to handle them:

Runner on second base, nobody out: Depending on the situation—the score and the man at the plate—the hitter might be trying to hit the ball to the right side of the infield, and the pitcher is trying to get a ground ball to the left side of the infield. Right side, the runner on second can advance to third base. Left side, the runner might have to stay put. If the hitter is a 3-, 4-, or 5-type guy, he might be trying to drive the run in himself. He might still be trying to hit the ball to the right side, but he's trying to *drive* the ball in that direction, not hit a twenty-seven-hopper to second base.

Runner on third base, less than two down: If the infield is in, the hitter needs to get the ball in the air to the outfield, and the pitcher needs a ground ball. If the infield is back, a ground ball might score the runner—depending on where it's hit. A fly ball to the outfield will also work. If the infield is back, the pitcher probably needs a strikeout or an infield pop-up to keep the run from scoring.

Double play in order: The pitcher wants a ground ball; the hitter needs to get the ball in the air.

Two outs, nobody on: In this case, you might see a power hitter try to get big: load up and hit a ball to the gap. If he can get to second base, one more hit might score him. Stay at first and his team needs at least two more hits to get him around the bases. In the National League, if the pitcher is on deck, a hitter just wants to get on base so the pitcher doesn't lead off the next inning.

Playing for your own numbers

Some guys don't know the situation. A guy who can't run hits a two-out single and is standing there thinking, *I'm hitting .304 now,* while his teammates are thinking how many more hits it will take to get him around the bases. There's so much more to the game than just pitching and hitting. Situational hitting is one of those small parts of the game that people need to work on: they need to know the situation and what they need to be doing at the plate.

When I was rehabbing from my shoulder surgery, I was working with some kids in the Kansas City Royals system. Granted, they were all young and this was their first taste of pro ball, but even if you're an eighteen-year-old professional, you're still a professional. I was in the batting cage, working on hitting the ball to the right side, when one of them asked, "Mr. Kendall, why do you keep hitting the ball to second base?"

"Dude, I'm not Mr. Kendall, I'm your teammate. And second—*really*? You're a right-handed hitter, the runner on first goes in motion, who do you think is going to cover second base? Probably the second baseman. If you know how to hit a ball on the ground to the right side, you can pick up an easy knock when you hit it through the hole where second was standing, and now your team has runners at first and third."

I don't care how young you are, you need to know this stuff; this is how the game is played. But now so many guys come up playing for their own numbers. You don't care about moving a runner so a teammate can get an RBI, *you* want the RBI. You're trying to put up numbers so you can get drafted or get a college scholarship. But if you play that way, you won't know the game. You won't know what it takes to win.

You'll see young guys at the major league level swinging for the fences, nobody on, down by 3 in the ninth inning. How do you hit a 3-run home run with nobody on? Instead of working the count and trying to get on base, which is what the situation calls for—especially if the pitcher has a history of wildness—a young guy will try to hit a home run. He's been taught to play for his numbers, not the team.

You don't win with selfish players.

The worst spot in the order

Nobody has it worse than an 8-hole hitter in the National League. Hitting in front of the pitcher? In baseball, that's the toughest spot in the batting order. Runner in scoring position, two out, first open, pitcher on deck: you *know* you're not going to get anything to hit. If you take your walk and bring the pitcher to the plate, now *he* has to drive in the run. If you expand your zone, chase something, and hit a little rollover grounder to the third baseman, now who's leading off the next inning?

As a catcher, I know I have an out in the pitcher's spot. The 8-hole guy knows he's screwed because the pitcher is hitting behind him. Early in the game, with a runner in scoring position, we won't give the 8-hole hitter anything to hit because the pitcher is on deck. And even though the 8-hole hitter is getting nothing to hit, he might swing anyway.

Foul balls

If the hitter fouls a ball off, that can give you valuable information. If your pitcher is throwing 95 and the hitter is late, he'll foul the ball into the stands on the opposite-field side. Why give the hitter a chance by throwing something off-speed?

I'd probably have the pitcher throw the same pitch—a 95-mile-an-hour fastball—but this time throw the pitch *down* in the zone. Give the hitter the same pitch down and he's probably going to hit a ground ball to second base—shortstop if he's left-handed. If the hitter pulls a pitch hard, that hitter is way too comfortable. I'd have my pitcher pop him right under the chin, put the hitter on his ass or at least make him uncomfortable. Now the outside corner of the plate has opened up.

Uncomfortable is a huge word in pitching; come up and in and make the hitter uncomfortable, and now you've opened up the down-and-away zone. If the hitter thinks you'll come inside, he's not so eager to lean out and cover that down-and-away pitch.

But these days everybody is so scared. A pitcher dumps a batter on his ass and the pitcher comes off the mound asking the batter if he's okay. If a pitcher has a ball get away from him—if he hits a guy, but it's not on purpose—he'll come off the mound and apologize. Even if it wasn't on purpose, hitting the batter can *still* send a message: the pitcher can use it to show the other team he's not afraid to pitch inside. You come off the mound and start apologizing and you send another message: you don't plan on doing it again—you're soft.

When you can bunt for a hit

Watch a pitcher's follow-through and you can see if he falls off to one side of the mound or the other. A pitcher whose follow-through has him falling off the mound is a target for bunting: a pitcher who falls off is in a poor fielding position. Fans can see this.

If it's a lefty and he falls off to the third-base side, bring the bunt with you: bunt it on the first-base side. If it's a righty and he falls off to the first-base side, bunt it to third. If the pitcher finishes in a bad fielding position—if it's as drastic as that of someone like Mitch Williams—guys who can bunt should take a shot.

Slumps

The media uses the word *slump* more than we do—we usually just say we *suck*. We might also say we're *scuffling* or *struggling*. *Slump* sounds so negative. If you're in a slump, you don't know how to get out of it, but if I'm scuffling? I'm scuffling *right now*, but I'll be all right. Baseball is such a negative game—you fail more than you succeed—why put more negative into it?

When you're scuffling—when you're in a slump—you're looking for anything that will get you back on track. One time, my dad helped me. I was struggling at the plate and he was coaching in Colorado. The Rockies came into Three Rivers and I told him, "*Man*, I'm scuffling." He told me to move in the batter's box.

Some of the best advice I ever got, and I got it from my dad.

At the time I was standing at the back of the box, back foot on the line. Dad told me to move one step up or one step back. I asked why and he said just do it. He's my old man, so I did it. I was already at the back of the box, so I moved up. I hit a home run in my first at bat, then got a couple more hits. After the game I asked, "Dad? Why? What's the philosophy behind it?" He started laughing and said, "I don't know, just change something up." I literally moved one foot, and mentally, it changed *everything*. I wasn't in my usual place. I didn't stay up in the box; the next day I went back to my old spot and got two more hits. If you're struggling, change something—*that's* how mental this game can be.

My dad's advice was pure genius: if you're scuffling, change something.

Breaking a slump the hard way

It happened in the Astrodome and I wasn't supposed to play that day. I was really scuffling, so the night before, my manager, Gene Lamont, told Dale Sveum, "Go get him drunk, he ain't playing tomorrow."

If you know you're not playing the next day, you relax; it's a mental break. The next day we had a day game. Dale and I stayed in the locker room until about four in the morning. We take a cab back to the hotel, grab our luggage—it was getaway day—and go back to ballpark. It's now about eight in the morning and I'm still feeling the effects of the previous night.

No big deal—I'm not playing.

For some reason the Astros changed pitchers, from whoever to a top-of-the-rotation guy. Gene Lamont decided he couldn't put our other catcher in against this new pitcher. The other catcher—Keith Osik—hadn't played in a while; Lamont didn't think it would be fair. Suddenly, I'm back in the game. I walk up to the plate—Tony Pena's catching for the Astros—and he says, "Jeez, you smell like a liquor store."

I was so worried about seeing the ball, I forgot about everything else. That got me out of my slump. I got three hits—I was *golden*. It just goes to show you: when you're scuffling, try something different.

Battling for every at bat

Some hitters are tough in every at bat; some are tough depending on the situation. But even if you're struggling, you battle. Do *some-*

thing to help your team out. Some guys—guys like Scott Hatteberg—never give away at bats. Guys like him battle *every* at bat. Other guys, when they're going bad, they get their heads down and start thinking they're not going to get a hit. This game is so mental: you think you're horseshit, so you're up there just *giving* at bats away.

I call bullshit on this. I call bullshit on guys whining that they can't find any holes. Hey, create your own holes: figure it out. If you're going to Nancy Kerrigan yourself—*Why me? why me?*—you're not tough. And you're not going to last long.

People whining about not getting lucky? Half of baseball is getting lucky. A hit's a hit; the next morning, a swinging bunt looks like a line drive in the box score. If you hit into bad luck, you can say woe is me or figure it will even out down the road.

A tough hitter's park

Every player has to deal with his home park. A home run in Camden Yards can be a fly ball on the warning track in Kauffman Stadium. What are you gonna do? Cry boo-hoo? You've got eighty-one games at home and eighty-one games on the road; that's just the way it is.

Everyone has to play eighty-one games in their home park. We're the ones that chose to sign a contract to play there. They're paying us pretty good; quit bitching about the ballpark, quit bitching about the conditions. They're all big league ballparks, and most people would give their left nut to play in one. We make a lot of money and nobody should be bitching about their ballpark. Big park, small park—deal with it.

When a pitcher is dealing

With some pitchers, you just can't let them get in a groove. Hitters have to find a way to upset a good pitcher's rhythm: take your time getting in the batter's box, then find an excuse to step out of the box. Adjust your batting gloves. Ask for the signs again. It might drive fans crazy, but the hitter isn't just being a pain in the ass. He might be trying to break the pitcher's rhythm. Hitters step out for a reason.

I'd do it just to piss the pitcher off. What's he going to do, hit me? I'm okay with that. If he gets bitter, if he tries to make his slider just that much nastier? Maybe he'll hang it.

When you see a pitcher working quick, *he's got it.* He's *on* that night and he's feeling good. If you step out, you slow him down, you frustrate him. It breaks up the rhythm that he's in. If the pitcher is showing a lot of comfort in the windup, find a way to get him in the stretch position. That might explain why you see someone bunt for a hit down by 4 runs; make the guy pitch with a runner on. It's even better if the guy who gets on can steal a base; he can force the pitcher to change his pitch selection or make him use a slide step—anything that disrupts what the pitcher's been doing.

It's why a pitcher can be sailing along and suddenly give up a big inning: something happened to change his approach. It's one of the reasons teams need to be able to play small ball. Trying to hit a guy that's dealing hasn't worked. Do something different: make the pitcher field a bunt, make the defense reposition themselves—anything that changes what's been happening.

Other mind games

Confidence is huge: believing you're better than the other guy gives you an advantage. When I stepped in the batter's box, I'd stare at the pitcher. If he wouldn't stare back, if he dropped his head, I'd know—I've got him. It may not be in that at bat, but at some point I *will* get him. It might be two months from now, but I'll get him—he's got doubt when he faces me. But if I stared at a pitcher and he kept his head up, if he stared right back at me? I'd think, *All right, game on.*

Another type of mind game a hitter might try is to pretend he's going to bunt for a hit and then pull the bat back. It's got to look as if the hitter is thinking hit—not sacrificing—for the move to do any good; just sticking the bat out there won't get the job done. On a 3-0 count you might sometimes see a guy stick his bat out there as if he were bunting, but that's a bullshit high school move. *Really,* dude? You think sticking a bat out there is going to shake up a major league pitcher? Not if he's any good.

When a guy's trying to steal, the hitter might hold his bat out there as if he were bunting, but all he's really trying to do is block the catcher's vision. In my opinion, that's another weak, bullshit move—which sometimes works. The ball's coming at 95 mph and you can't see it? It's hard for a catcher to get off a great throw under those conditions.

Most of the time when you see a guy act as if he were bunting for a hit, he's just trying to pull the third baseman in. If you see a third baseman playing in on the grass, any ground ball hit between third and short is going to be a base hit. Of course, some guys can show bunt and the third baseman ain't ever coming in. If Billy Butler or Adam Dunn wants to bunt for a hit, most third basemen will say be my guest.

I tried showing bunt all the time to pull the third baseman in, but the guys who knew me wouldn't buy it; they knew I didn't bunt for a hit that often. Aramis Ramirez would set up back on the outfield grass and yell, "C'mon, let's see it—you ain't gonna do it." So I'd try to bunt for a hit just to make a game out of the game, and I'd always end up 0-2. I could sac bunt as well as anybody, but drag bunting for a hit? I wasn't very good at it.

Another mind game hitters use is to try to influence the umpire. Say we get a strike called on the outside corner and the hitter asks the umpire if that's as far as he's going to go. The hitter wants to know if that's the limit of the outside corner or if the umpire will extend the zone even farther. The hitter is trying to get the umpire to establish a strike zone and stick with it. If the hitter was a guy I knew—a guy I played with—we might bicker about it; but if I didn't know the guy, I'd tell him to shut up.

Catchers have more leeway when they hit because of their relationship with the umpire. Catchers can say more and get away with it. If I get a borderline pitch called against me when I'm hitting, I might say, "I don't like the call, Wally—that ball's out." Of course tone is a big thing: if you want to maintain a good relationship, you've got to show respect. As a catcher, the relationship you develop with umpires *totally* works in your favor when you're hitting. You see a catcher blocking pitches with nobody on, he's making sure the umpire doesn't get drilled by a pitch in the dirt.

You don't think umpires appreciate that?

A borderline pitch might be a ball when a catcher is hitting and a strike for someone else. Most of the time, hitters are only up at the plate four or five times a game; they don't have the same chance to develop the kind of relationship with umpires that catchers have. Granted, the umpires rotate: one day they're behind home plate and the next day they go to third, then second, then first. That's when the infielders—at least the smart ones—try to develop a relationship with umpires. Outfielders get screwed—they get no face time—but in between innings on the way to the outfield they still try to say hi to the umpires.

Some managers try to influence umpires from the dugout by yelling at them when they don't like a call. They're hoping to influence the umpires as well: maybe if they bitch about that close call, the next one will go their way.

Bottom line: everybody is looking for an advantage—everybody's playing mind games.

Stalling

It's a mistake for a hitter leading off an inning to be waiting at the plate for the inning to begin. Guys leading off an inning want to slow the game down; that gives their pitcher a breather. Leadoff hitters should stay near the on-deck circle until the umpire calls them. In the National League, if the pitcher makes an out, the leadoff hitter will take his time getting to the plate. And 99 percent of the time, he'll take the first pitch. The pitcher has just hit, and if he put the ball in play, the pitcher ran to first and he's just now getting back to the dugout to sit down and rest.

Fans can look for this: Watch how slowly the leadoff hitter comes to the plate. The umpire is yelling at the guy on deck to get moving, but he's stalling. Fans might get frustrated, but it's strategy.

When numbers don't count

Spring training stats mean nothing unless you're a rookie trying to make the team. The veterans use spring training to get ready for Opening Day and that's about it.

Spring training hits make you feel good when you go home at night, but they don't mean anything. If I get a hit in a spring training game, am I happy? Yeah. If I make an out, am I pissed? Yeah, but neither one means anything. If I take an 0-fer, I'm not going home depressed. I was never a good practice player; I just wanted the season to start. Established players can take that attitude: you know what you have to do to get ready for the start of the season. You want to win every time you step on the field, but if you had solid at bats, if you played good defense, that was all that mattered.

The same thing goes for pitchers: the guys trying to make the team need to show something in spring training, but veterans are just working to be ready when the season starts.

Some veteran pitchers don't throw all their stuff in spring training.

If we have a spring training game against a team in our division? I'll call a totally different game from what I will during the regular season. I'm not going to let a divisional opponent see all my guy's pitches. I'll call the game completely the opposite of how I'll call the game during the season. I'll tell the pitcher we're going to work on one of his pitches, and we'll throw a shitload of them. I won't worry about the results. But if I look at the schedule and we've got a team we won't see in interleague play, we'll throw the real deal. Let's throw your game and see what we've got, how you would attack a lineup.

Fans shouldn't get too worked up about spring training numbers. The same goes for the numbers put up in the minor leagues.

Fans get giddy about a guy doing well in Triple A, but it's a different world in the big leagues. I'm not saying that a minor league phenom won't be a good player, but it *is* two different worlds. Minor league parks are nice, but when the lights come on in a big league park and you look up and see forty thousand people, it can be intimidating. And the players are better—they're the best players in the world.

A guy's hitting .300 down there, get promoted but starts pressing, and pretty soon he's hitting .210 up here. When a guy starts playing pro ball, it might be the first time he's seen players as good as he is. That's when the mental game needs to kick in: How good *are* you? Because now, *everybody*'s good. How are you going to react? You can be tough or weak—some guys get tough, some guys fold.

The players in Triple A are good, too, but they might see a starting pitcher with major league stuff once a week. Those numbers fans get so excited about are put up against minor league competition. Sometimes those minor league numbers translate into similar major league numbers, sometimes they don't. Ask a big league rookie what he has to say about big league pitching and he'll probably tell you that *every* at bat is hard. And it's not just the competition that's different: suddenly you're giving interviews, you're signing autographs, everybody wants to be your friend—it's everything else that comes with being in the big leagues.

Like I said—up here, it's a different world.

Is hitting contagious?

People are always saying hitting is contagious, as if it were the flu. I'm not sure if hitting is contagious, but I'm pretty sure bad pitching is. If everybody's hitting or nobody's hitting, it's probably because of the pitcher. But even when you score 13 runs and everybody else is getting hits, there's always that one guy who takes an 0-fer—so hitting can't be *too* contagious.

Being that guys sucks. Everybody's got two or three hits and you look up at the scoreboard and you've got a zero next to your name. It's up there and everybody can see it. You're winning and that's good, but watching your average go down while everyone else is getting hits sucks.

Seeing the ball

Keeping the head still while you're hitting is the biggest deal in baseball. Your eyes are everything—it's common sense: if your head is moving, your eyes are moving, and then you've got no chance.

People get caught up in a hitter's batting stance, but all hitters will get to the same place. No matter what stance they start in, they all move to a proper hitting position: weight balanced, hands back, and head still. Good hitters keep their head down—keep it still—throughout the swing. If your head is still, you can have whatever stance you want.

The toughest pitcher I ever faced

People ask me that all the time: Who's the toughest pitcher you ever faced? Chad Bradford gave me a tough time, but I usually say the same thing: any guy I hadn't seen before. If I don't know what a guy does—how his stuff moves, how he likes to use it—I'm at a disadvantage.

There was some pitcher I faced—back when I was with the A's—and I had no idea who this guy was. I went to the plate and there it was on the scoreboard: I was something like 0 for 25 off this guy and I didn't even know his name.

Hell, I *still* don't know his name.

I stepped out of the box and thought, *Shit, I got no chance!* I stepped back in the box and hit a line drive—off his shin. It bounced to the second baseman; he picked it up, threw it to first, and I was 0 for 26.

If you look up at the scoreboard or see the matchup numbers—which a lot of ballparks show these days—and you're 10 for 18 off a guy? You're going to get him. You look in the newspaper and see you're facing a guy you hit well and you're thinking you're going to the ballpark and getting two hits that day—for whatever reason, you hit this guy well. They might be line drives, they might be little duck farts, but you get your hits. You look at the game notes—all the related statistics—and see you're facing someone tough on you? You think, *Oh, shit, I'm 0 for 30 off this guy.*

Of course, in my mind, if I'm 0 for 30 off a guy, I'm *due.*

Armor

Everybody wears so much armor up at the plate now—elbow pads, shin guards—I did it, too. Guys are a lot softer these days. If they get hit by a pitch, they're worried they may be out six weeks. I *get* it: it hurts.

I eventually started wearing an elbow pad and learned how to use it. Before the elbow pad I had a lot of contusions on my left biceps because I got hit by so many pitches. Guys would pound me in to get me off the plate and I wouldn't move. I would dive to cover the outside corner, so pitchers would throw inside; but if they came too far inside, they'd hit me and I'd take my base.

My biceps actually looked great: it was *huge* from being hit so much. Finally, they told me to start wearing an elbow pad. It took a lot of people to convince me to do it. I wore it and the first night I went 0 for 3; I took it off after that. About a week later I put the elbow pad back on because I got hit again and it [bleeping] hurt. The next night I had three hits. After a while it got to the point that if I didn't have my elbow pad on, I wasn't comfortable. Hell, I'd wear it facing Tim Wakefield. The guy *might* be throwing 60 miles an hour. Tom Candiotti, another knuckleballer—same thing. Are these guys going to hurt me with a knuckleball? No, but it became part of my being comfortable: it was part of what I did.

You also see guys come to the plate wearing a shin guard after they've fouled a ball off their leg. If a guy tends to foul down-and-in pitches off his leg, he might start wearing a shin guard as protection. It might be part of what makes *him* comfortable at the plate.

If I fouled a ball off my leg, I'd get right back in the box; I didn't care if my leg was broken. I did it my whole career. Get right back in there and nine out of ten times you'll get a hit. Stay in the box, don't let anyone know it hurts. You don't want the fake ambulance—the trainer—coming out there. You see guys go through all this acting hurt, then jump back up, hit a double, and take off running. Hey, I thought you were *dying* five minutes ago. You see guys collapse on the ground, get help from the trainer, go down to first base, and then steal second on the next pitch.

A guy fouls a ball off his leg and collapses on the ground? Get up; don't waste my time. If the leg's broke? My bad—sorry I yelled at you. But you see these guys hobble around for a while and then announce they're okay. If a guy fouls a ball off his leg and makes a big production of it—if he lets us know it hurt—guess what?

We're throwing the ball right back in the same spot. Oh, *that* one hurt? Here's another one in the same place.

Fouling a ball off your leg hurts a *lot,* don't get me wrong—but you still get right back in the box. Show them it doesn't bother you. You get hit with a foul ball and dance around? You look soft *and* silly. Get back in the box and hit. It's your job.

Emotion

Emotion is a huge thing in baseball—but you have to learn to control it. Throwing helmets, trashing watercoolers, snapping all the time? That's not the way to play the game.

A guy hits a single, claps his hands, and points to heaven? Getting hits is his *job,* that's what he was supposed to do. Why doesn't he do it when he strikes out? Wasn't that part of God's plan, too? You only thank Him when you get a hit? If God's with you all the time, wasn't He with you when you chased that slider in the dirt?

If you play all year, you're going to make 400 outs. Are you going to snap and throw your helmet 400 times? I was too emotional for the first eight years of my career. It takes a while to learn control. I couldn't tell you how much I had to pay for all the stuff I broke. When you're in your early twenties, you're still a kid—people forget that about ballplayers. One night I got mad, punched a wall, and broke a finger; *that's* when I stopped snapping. Watch the guys who are true pros and you won't know if they're 0 for 20 or 20 for 20.

You have to control your emotions unless you do something *really* big. You get a game-winning knock, make a huge play in the play-offs, or do something big for your team? Go nuts—*that* shit is hard to do. But if you hit a triple in the first inning, slide into third base, and jump up clapping, you gotta be kidding me. We've got twenty-seven outs to go.

Harder than it looks

Hitting is so damn difficult.

But now I watch it on TV? It looks so easy. Fans can't understand how a guy can swing and miss. But on TV you can't see how much a pitch sinks or cuts. The ball looks straight when you see it on TV. Every fan should get the chance to step in the box and face one four-seam fastball—and that's not even a pitch with movement—then they'd know how hard hitting is. You'll never know how difficult it is to hit a baseball unless you face a big league pitcher. And you need to face that pitcher in a full stadium. You get used to it after a while, but at first? The ballparks are overwhelming: you can't believe how many people are watching. On TV, hitting looks so easy, I see why fans get frustrated.

USA Today did a story on the ten hardest things to do in sports, and hitting a baseball was number *one.*

They won't get any argument from me; hitting is *damn* difficult.

7
THE BASE RUNNER

BASERUNNING IS the most ignored part of baseball.

Watch how a guy comes out of the batter's box—you should always see him hustle. If a guy stands there and flips the bat in disgust because he hit a pop fly, that's a bad sign. Loaf out of the box because you think you just flew out and you'll be embarrassed if the ball drops. Give up on a ground ball halfway down the line and you'll look bad if the first baseman drops the throw. Ease up because you assume you just hit a single and you'll miss the chance to advance to second base if the outfielder kicks the ball around. Fans tend to watch the ball and don't usually see it when a hitter doesn't bust ass out of the box. The hitter stands there and watches because he thinks the ball is out of the park, but it hits off the top of the wall and now the guy has to scamper to make it to second base. He gets thrown out, and—because they were watching the ball—fans miss that it was the hitter's fault; he didn't break hard out of the box.

Same thing with secondary leads: fans don't notice that a guy is doing a half-ass job of extending his lead once the pitcher throws the ball to home plate. The guy at the plate singles and the runner who was taking a lousy secondary lead gets thrown out going first to third. If you didn't notice the guy's secondary lead, you won't know it was his fault he got thrown out at third.

Here's another one: a guy hits a pop fly and doesn't run it out—99.9 percent of the time, they're going to catch the ball. You hustle down the line and run it out because you want to be ready for that one time they drop the ball. You don't run it out and you only make it to first base when you should be on second? You just made a complete ass out of yourself; you also embarrassed your team. The next guy gets a hit and you don't score because you only made it to first base instead of second? That run might be the difference in the game. Miss the play-offs by one game and that run might be the difference in the season.

Guys who hustle give themselves a chance. Everybody has that one-second temper tantrum when he hits the ball poorly; you're pissed because you made an out. But after that, you bust ass down the line.

Being prepared

Being prepared to play means you know the situation: you know the outs, the score, the inning, the strength of the outfielders' arms, whether the outfielders are right- or left-handed, and what the ball will hit if one of the infielders overthrows first. Any one of those things can change the way you run the bases.

The great base runners have great instincts: if they think they can make it, they're gone. I was never the fastest guy, but I knew what I could and couldn't do. If you're on first base and the ball is hit to right field, you should *know* whether you can make it to third without looking at the third-base coach. If you need to look at the coach to see if he's going to wave you on, you're not a good base runner. You should have looked around before the ball was ever put in play. There's no reason for a big league player to have to look at the third-base coach while going first to third. You should already know where the right fielder was playing, what kind of ball was put in play, and what your chances are of taking the extra base. The guys who have to find the coach to be told to go first to third are losing steps.

Once you make the turn at second base, it's different. Your back is to the outfield and now the third-base coach can help you with the stuff you can't see. Did the outfielder bobble the throw or come up with a great one? Maybe the center fielder made an unbelievable play off the wall, maybe he dropped the ball—that's the stuff you can't see. But if the ball is down in left field and I can still see it, I can make my own decisions—I don't need the coach.

As a base runner, if there's one down in the ninth and someone puts a ball in the gap, I should know if I can score from first base. You should know how hard the ball was hit, where the outfield was playing, and how good the outfielders' arms are. The good base runners have good instincts and know what they have to do: they understand the situation. The good base runners make it to the next base when it matters; they have that extra step because they get a good jump. The other guys can be better if they work at it, but they have to be prepared.

Base runners need to know the situation:

The score: Why take a chance of getting thrown out if your run means nothing? If you're down by two late in the game, you're not going to risk getting thrown out trying to take an extra base. If you're the tying run, the winning run, or a tack-on run, that's different.

The inning: Early in the game you might take more chances on the base paths. If you're down by 3 early, you might take a chance to score one now and hope to get the other two runs later. But late in the game you don't have many outs left—don't run into one.

The outs: Don't make the first or third out at third base. You don't want to make the first out at third because you're already in scoring position—second base—and you still have three outs left to get the run home. You don't want to make the third out at third because you're already in scoring position and one hit might do it. But if there's *one* down, getting to third can be a priority: a runner on third with one down can score without a hit. A fly ball or grounder in the right place will get the job done.

With two outs the runner might take chances to get to second base or home: home because if he holds up at third base, his team will need another hit to score him, and second base because he's then one hit away from scoring. Stop at first base and his team will probably need two more two-out hits to get him across the plate.

Exceptions to the rules

All this stuff can change, depending on the situation. The better the other team's pitcher, the more chances you take on the base paths. If you're not going to get a ton of hits, you've got to make the most of the ones you have. Being conservative on the bases and hoping for another hit might be a bad bet.

Say there are two down, a runner heading home on what looks to be a bang-bang play at the plate, and a trail runner sees a chance to make sure the runner scores. Trail runners will sometimes take off for the next base right in front of the cutoff man. The runner is offering the defense an easy out. If the trail runner can get the cutoff man to catch a ball headed for home plate and redirect it to another base, the runner has traded an out for a run, as long as the runner crossing home plate touches it before the runner drawing the throw gets tagged.

And what if you're in Fenway? Ballparks can change the way you run the bases. The left-field wall in Boston changes the baserunning rules. Now a runner can't be sure he'll score from second base on a single—the Green Monster's too close to home plate. In Boston, base runners need to take more chances to get to third base. There are exceptions to the basic baserunning rules, but *most* of the time, when you see a guy hit a two-out double and he tries for third and gets thrown out, he's going to hear it from someone when he gets back to the dugout.

Pay attention and see who gets thrown out on a dumb play.

The rain delay

Is the outfield grass wet? If there's been a rain delay, the grass may be soaked. That might not affect a fly ball, but a ground ball will be dripping by the time it gets to an outfielder. He'll be throwing a wet ball, and that's not ideal. And a one-hop throw that hits wet grass can skip and give the infielder on the other end a tough ball to handle. Watch for base runners to push it anytime the outfield grass is wet and the ball gets down on the ground.

The outfielders' arms

You have to know the personnel on the field; you should know not to run on certain guys. Arm strength matters; if a guy's got a cannon out there, a base runner needs to know. That's why some of the best-throwing outfielders don't get many assists: nobody runs on them. But *which* arm an outfielder throws with also matters.

Anytime an outfielder fields a ball on his throwing side, he'll come up with a better throw. Fielding the ball backhand—on the throwing side—closes up the fielder's front shoulder and puts his feet in the right throwing position. The throw will take less time. Field a ball on the glove side and the outfielder needs to turn around and reset his feet before making the throw. That takes time and loses momentum.

That's part of what I mean by being prepared to play: you should already know the left fielder is right-handed and will come up with a weaker throw anytime he fields a ball going toward the left-center gap. You're not going to figure all this out while you're running from first to second. Before the ball is ever put in play you need to mentally run through different scenarios and know what you're going to do.

Look around

If you see someone point to his eyes and then swirl his fingers in the air, he's reminding a teammate to "look around." Once again, a big league ballplayer shouldn't need this reminder. Looking around should be second nature. A base runner needs to know where the defense is positioned before the ball is ever put in play.

If a runner on first base checks the outfield's positioning and notices the right fielder is playing over toward the right-center gap and then the batter hits a flare over the runner's left shoulder, the runner can take off immediately. The runner knows the right fielder can't get to that ball and doesn't have to see the ball fall before going first to third. A runner who didn't check outfield positioning will have to wait, turn, and see if the ball will be caught. When it's clear the catch won't be made, he can then start running; but the delay might cost the runner a step or two, and that step or two can cost another ninety feet. The runner might not make it to third base.

If you don't want to be behind the game, you've got to think ahead.

Decoys

Deke is short for "decoy" and refers to anything a player does to fool the opposition. This stuff goes on all the time. Outfielders will try to deke runners by pretending they're going to catch a ball that's out of their reach or pretending they *won't* catch a ball that's within their range. Torii Hunter would pretend to lose a ball in the sun when he had it all the way. Larry Walker was one of the best at deking.

These guys might pretend they were going to catch a ball near the warning track when they had no chance: the ball was actually going off the wall. Runners would hold up when they thought the catch would be made, and that one step might make a difference. That kind of decoy can cost a runner ninety feet and keep a run from scoring. If the deke can make the runner hesitate, it might be the difference between scoring standing up and being out on a bang-bang play at the plate.

With a runner on second base, if the batter hits a flare to right field and the right fielder is charging forward, but realizes he won't get there, he can try to freeze the runner by holding his glove up as if he were going to catch the ball. If the runner buys the deke, he might stop—see the ball fall—and then advance. Once again, that pause might mean the runner can't score. A great deke can even convince a runner to go back and tag the base.

Outfielders aren't the only ones that try to deke runners. On a ground-ball single with a runner on first, middle infielders will sometimes pretend to turn a double play when the ball is actually in the outfield. If they can get the runner to slide to break up the nonexistent double play, the runner's chance to go first to third is gone. But let's face it: If you fall for a double-play deke when there's no ball in anyone's hand, you're not very bright. You deserve to be deked.

A middle-infield deke should never work on a big league base runner. Balls in the outfield are hard to read, so outfield dekes can work. But a base runner should not get fooled by a middle-infield deke: as a big leaguer, you should always know where the ball is. If you're running the bases and you take off for the next base, you always want to take a little peek in at the plate, especially if you hear the sound of a bat hitting a ball. You should know if the ball is in the outfield or still on the infield. If you get deked by a middle infielder, you're not doing your job as base runner.

I've seen guys steal 1-2 and not peek in to home plate; they'll run with their heads down. With two strikes a hitter can't take a close pitch, he'll have to swing. I've seen runners almost get killed when they tried to steal a base, didn't look in, and a line drive whistled past their head. Base runners better take a glance at the plate and make sure the hitter didn't put the ball in play. And if the hitter *did* put the ball in play, the runner needs to know where the ball is. Middle-infield dekes are the kind of thing you do in college ball—up here, base runners should be better than that.

But dekes still work.

I deked runners all the time. When there was going to be a play at the plate, I'd stand there like nothing was happening. Guys would come around third, see me standing there like there was no play, and ease up. I could wait to the last second and then move to catch the ball and apply the tag. Not everyone can do that. I have good hands—good enough that I didn't have to get into position to field a short hop. If I could get a runner to slow up and come in standing, I could steal an out. All I needed was for a runner to slow up a step; that one step might be the difference.

Just like the middle-infield deke, a deke at home plate shouldn't work. If the on-deck hitter does his job—moves into position behind home plate and signals the runner to slide or come in standing—the runner should know I'm deking. But watch on-deck hitters and see how many of them hustle up to the plate and do their job; not many.

A deke shouldn't work at third base either. Kansas City third baseman Mike Moustakas is great at deking runners, but right behind him is a third-base coach signaling the runner to get down. Runners get visually locked in on the third baseman or catcher and don't look at the third-base coach or the on-deck hitter right behind the defender.

If a base runner gets deked into giving up an out, it's his own fault.

Slides

The headfirst slide is faster, but it not only allows infielders to block the runner off the base by dropping a knee or putting a foot in the runner's way, it can also injure a base runner's hands. I slid headfirst all the time, but once I screwed up my thumb, I went feetfirst. Even if the infielder doesn't drop a knee, base runners can injure their fingers or wrists when they get jammed into a base. That's why you see some base runners carrying their batting gloves on the base paths: it forces them to clench their fists and that protects their fingers. Other guys will grab two handfuls of dirt when they get on base. That also forces them to keep their hands closed when sliding into a base.

A base runner sliding headfirst into home plate is a catcher's dream. If you want to, you can put a shin guard in their face. For a catcher, a headfirst slide, instead of getting run over, is like having filet mignon instead of a hamburger.

The angry base runner

If a guy gets hit by a pitch, there's a pretty good chance he's stealing second within the first two pitches—he may try it even if he's not a base stealer. If he's a guy who does not normally go in hard to second base to break up a double play, now he will.

Pay attention to a guy that gets hit with a pitch: watch how differently he runs bases. The guy's pissed off and he's looking for payback. He's going after somebody, he'll look to get even as soon as he can—if he's any good.

The base stealer

Speed helps—speed helps a *lot.* If you can outrun a baseball, you don't have to be that smart or have great instincts; but if you have that kind of speed and add smarts to it—now you've got something. The best base stealers aren't just fast, they work at it: they study video of the pitchers to see their pickoff moves and look at stat sheets to figure out the best counts to run on. Nowadays too many guys let the coaches do everything for them: they let the coaches study the video and wait for the coach to tell them when to run. But if you do that, you're never going to be as good as you could be.

Good base stealers not only have to work at it, they can't be afraid. If you've got the green light, you've got to have the balls to use it. If you're scared to get picked off, you'll never be a good base stealer. When everyone was hitting the long ball, more base runners were standing around waiting for someone to hit a home run. Nobody wanted to get thrown out, then have the guy behind them hit the ball in the gap or over the fence. Good base stealers have to use common sense: there's a right time to go and a right time to stay put—but if it's the right time to go, you have to have the balls to take off. That means teams and managers have to accept that once in a while a base stealer will get thrown out. If you get second-guessed by the staff, then everybody's scared. Guys will shut it down so they won't get criticized.

You don't see guys stealing 100 bases in a season anymore, and people say that's for a lot of reasons: focus on the long ball, not as many stadiums with artificial turf (which is a better running surface), more pitchers using the slide step and varying how long they hold the ball in the set position—more emphasis on stopping the stolen base in general.

That's one way to look at it, but here's another way: Nowadays players are too soft. Too many players are worried about getting hurt.

Not only do some players not want to get criticized or to do the homework required, they don't want to get banged up. Stealing bases beats you up: sliding is hard on your body. Taking off like a sprinter can pull a hamstring, and you can get a hand stepped on by a middle infielder if you slide in headfirst. There's just too much money to be made these days, and you can't make it if you're getting hurt all the time.

Why risk all those injuries by stealing bases?

Because speed is one of the most disruptive forces you can put on a ball field. Catchers call for more fastballs, those slide steps pitchers use can leave the ball up in the zone, middle infielders have to position themselves closer to second base, and when a runner takes off, holes open up all over the infield.

The stolen base can pay a lot of dividends, but you've got to have the balls to use it.

The stolen base and the stopwatch

If a pitcher takes more than 1.4 seconds to deliver the ball to home plate from the set position, and a runner on first base tries to steal second, catchers don't have much of a chance at throwing out the runner. If the pitcher can deliver the ball to home plate in 1.3 seconds or less, catchers have a shot. Of course the runner, his jump, and the ball you get to handle also matter. With some runners the pitcher can get the ball to home plate in 1.3 seconds and you still can't get them. You throw out the guys that you can.

When a hitter makes it to first base, you'll see the first-base coach lean in and talk to him. The base coach reminds the runner of the pitcher's delivery time to home plate. The runners know what time they can beat. That's why first-base coaches carry stopwatches: they're double-checking the pitcher's delivery time to make sure he's not any faster or slower that night. Everybody has timed everybody else. The defense knows how fast the runner is and the offense knows how quick the pitcher is—every tenth of a second matters. That's what all the throwing over and fighting for leads is about: shave or add a tenth of a second to the runner's time and the balance has shifted.

Fans can simplify all this by checking the scoreboard. Y'know where it says SB? If it's August and the number next to SB—stolen bases—is one, the catcher doesn't have much to worry about. The guy probably stole a base on the back end of a double steal. But if the number next to SB is 28, the catcher has to be more aware of the runner.

You don't have to carry a stopwatch to know whether the pitcher is fast or slow to the plate—just watch his front leg. The bigger the leg kick—the higher the pitcher's front foot gets off the ground—the slower the delivery to home plate.

Just remember: for a catcher, game calling is ten times more important than throwing out base stealers.

Patterns

Good base stealers will check the stats and look for breaking-ball counts: When does the pitcher like to throw off-speed? If they see that a pitcher throws a slider in a 1-0 count 75 percent of the time, they might roll the dice and go in that 1-0 count. If a pitcher has thrown a slider in a 1-0 count ten out of fifteen times in his last five starts, a runner should know that before the game starts. Pitchers need to stay out of patterns that give the offense an edge.

A good baserunning coach—a guy like Kansas City's Rusty Kuntz—is at the ballpark as early as I am. He's watching video so he can give these types of stats to the base stealers. If you don't have a coach like that, a coach as good as Rusty, base stealers need to do the research on their own. They ought to be doing this work on their own even if they *do* have a good coach working with them.

Everybody's looking for patterns, including catchers. When a team comes into town, I'll check what counts their base stealers have been using to steal bases. If a guy likes to run 1-2 because he thinks that's a breaking-ball count, then I need to know that.

Everybody is looking for patterns; smart ballplayers stay out of them.

Stealing third

With a runner on second base trying to steal third, the math changes: catchers can deliver the ball to third base in less time—it's a shorter throw. But runners on second base also get a bigger lead. Pitchers can take a little more time getting the ball to home plate because the catcher has that shorter throw, but still need to vary their looks. If the pitcher keeps holding the ball in the set position the same amount of time, the runner will time him and get a huge jump. If the pitcher varies how long he holds the ball—how many time he looks back at second—he cuts down that jump. Keep an eye on a pitcher who keeps the same pattern. Even a guy who is quick to home plate, but keeps doing the same thing on every pitch, allows the runner to get a better jump.

Because you don't want to make the first or third out at third base, you'll often see attempted steals of third with one down. I'm not saying you'll never see it with nobody out or two outs, but the guys who do that—steal third with no outs or two outs—better be safe.

Stealing third with two outs

Sometimes this is a good play, sometimes it's a bad one; it depends on the situation. The pitcher, the batter, the runner, the score, the inning—all this stuff matters. A runner on second base is already in scoring position: if the runner steals third base with two outs just so he can pad his stats, that's a bad play. If the pitcher is wild as hell, if he's throwing balls in the dirt, if he's afraid to throw a breaking pitch with a runner on third—and if the run means something—stealing third with two outs can be a good play.

With two outs, a runner on second, and a right-handed hitter at the plate, the third baseman might not cover third on a stolen base. The catcher will let the third baseman know that he's not going to throw the ball if the runner on second takes off for third. The defense is giving third to the runner because they want the third baseman to stay where he is—if a right-handed batter hits a grounder, it's got a good chance of going through the hole where the third baseman was standing before he moved to cover the bag. Covering the bag can open up the left side of the field.

Runners know this, so it goes back to the unwritten rules:

It's an easy bag to steal, but if the guy stole the base in a blowout just because he knew he could pad his stolen-base total, the next time we see him—his next at bat or two months later—we won't forget what he did. He'll pay the price.

If the run mattered, if the pitcher was throwing balls in the dirt and the defense was giving the runner the base, we get why the runner stole third—one more wild pitch and he scores. And some pitchers are afraid to a throw a slider with a runner on third; some catchers are afraid to call one. A runner on third might get the hitter a better pitch to hit. So there could be good reasons to steal third with two outs.

You got some dude on the mound that's all over the place, it's a 3–1 game in the eighth inning, and you got a closer coming in? If they're giving me third and I'm on second base, I'm gone. I know we've got the closer coming in and things are about to get a lot harder. If I'm on third and the pitcher throws another one in the dirt, it's a run. Now the score's 3–2 instead of 3–1: you cut the deficit in half. Now you only need *one* run off the closer in the ninth. But you have to know the situations when stealing third base is a good play.

These days, too many ballplayers don't know.

Peeking in

If you're watching a game on TV and they show the runner at first base, watch his eyes. If they're darting back and forth, the runner is probably peeking in at the plate, trying to steal a sign. If a catcher gets sloppy and leaves his knees too far apart, the runners on the corners—and the first- and third-base coaches—can see the signs. If the runner on first can pick up a sign for an off-speed pitch, that's a good time to go: an off-speed pitch takes longer to get to home plate.

But the runner might also be looking for the slide-step sign. A lot of teams use the same sign: if you see a catcher slide his hand down the inside of his thigh, he's telling the pitcher to slide-step. The catcher wants the pitcher to deliver the pitch while barely lifting his front foot off the ground. A pitcher who is a 1.5 in his normal delivery might become a 1.3 with a slide step. If the runner knows the pitcher is using his slower delivery—no slide step—that's another good time to steal.

The runner might also look for the catcher to give the pickoff sign; that one looks like the catcher is flipping a coin with his thumb. Ninety percent of all pitchers won't throw over to first base unless they get a sign from the catcher. If a runner can see the catcher's signs and doesn't see the slide-step sign or the pickoff sign, he may be going.

Most pitchers are more worried about executing their pitch than about the runner on first base—as they should be. That's why catchers need to remind pitchers to mix it up, especially if a guy is slow to home plate. Pitchers get in a rhythm and tend to hold the ball in the set position for the same amount of time on every pitch. Then all a runner has to do is count, "One thousand one, one thousand two," and break for the next base at the right time. A pitcher can be getting the ball to home plate in 1.2 seconds, but if he keeps the same pattern, a runner can time him and still steal the base. Catchers need to make sure the runner at first can't see the signs, and pitchers need to mix it up.

Otherwise, someone's going to steal a base.

The pickoff sign

That sign—flipping the thumb for a pickoff—used to be the sign the catcher gave the pitcher when he wanted the pitcher to hit the batter. Now there's so much TV coverage, catchers don't use it anymore; it's pretty obvious and easy to see. I'm not sure the sign changed because of TV, but it seems likely. With so many cameras around now, not much gets missed.

Instead of giving a sign for the pitcher to hit the batter, I'd go to the mound and tell the pitcher what I wanted: hit this guy on the third pitch. Waiting a couple pitches puts some doubt in people's minds; if you hit him right away, it's pretty obvious what the mound meeting was about. On the other hand, if you want to make a statement, the first pitch is the best time to do it.

When I could no longer throw because of my arm, if I had a base stealer on, I'd give the pitcher the pickoff sign over and over. Sometimes I was trying to tire the runner out, but other times I was just dicking with the crowd. Hell, I'd have the pitcher go over to first base six times. People would boo and I'd get a kick out of it. I screwed around with the crowd all the time. I'd have the pitcher go over and the crowd would boo. I'd think, *This is kinda cool, let's do it again.* Every time I'd signal for another pickoff, the crowd would boo louder. I thought it was funny—they weren't booing me, they were booing the pitcher. I'm making him go over and he's thinking, *Goddammit, don't make me throw over there again.* The pitcher's wearing it: everyone thinks he's a jerk for trying five or six pickoffs in a row, and I'm behind the plate cracking up.

It's a long season; you do what you can to amuse yourself.

The runner on second base

Runners on second base can see the catcher's signs and—if they can decode the sign sequence we're using—pass that information along to the hitter. Guys at the plate want to know if the pitch is a fastball or something off-speed. Slider, curve, change—it doesn't matter—they just want to know if they need to be quick or wait back on the pitch. A runner has so many ways to signal the hitter: tug on your pants once it's a fastball, two tugs it's off-speed. Two looks back at the shortstop, off-speed; one look, it's a fastball. Fans can watch a runner's mannerisms and begin to pick up patterns.

A runner on second base might step forward as he takes his lead to signal one kind of pitch. If he takes his lead by stepping straight toward third, it's something else. Which foot he uses to start his lead might be the signal: If he takes his lead left-foot first, it's hard. If he takes his lead right-foot first, it's soft. Most of the time I wasn't stealing signs, but when I was, I might take my helmet off with my left hand if it was a fastball and with my right hand it was off-speed.

A runner can signal the hitter what's coming in so many ways—but if we catch you doing one of them, we'll drill you.

First movement

Left-handed pitchers can be hard for a runner on first base to read: if the guy's got a good move, it's hard to tell if he's going to throw the ball to home plate or over to first base. With some lefties you might have a key, something that tells you what he plans to do. For example, if he starts his motion and the toe on his front foot is up, he's coming over to first—toe down, he's going home. Base runners and baserunning coaches spend hours watching videos looking for that kind of key.

But if you don't have a key and still feel the need to run, you can go on *first movement*. Running on first movement is a roll of the dice: the runner doesn't try to read what the pitcher is doing—he breaks for second on the first movement the pitcher makes from the set position.

But before you go on first movement, you better know if the lefty's a *reader*. A reader is a left-handed pitcher who can lift his front foot, let it hang, and *then* decide whether to throw the ball to home plate or attempt a pickoff at first base. He "reads" what the runner is doing and then decides what he wants to do with the baseball.

Those guys are athletes.

You should already know before the game starts—guys like Andy Pettitte, Mark Buehrle, and Jamie Moyer are really good at it. Their moves are amazing. You don't steal off them—they'll hang and read you. Most pitchers can't do that. Most pitchers have to decide what they're going to do with the ball before they ever pick up their front foot. A lot of pitchers mentally commit to going over to first base or throwing the ball home, and once that movement is started, they can't change. When a runner going on first movement guesses right, it works great. When a runner guesses wrong, it looks awful—but it might have been a calculated gamble that didn't pay off.

Early in my career I was on first base and lefty Terry Mulholland was on the mound. I was just starting to extend my lead when Mulholland tried to pick me off. I was caught in between, quickly changed direction, and got back to first base—but I pulled my hammie. I was too embarrassed to tell the trainers how I'd done it.

My hamstring was black-and-blue from my ass to my calf, but I didn't want to admit I'd hurt it when a lefty with a good move tried to pick me off.

The walking lead

The walking lead is such a great play. Former catcher John Wathan showed me how to do it. You take a short lead. The pitcher looks over and you're one step away from first base: nothing to worry about. When the pitcher looks over, I'm on top of the bag.

Then the pitcher decides to go home.

I start walking, walking, walking—then boom, I'm gone. I stole 12 bases my last season and I think I stole 9 of them standing up.

The pitcher would start to deliver the ball home and I'd already be halfway down to second. Everybody would be screaming for the pitcher to step off the rubber, but the pitcher had already decided to throw the ball to home plate and couldn't change what he was doing.

The walking lead is a gamble: it takes guts. If the pitcher looks over twice, you're screwed; but they're such creatures of habit, you can take advantage of them.

The one-way lead

A base runner sometimes takes a *one-way lead*. That means the runner takes a big lead but doesn't intend to break for second base. The runner takes a big lead with every intention of going back to first base.

The runner might be doing this for his own benefit: he wants to see the pitcher's pickoff move live. Or he might be doing it for the first-base coach's benefit: the coach wants to see the pitcher's move live. They've seen the video, but want to see what it looks like in real life. A runner who takes too big a lead *forces* the pitcher to throw over to first base: the pitcher can't deliver the ball home while the runner is that far off the base.

The crowd is booing the pitcher for going over to first base again and again, but it might be the base runner's fault.

The secondary lead

You can tell something about a base runner by how he takes his secondary lead. When a runner leads off a base while the pitcher still has the ball in his hand, that's the primary lead. When the pitcher delivers the ball home, the runner takes a couple shuffle steps toward the next base: that's the secondary lead. Runners take secondary leads to get a head start toward the next base.

Lazy runners won't push it on the secondary lead—they'll get off the base, but not that far off. Some of these guys are just standing there digging themselves. They're thinking about the hit they just got and what their batting average is after getting that hit. Their mind is not on baserunning; they don't take it as seriously as they should.

What's the cliché? Baseball is a game of inches?

It really is. A guy takes a lousy secondary lead and then gets thrown out by a step at home plate? That guy could have been safe if he'd been working harder at his baserunning. Pay attention and you can see the guys who work at getting a good secondary.

The third-base coach

Third-base coaches have a tough job. If they send a runner home and the runner's out on a close play, the crowd thinks the base coach screwed up. If they send a runner home and the runner's safe on a close play, the crowd thinks it was a great slide.

Coaching third requires a lot of information. Before the coach decides to send a runner home or hold him at third, he needs to think about the inning, the score, the number of outs, the runner, the on-deck hitter, possible pinch hitters, relievers warming up in the other team's bull pen, the type of ball in play, the outfielder's arm, if the outfielder is left-handed, if the outfielder is moving laterally or toward home plate, if the throw is coming from right field, if the grass is wet and how good the other pitcher is—and that's just for starters.

Ask a big league third-base coach like Eddie Rodriguez what he's thinking about when he decides to send a runner, and he'll give you an incredible list:

Inning: If it's early in the game, the manager probably won't hit for the on-deck hitter, and the opposition manager probably won't bring in a reliever. Later in the game, the third-base coach needs to consider possible pinch-hitter/reliever matchups and keep an eye on the other team's bull pen. The third-base coach needs to know who is getting ready to come into the game and how that changes things.

Score: The third-base coach needs to know what an extra run means. If it's the tying run, that can mean one thing; if it's the winning run, then that can mean another. But it can get even more complicated. If you're up by one run in the bottom of the eighth and sending the runner home will put you up by two runs, that means your defense won't have to guard the lines or play no doubles in the top of the ninth. The insurance run means better defense during a crucial part of the game. That extra run also means the pitcher can be more aggressive; he doesn't need to worry about giving up the lead on one swing of the bat.

Outs: If there are two outs and the on-deck hitter is not a good matchup with the pitcher, expect the third-base coach to be aggressive about sending the runner home.

The runner: How fast is he? If there's a play at the plate, what kind of slide can you expect? Is the runner a bulldog or a guy who's soft?

Positioning of the outfield: Is the outfield playing shallow? If the outfield is shallow and a ball gets into a gap, a runner on first base might have a chance to score—the outfielders have a long run to the ball. If the outfield is backed up playing "no doubles" when the ball is hit to the wall, a runner on first base might not be able to score—the outfielders are deep and have a shorter run to the ball. If a ball is hit hard—right at an outfielder—a runner on second base might be able to score if the outfielder was playing deep and might have to hold up if the outfielder was playing shallow.

Type of ball in play: If there are less than two outs and the ball in play is a low line drive, the runner is going to get a lousy jump—he has to wait to see if the ball will be caught. If the ball in play is a grounder, most of the time the runner gets a good jump; he can leave right away—unless he was on second base, the ball was in front of him, there was no force, and he had to hold up to make sure the ball got through the infield.

If a ball splits a gap perfectly, both outfielders will have a long run to the ball. If the ball hits the chain link on a bull-pen gate or covering an outfield scoreboard, it will die and drop straight down. If it hits a solid wall, it will come back to the outfielder quickly.

The outfielder: Does he have a good arm? Is he moving back, laterally, or toward home plate? Is he fielding the ball on his glove side or throwing side? Is he right- or left-handed? Thrown balls can tail to the arm side, whether it's a lefty or a righty. So a throw home from a lefty might pull the catcher into foul territory, while a throw from a righty might pull the catcher up the third-base line.

If a guy throws from over the top, the ball will be straight, but if the outfielder has a lower arm angle, the ball will have lateral movement. Coaches need to know if an outfielder has that kind of movement on his throws. Will that movement pull the catcher away from the plate and be enough to allow the runner to slide in safely?

If the throw is coming from left field, the catcher can see the ball and the runner at the same time. If the throw is coming from center field, the catcher can see the ball and the runner out of his peripheral vision. But if the throw is coming from right field, the catcher will lose sight of the runner while fielding the throw and will have to turn back to the plate to make a tag.

A third-base coach can be more aggressive about sending a runner when the throw comes from right field—especially if the right fielder is left-handed.

Playing conditions: If the outfield grass is wet, a ground ball will also be wet and the throw will not be as strong. A ball caught in the air won't be affected.

The pitcher: If there are two outs and CC Sabathia's on the mound, you might want to send the runner. Most of the time, counting on another hit off him is a bad bet. If you see a lights-out reliever warming up in the pen, same thing; if the run matters, the lights-out reliever might come in to shut the door.

When you're coaching third, there's a lot to think about and the decisions have to be made before the third-base coach knows how it will all turn out.

Aggressive baserunning

In baseball, anytime you rush, it's not a good thing—and aggressive baserunning makes the other team rush. Pitchers have to speed up their delivery to the plate, catchers try to be quick getting the ball down to second base, outfielders make bad throws when they get in a hurry, and infielders bobble the ball on the relay because they know the runner is headed home.

If I were a third-base coach, I'd send runners home all the time. People don't know how hard it is to do all that: field the ball cleanly in the outfield, hit the cutoff man, catch the ball again, accurately relay the throw home, catch the ball a third time with a runner bearing down on you, block the plate, and make the tag.

The odds are with the runner.

The alternative to aggressive baserunning is conservative, station-to-station baseball. Advancing one base at a time puts tremendous pressure on the offense: they may have to get three or four hits to score a single run. And station-to-station baseball takes pressure *off* the defense. If they don't have to worry about the stolen base, the pitcher can take his time delivering the ball home, the catcher can call more breaking pitches, and the middle infielders don't have to stand closer to second base. If they don't have to worry about a base runner taking an extra base, the outfielders can take their time getting the ball back to the infield. Everybody relaxes.

Some fans get upset when their team gives away outs on the base paths. But making outs is an occupational hazard—it's the main thing a hitter does. Sometimes it's better to push it on the bases than to count on a hitter to get the job done, especially if the other team's pitcher is Chris Carpenter.

It all depends on the pitcher, the hitter, the runner, and the situation.

8

THE MANAGER

THE BEST part of a manager's day starts at 7:05—game time. Until then, the manager has to deal with all the other parts of his job: the media, the front office, the clubhouse, the grounds crew, the coaches, and the support staff—all the stuff that goes into managing a baseball team that most people don't think about. Once the game starts, the manager can forget all that and just worry about baseball.

Good managers go over scenarios: Who are the starting pitchers? What's their history? What kind of performance can be expected tonight? What do we do if we grab an early lead? What do we do if *they* grab an early lead? Which relievers are available in our pen? Which relievers are available in *their* pen? Who's on our bench? Who's on *their* bench? What are the likely late-inning matchups? If they bring in this reliever, what pinch hitter do I send to the plate? Is anyone banged up? Do we have a defensive replacement available if needed?

Managers should think about this stuff before the game ever starts. Then, when that situation pops up, the manager doesn't hesitate; he's already thought about it and knows what he wants to do.

If a manager doesn't think about these things in advance, he'll get caught flat-footed by some situation he hadn't considered.

Good managers manage ahead of the game, bad ones manage behind the game.

Small ball versus the big inning

You can manage to score one run or to play for the big inning. When you play for one run, you're willing to use your outs to advance a runner around the bases: you bunt, you hit-and-run, you steal. You're happy if you scratch out a single run. When you play for the big inning, you let the guys hit away and hope to put a crooked number up on the scoreboard.

Based on the starting pitchers, you already have an idea of what kind of game you'll be in that day. If you're facing an ace—a Félix Hernández—you're going to play to score one run and to *prevent* one run earlier than normal. There won't be a lot of scoring today. If you're facing a bottom-of-the-rotation type pitcher, you're probably going to play for the big inning.

How you manage depends on who's pitching.

Early in the season, the number one starting pitcher on your staff will face the number one starting pitcher on the other team's staff—the pitching rotations match up. That might happen the first month of the season. As the season goes along, teams are rained out and have off days; rotations are no longer in sync. Now your number four starting pitcher can be facing their number one starting pitcher. If that's the case—and their number one is dominant—you don't want to get behind early; he'll bury you.

If their starting pitcher only needs three runs to win, you better make sure he doesn't get those three runs. You have to bring the infield in earlier in the game to prevent a run from scoring and push it on the base paths, going first to third, second to home, or stealing a base. In those types of matchups, you have to do things a little bit differently. If you've got your number five guy facing a Cy Young Award winner, you *better* not manage by the book—you'll get your ass kicked. You don't match up well. And if doing something outside the box backfires, you have to be willing to handle the media afterward. If you do a hit-and-run with runners on first and second with one down, that's a great play: the third baseman will cover third and open the left side of the infield. A routine grounder to third base will score a run. But if it backfires, you've got to answer questions.

In a bad matchup, you should play for the early runs: try to put a couple up on the board as quickly as you can. Getting your number five guy an early lead can build his confidence. You're going to need a cushion—try to score a couple runs in the first few innings. Sitting back and playing for a big inning when you're facing an ace is bad strategy: if he's on—and you'll know fairly early—the big inning is just not coming.

The stadium you're playing in can also change your strategy: you're more likely to play for a big inning in Camden Yards than in Kauffman Stadium. How you manage changes game by game, inning by inning, pitch by pitch. The score, where you are in the lineup, who's on the mound—your strategy depends on a lot of factors, and those factors change all the time.

Strategies

Hit away, hit-and-run, bunt-and-steal. People make it so complicated, but there aren't that many options, and the players involved dictate the moves. If the guy at the plate can't bunt, why call it? It might be the right move most of the time, but tonight—*right now*—it's not. If the guy at the plate can't hit the guy on the mound, why hit away? If that's the case and you have a runner on and the situation calls for it, then you might want him to bunt the runner over. The people involved change the strategy.

Here are some common strategies a manager can use:

The bunt: Making outs is what hitters mainly do, so make some productive ones. If a runner's on base and nobody's out, move him, especially when you're in a bad hitter-pitcher matchup. If the guy at the plate can't hit this pitcher anyway, use him to move a runner—as long as the run matters.

But where you are in the lineup can change your strategy. The guys at the bottom of the order need to be able to hit to the situation of the game. If the situation calls for a bunt, a hit-and-run, or moving the runner over—the guys at the bottom of the order need to have those bat-handling skills, that's their job.

The guys in the heart of the order need to hit; you're not asking those guys to lay down a bunt. Guys in the middle of the order have to do some damage; let them hit away. The 3, 4, and 5 guys have to hit and drive in runs. The better teams go even deeper than the five-hole with good hitters.

Most of the time, you want to use the bunt later in the game, unless you're in the National League and the pitcher's at the plate. You might use the bunt earlier in the game if you're facing a Roy Halladay–type pitcher. Then you're just trying to get an early run on the board.

The hit-and-run: You hear a lot of rules for using the hit-and-run, but I'd say use it when you feel it. It just depends on who's hitting and who's pitching; I've done it with two strikes before. If the guy at the plate can handle the bat and the pitcher's around the plate, it can work; it just depends on the people involved.

I'd do it with three balls—why not? In certain situations, it could be a good move. If the manager trusts the hitter, you could make it work. If the count's 3-0, everybody knows the hitter's taking. What if he doesn't? If you put a runner in motion and the pitcher grooves a fastball, there are going to be holes all over the infield. If it's a strike, you swing; if it's a ball, you take. The manager has to trust the hitter to do that. But if you have the right person at the plate, you can get away with a 3-0 hit-and-run. You have to be willing to take chances. If the hitter swings and misses, you're going to look like an idiot. If it works, you'll look like a genius. As a manager, you need thick skin.

I loved moving the runners; put runners in motion and holes open up. I'd also put a hit-and-run on if a guy's struggling at the plate. If it works, you build the hitter's confidence: you might get him out of his slump. When a guy's scuffling, he's looking for something positive. When you're scuffling and you *do* hit a ball hard, it's right at somebody. Put runners in motion and you open up so many holes on the infield for the hitter. Giving a guy who's scuffling a hit-and-run sign can also clear his mind. You take the decision to swing the bat away from him; he's swinging, no matter what. In that case, he can quit worrying about pitch selection and concentrate on making contact.

The stolen base: Be unpredictable. Whenever a team came into town, I'd look at the counts in which their leadoff hitter ran. I wanted to know in what count the runner had the most steals. Some base stealers like to run in certain counts, others like to do it with a certain number of outs. Base runners fall into patterns, just like pitchers. If you're 10 and 0 stealing in a 1-0 count, you're probably going to keep running in 1-0 counts. If you're 2 and 8 stealing in 2-1 counts, you're probably not going in that count. Catchers need to know when a base stealer's success rate is good and when it's not so good. By being predictable, base runners gave me a better chance to throw them out.

If the runner falls into a pattern—using the same counts, stealing in the same situations—he gives the defense an edge. If the pitcher and catcher fall into a pattern—using the same pitches in the same situations, holding the ball for the same amount of time in the set position—we give the runner an edge. If the only time a manager uses the hit-and-run is in a 2-1 count, we know that and we'll pitch out.

You can't fall into patterns.

The 3-0 green light: With a tough pitcher on the mound, a 3-0 pitch might be the best pitch the hitter will see. If the guy's got nasty stuff, this might be the hitter's best chance. I'd mainly use it when a guy with power was at the plate, but I might also use it with a contact hitter and a runner in scoring position.

You use it with a power hitter at the plate because he might drive himself in. Some power hitters take a walk and all they do is clog the bases. If the walk came with two outs, you might need two or three more two-out hits to get the run home. It might be better to let the power hitter see what he can do with a 3-0 green light. A contact hitter is more likely to hit a single, so with him you might use the 3-0 green light with a runner on third and less than two outs. This might be the best chance to get the run in. In the National League you can use a 3-0 green light with a runner in scoring position and the pitcher on deck.

Hitting 3-0 is all about picking a zone: if the ball's not there and it's not a four-seam fastball, shut it down.

I couldn't hit 3-0; I just wasn't comfortable doing it. Some guys can hit 3-0, some guys can't. Some guys get too big—they overswing. They *know* they're getting a four-seam fastball down the middle of the plate and they try to hit a home run. That's one of the reasons catchers might call something other than a fastball 3-0. Overswinging in a 3-0 count is similar to what happens to hitters with runners in scoring position: some guys can keep everything the same and some guys try too hard. The manager needs to know who can handle a 3-0 green light. The guys who can hit 3-0 are the same guys that can hit in the clutch: the guys who keep everything the same 3-0 or 0-0, first inning or last, tying run on second or bases empty.

The squeeze play: In a suicide squeeze, the runner sprints for home when the pitcher's front foot comes down. If the batter doesn't get the bunt down, the runner will be out. In the safety squeeze, the runner has to make a judgment call about breaking for home. If he thinks the bunt is good enough to score him, he breaks for home; if not, he stays on third.

The manager on the defensive side pretty much knows when a squeeze is coming. He sees the same things the manager on offense sees: right guy on third, right guy at the plate, right guy on the mound, the score, the inning, the number of outs. Defending the squeeze is all a matter of picking the right pitch to pitch out on.

I don't like the safety squeeze. In fact, I can't *stand* the safety squeeze. It's a way for a manager to cover his ass. He doesn't want to get out on a limb by committing the runner to go home. If you're going to squeeze, use the suicide. If the defense sniffs out a suicide squeeze and pitches out, the suicide squeeze looks bad. But if you get a good pitch to bunt, the suicide is easier to execute: get the ball down on the ground *anywhere* and the runner will be safe.

A safety squeeze is trying to split the difference: you're not committing the runner to break for home, but the bunt's got to be better. It has to be placed just right to give the runner time to see that it's a good bunt and then break for home. A lot can go wrong, and the safety squeeze puts a lot of pressure on the players to get it right. If they don't, the manager can fault the execution.

Use the suicide squeeze; you either get the bunt down and score the run, or you miss the bunt and the runner's out—keep it simple. In my opinion, the safety squeeze is a terrible play; but some people like it.

Managing a baseball team is easy when the team's hitting: just send the guys to the plate and let them hit away. When the lineup's scuffling, the manager needs to be creative and use some of the strategies listed above. When your team is scuffling, you need to think outside the box. Change something up; get them out of the rut they're in. If you've lost six games in a row, what you're doing isn't working.

Do something different, take a risk.

Less talent = more risk

A lot of managers manage on the safe side; they'll go by the book because they don't want to deal with the media questions after the game. If they go outside the box and do something different, the media will be all over them if the move fails; take a chance and you're out on a limb. But if you're going to manage by the book, you better have the Yankees on the field; you better have the pitching. If you don't have the studs you need, you better take some risks.

Look at a bad team—how do you change that?

By doing something different. Playing by-the-book baseball against better teams hasn't worked. So you have to take chances; but after you take a chance, you have to behave the same way whether the move succeeds or fails. You have to be the same guy—you can't panic. Face it: manage long enough and you *are* going to get fired.

If you're lucky enough to have future Hall of Famers all over the field, let them play. But if you've got less talent, take advantage of the talent you *do* have. As long as you believe the man at the plate can make contact, go ahead and put on a 1-2 hit-and-run. Catch people by surprise; be unorthodox. When you don't match up well, going toe-to-toe with the other team is a good way to lose. Fear is not an option: you can't be afraid to be criticized for the moves you make.

Pressure

You always want to push the other team to make plays. If I were a third-base coach, I'd send everybody because throwing a runner out at the plate is hard. If the defense makes the play, tip your cap. Pressure changes the thought process of the whole game. If you never take an extra base, steal, bunt, or hit-and-run—if there's no pressure—the other team relaxes. They stand where they want, make the pitches they want, and play at the pace they want. Some teams can get away without ever playing small ball or trying to apply pressure, but if you do that, you better have some boppers in the lineup.

Speed changes the game; speed gives you options. Speed drives the other team crazy. The pitcher has a base stealer on first? The pitcher knows that if he throws a breaking pitch and that runner takes off, his catcher has no chance to throw the runner out. Now the hitter knows a fastball is coming.

If you're on a roll, keep going: go, go, go. Pressure the other team. Put a hit-and-run on, steal a base, drop a bunt. If there's a distraction, an argument, a delay of some kind—anything that has the other team focused on something other than the game—put a play on. Keep coming at them. Jump on them. If there's a scuffle on the field—nowadays they're just out there hugging each other—put a play on the next pitch. The other team will still be thinking about the fight.

If you get to the play-offs, you gotta do everything: play for the big inning *and* manufacture runs. Look at the World Series champs—most of the time they're teams that can scratch for a run when they need to. You need to play that way during the season if you want to be able to play that way in the play-offs. If you wait until the play-offs and *then* decide you need to manufacture a run, people won't be comfortable. Make that part of your game, starting on Opening Day.

You can't be scared; you have to be willing to take a risk. Let it ride; leave it all on the field. You can't care what people think about you.

Lineups

In the American League, you build your team around the DH. Look at who they are: David Ortiz, Billy Butler, Adam Dunn. The DH should be hitting third, fourth, or fifth. If you see a DH hitting seventh or eighth, you're probably not looking at a very good team. Once in a while you might see an exception to that. Paul Molitor comes to mind, but that's Paul Molitor—a Hall of Famer.

The leadoff hitter needs to get on base, the 2-hole hitter needs to handle the bat and be able to move the leadoff hitter over, and the 3-4-5 guys need to do some damage. If you can go deeper than the 5-hole with good hitters, that's great. After that, the bottom of the order needs to hit to the situation and handle the bat.

But before you make out a lineup, you've got to know a guy's makeup. Can he hit in the 3-hole? Has this other guy got the mindset to lead off? The 3-4-5 guys have to have the right temperament. Some hitters are *unbelievable*—until big-game situations. You have to know who responds well to game-on-the-line situations and who folds. A guy may be great *before* a big situation comes up—he puts up all kinds of numbers—but then he's not the guy you want up at the plate with the game on the line. You might be better off with a .275 hitter at the plate than a guy hitting .300, depending on the guys involved. When he makes out the lineup, a manager has to know who's mentally tough and who's not.

Once a manager identifies who he wants in what spot in the

order, the biggest thing is set roles. Let the guys get comfortable. Players perform better in set roles. Guys perform better if you don't keep jerking them around; let them know their job. The game is so mental you don't need to throw anything else their way.

Once in a while—when the whole lineup is scuffling—you'll see a manager flip things around. He's just giving guys a mental break from what they've been doing, but if you're going to do that, let the players know in advance.

When players know their roles, they know how to prepare. If possible, the best thing a manager could do is post the next day's lineup after a game. If a guy's getting a day off, tell him in advance. If a bench player is going to play, let him know the night before. Let the players get mentally prepared for the next day. That way, a guy doesn't come in the next day, see his name is not in the lineup, and wonder why. The worst thing you can do is tell people what they're doing right before a game. I might do something different in certain situations—like the play-offs—but over the long haul, guys perform better in set roles.

The banged-up player

A player may be banged up—hurting—and nobody outside the team knows it. The trainer might come to the manager and say this guy has a sore hamstring; you can't run him tonight, he's getting ready to blow. Despite the fact that the player's not 100 percent, the manager might still want him in the lineup. A star player's bat and presence can change the game.

A star player can get better pitches for the guy hitting in front of him just by standing in the on-deck circle. If they pitch around the star player—*they* don't know his hammie's sore—the star player might to do the same for the guy hitting behind him. And nobody will ever know this guy is playing in pain. Fans and the media might wonder why this guy didn't steal a base or go first to third or why he let a ball drop in front of him. Even though he's playing at less than 100 percent, he might still be better than the alternative.

People sometimes wonder why teams get so secretive, but they might have a banged-up player on the field and the manager doesn't want the other team to know.

Blue-collar players

Some guys are in the big leagues because they do one thing great. Other guys are in the big leagues because they do a lot of things well—and those players give you options.

Everybody knows the superstars, and you need as many of those as you can get. But after that, you need the guys who can do a variety of things, the guys who have worked hard at developing different skills and can do the little things that turn into big things; you need these blue-collar players. Every team needs one or two guys who can handle a bat, play solid defense, and make good decisions on the base paths. It's probably more important to have these players in the National League, but every team needs to have at least one. These guys change the game and nobody notices.

They can change the game by going first to third, bunting a runner over, backing up a base, hitting the ball to the right side, hustling down and breaking up a double play, or hanging in and turning a double play on defense. These guys know what they can and cannot do. They know their roles. They're the feisty players, the guys who have ten-pitch at bats to give their pitcher a chance to rest or let their teammates see what the other pitcher has that night. They hit the ball where it's pitched. They make the defensive plays. They're smart. They get the most out of the talent they have.

These guys stay around a long time. Everybody comes to see the stars and manages to miss some of the most important players on the field: the blue-collar guys. They might be hitting .240, but they still change the game. They get it done when it matters because they've done their homework. They might not hit .300 or drive in 100 runs, but they're still valuable players. You have to have these guys on your team.

All these blue-collar guys could manage a game right now; they're always thinking ahead. They make your job as a manager so much easier because they allow you to get creative: they have a lot of different skills and you can use them in every type of situation. Chris Getz, Jeff Blauser, David Eckstein—perfect examples. Look at any one number and these guys won't blow you away, but look at the variety of things they can do and you want these players on your team.

These guys make a team better, they're true gamers.

Bench players

Bench players might get into a game when a starter needs a day off, gets hurt, or the game's a blowout. Even though they don't usually get into a game until the later innings, bench players need to stay ready all game long. If a guy pulls a quad running down to first base, the bench player can't come out on the field and start doing jumping jacks to get warm—he's got to be ready to play right now. The smart bench players warm up every few innings. They stay loose and ready. The good bench players—guys like Mitch Maier, who played with me in Kansas City—are real pros. They know they're not going to start, but they also know they can't goof around during the game. If they're going to be any good, they've got to pay attention to everything that's going on.

A guy fouls a ball off his leg and decides to leave the game during an at bat? The bench player better know what the pitcher's been throwing with two strikes. A guy gets hit by a pitch and leaves the game? The bench player better have a good idea of what the pitcher's pickoff move looks like. Bench players have to pay attention to every pitch. They need to understand the game situation and how they might be used. If the manager plans to use the bench player to pinch-hit for his second baseman if the other manager brings in a left-handed reliever, the bench player needs to know that and be prepared. The manager should tell the bench coach to tell a player to get ready, but a good bench player has been thinking along with the manager and should be mentally prepared whenever his name is called.

Sometimes bench players get to play when a starter needs a day off—then the *starter* becomes a bench player. Some starters get the day off and treat it as if they have the *whole* day off, but they need to fill the bench player's role: be ready to play. If a guy's sitting there bullshitting and spitting sunflower seeds, he isn't ready for a key at bat if the manager calls his name. A major league player should never be caught with his pants down. Even a starter with a day off should be in the batting cage taking swings to get ready, just in case he's needed. A coach should remind the player to prepare, but a player should assume he'll be needed and stay ready.

A manager calls on you and you're *not* ready?

That's a good way to get shipped out.

Know your pitchers

If I were a manager, the first week or two of spring training, I'd catch all my pitchers. As a manager, I need to know what they have—and you can't tell without catching it. Granted, I have an advantage because I can catch. If he can't catch, a manager needs to get behind the backstop and watch a pitcher's stuff. You need to know a pitcher's quirks; you need to know the movement of all of his pitches. How much does his fastball cut? What kind of sink does he get on his two-seamer? How nasty is his slider? You need to know this stuff to make good decisions.

One year, late in the season—I think it was August—we had a mound visit by the manager. The pitcher had a situation going, so the manager suggested the pitcher throw a couple sinkers and get out of the mess he was in. One problem: the pitcher didn't throw a sinker. It was August and the manager still had no idea that the guy on the mound didn't throw a sinker?

If I'm managing, I need to know exactly what every pitcher has. You can't tell a pitcher to get out of a mess with a pitch he doesn't throw. You need to know exactly what each guy throws and how it can be used. If one guy has more sink on a ball and another guy has more run, if I need a ground ball, I'm going with the guy with more sink. As a manager, I want to know that. If I *don't* know that, I'm not doing my job.

Pulling the starter

You can't treat a rookie like a veteran. You might want to avoid having a rookie take a loss, so you pull him while he's still ahead. A veteran you might leave in; he can handle losing. He's been around and it won't shake his confidence.

When the manager pulls the starter depends on the situation in the game. Here's the simple version: If a starter is letting the game get out of control, if he's giving up hits and walks, if runs are scoring on him—get him out. If a starter is getting outs—let him go.

When a pitcher starts getting tired, he'll get the ball up in the zone. A pitcher's got to be honest: if he's getting tired, he needs to let people know. If *he* doesn't let people know, the catcher better say something. Nobody has a better idea of what a pitcher has left than the catcher; managers should be talking to their catchers throughout the game. If the pitcher or catcher doesn't let someone know the pitcher's gassed, the hitters will: if the ball's up in the zone, they'll start knocking the crap out of it.

Managers want to get their starters wins and will try to get them through the five innings required to qualify for one. But the manager needs to know the pitcher's makeup. Some guys can start to scuffle and get it back. Some guys, once they start losing it, they're done—get them out right now. It all depends on who it is. If it's a top-of-the-rotation guy, you let him fight through it, he's your horse—he's earned it. Bottom-of-the-rotation guys are a little more hit-and-miss. Leave those guys in and it might get loud.

Matchups

If you have the right personnel on the field, all you really need to worry about is the bull-pen matchups later in the game. If the other team has a Tom Glavine on the mound, you better scratch and claw—do some managing, play some small ball. Otherwise, let your players play for the first five or six innings; after that, you manage matchups.

Once the starter leaves, everyone in the bull pen has a role. The score dictates everything. If the score's 10–0—whether you're winning or losing—you put your long reliever in the game and have him go as far as he can. If the score's 1–0, you might use every reliever in the pen. If it's a tight game—after the starter leaves and until you get to the back end of the bull pen—it's all about those matchups. Once you get to the back end of the pen—the eighth-inning setup man and the ninth-inning closer—things get easier. Until then the manager earns his money by mixing and matching, trying to get the best reliever-hitter matchups possible. So many games are won or lost in the sixth and seventh innings because of matchups.

In the American League, that's the main thing a manager does: he tries to get good matchups from the time his starter leaves until he gets to the back end of the bull pen.

Some matchups are obvious. If you've got a left-handed reliever down in the pen and two left-handed hitters are coming up next inning, the left-hander is probably going to get the ball. Anytime you see a left-handed reliever warming up, look at the other team's lineup for left-handed hitters—now you know when the reliever is coming into the game.

Other matchups are less obvious. I'm not that big on the righty-lefty stuff. Look at the matchup numbers—a pitcher's record against individual hitters—and you'll see certain right-handed pitchers can get certain left-handed hitters out, and vice versa.

If the other manager has two left-handed hitters in the lineup, he can stack them—have them hit back-to-back—or sandwich them—put a right-handed hitter in between the two lefties. You see a manager use three relievers to get through those three hitters in one inning—lefty, righty, lefty—it looks like great managing, but the bull pen is being chewed up. It might be worth it—depending on the situation—but what if the game goes fifteen innings? You used three guys to get through the eighth.

Some guys like to overmanage—it shows how smart they are. Myself? I hated it. You're bringing in three guys to get three outs, and we all have to stand around for another ten minutes while this guy warms up? Fans think you're managing the hell out of the game, but you're wearing out your pen and putting your defense on its heels. If you think your left-handed reliever can do the job, you leave him in to face that sandwich guy—the righty. That's how you avoid burning up your pen.

The only time I might get tricky with my bull pen is in the play-offs. If the other team's 3-4-5 hitters were coming up in the eighth inning and I knew my closer had crushed them in the past, I might bring him in early. Over the long haul I believe in set roles, but in the play-offs, it's all hands on deck.

Over 162 games the bull pen needs set roles, but in the play-offs, it's balls to the wall. You might send a starting pitcher down to the pen just in case he's needed. If you have to win tonight or go home, you might do some things in October that you wouldn't do in July. So if my closer has had unbelievable success off the 3-4-5 hitters and they're due up in the eighth, I might bring him in right then—but I'd let all my players know in advance so they could mentally prepare for the new situation. "Here's the deal, guys: Roles are out the window tomorrow night. If I got a situation where I need you early, I might go to you early."

If you're going to do something different—and in the play-offs you might have to—the key is letting the guys know that in advance.

Protecting your players

Players want to be protected and a good manager does that. If a guy screws up, you don't air him out in the dugout when everybody is watching. If a player needs an ass chewing, you call him into your office and do it in private. If you think it can't wait, you take him up the tunnel and do it out of sight of the fans and the cameras. You don't embarrass your players publicly. If you throw them under the bus, they may not hesitate to throw *you* under the bus.

You've got to have their backs—or at least *appear* to have their backs.

When you see a manager with his finger in an umpire's face, it looks like he's backing up his player. Sometimes he is, but sometimes he's saying, "You're absolutely right, my guy *was* out! But I'm looking out for my player!" The finger waving is an act. In public, you always back your players; in private, you may have your differences.

Mental mistakes piss off a manager. A base runner shouldn't make a dumb out because he didn't know the situation; this is the big leagues. These are grown men; they should know what to do. *Physical* mistakes will happen: a guy pops up a bunt or lets a ground ball get through. A manager should never, *ever* forget how hard the game is, although some managers do. No matter how hard he tries, a player will still suck some nights. But as long as a player busts his ass and gives a good effort, that player can look himself in the mirror.

But some players *don't* give a good effort. They'll hit a fly ball and start jogging because they think they've made an out. I don't care who it is. If a superstar hits a fly ball and doesn't run it out, he should be benched. Don't let anyone disrespect the game. The same goes for everybody on the roster. You can't have two sets of rules, but today some managers will not call out a superstar—there's too much money in the game now. But if you let the superstar get away with that stuff, every player sees it. That's why you've got to nip it in the bud right then and there; otherwise the other guys begin to think it's okay to not run out a fly ball.

Now you've got a real problem.

Letting them play

Most fans would be surprised by how often big league ballplayers are doing things on their own. You always check with the manager first: ask him if he's cool with you putting on your own plays. Me and Mark Kotsay put on our own hit-and-runs all the time: if he was on first and I was at the plate, I had a sign I could give to put him in motion.

This isn't Little League, these are professional ballplayers. The catcher calls the pitches because he can see things no one else can. If a base runner has the green light, he can steal a base whenever he thinks it's a good idea. The manager might have a sign to tell the runner *not* to go or a sign that tells the player he *must* go on the next pitch, but the rest of the time, if the player feels it, he goes. This kind of freedom goes to the guys who earn the privilege. Guys need to show they can handle the responsibility.

A player with good bat control might be on his own when moving a runner from second to third. He's the one facing the pitcher and has the best idea of what will work in this particular situation:

bunting or hitting the ball to the right side. Fans might be yelling at the manager for having a hitter bunt when it was the hitter's idea.

On the other hand, guys bunting on their own might get selfish: "Hey if I lay down a bunt to third base and it works, I get a hit. If it doesn't, I get a sacrifice and it doesn't hurt my average." Everybody on a team knows which players are selfish and which guys are team players, but nobody wants to call anybody out. When a manager finds himself with a selfish player, he needs to confront him—do it in private—but tell him you know why he bunted off Randy Johnson: he's 0 for his last 25 off him. If a manager doesn't put a stop to selfish play, it'll keep happening.

A player thinking like that—playing for his own numbers—is not good for the team. A manager needs to stop that shit right away, not let that stuff get started. If a manager sees selfish play, he's got to clean it up, nip it in the bud. The guys who make good decisions should keep the privilege; the guys who make bad ones lose it.

Keeping it simple

The game is so complicated, whenever a manager has the chance, he needs to keep it simple—and the smart ones do. In certain situations, they keep it *really* simple. You might see the third-base coach give twenty-seven different signs when it's a coach in the dugout who's telling the runner what to do: hat on, the runner stays put, hat off, the runner is going. The third-base coach's signs mean nothing.

A manager might tell the on-deck hitter that if the guy at the plate gets on, they should hit-and-run on the second pitch. People are watching for signs, and the play was put on before the inning even started. Cameras will show the manager making a bunch of complicated signs when the real sign may be where someone in the dugout is standing or whether a coach puts one or two arms on the dugout rail. The simpler you make it, the better. Confused players don't play well. The game is complicated enough; the manager's job is to make it as simple as possible for the players.

The smart managers find a way to simplify the game.

Taking charge

These days, too many managers don't take charge. Some managers worry too much about the media; these managers are more worried about their image than managing their team. Too many managers let the coaches run the game; the managers have been worrying about all the off-field shit and don't know what to do when a situation comes up.

Taking charge also means a manager needs to let his players know that if they don't buy into his shit, they're out of there. A manager needs to get in a guy's ass when he's embarrassing the team—when he's not running balls out, when he gets a take sign and swings away. You protect him, you don't let the public know what's going on, but you still get in his ass. If a guy still doesn't get it, if he's still not buying in? You send the player a wake-up call.

What's a wake-up call?

In my mind it's one of two things. Number one, you bench the player. You can't perform if you're on the bench. You lose your playing time and women aren't so impressed with you. People you meet in the street ask you why you're not playing. The manager might make up an excuse to give the press—tell them the player's got a sore leg—but the player knows and so do his teammates.

Everybody digs himself. You know what being benched does to a player's ego? You mope and throw shit? You don't run out ground balls? You got a tired act? Sit down for three days and figure things out. You know how embarrassing that is for an everyday player?

Now the guy's saying, "I'm going to the ballpark and I'm not playing? I better get my shit turned around."

The second thing you can do is send a guy down to the minors for two weeks. By sending him down you let him know he can lose everything: being a big league ballplayer is not guaranteed. The manager and the GM know the guy's getting called right back up, but you want to talk about a wake-up call? You're in the big leagues thinking you're a golden child, but someone calls time out and says, "You better pull your shit together if you want to play up here." Now *that's* a wake-up call.

Unfortunately, wake-up calls don't happen that much anymore.

Managers

I've had good ones and bad ones. I enjoyed playing for Gene Lamont. If someone asks me about Lamont, I'll tell them that's your manager, right there—hire the guy. I only played for Jim Leyland for one year, and it seemed like he turned over a table of food about once every two weeks. Lloyd McClendon got mad when I was called out on a bang-bang play at first and came out, pulled the bag out of the ground, and left with it—it was hilarious.

I never played for them, but I was in the game a long time and never heard a bad word about Bobby Cox or Ron Gardenhire. Now that's saying something.

To be totally honest, I feel like I managed for the last ten years of my career. While I was still playing, in between innings, some of my managers would ask me what I thought they should do. That's not a bad thing: smart managers *should* be talking to their catchers all the time—nobody has a better feel for what's going on during a game than the guy behind the plate. Nobody has a better idea of how much a pitcher has left. But if you want to know what advice I'd give to a manager these days, here's my answer:

Do it your way

A manager is only as good as the players on the field. A good manager gets the most out of them, a bad manager gets less. A good manager understands his players, what they can do and what they can't do. A good manager knows his players and puts them in a position to succeed. A good manager communicates with his players; it's the key to winning.

But no manager is perfect.

A manager takes his best shot; sometimes it works, sometimes it doesn't. Just because something didn't work, it doesn't mean the manager screwed up. He looked at his options, took the one with the best chance of success, and it didn't work out. It's a game of failure. You lost tonight; you go get 'em tomorrow.

A good manager trusts his instincts. Gut instinct is your subconscious and your baseball knowledge talking to you. Your first instinct is almost always right. You can follow the scouting report and cover your ass, or you can follow your instincts. A scouting report can tell you about the past, but something is going on tonight that tells you to do something different. Ignore your gut instinct and you're in trouble.

Eventually *everybody* gets fired—you might as well do it the way you want to.

9
THE OTHER STUFF

The media

Ballplayers see a big difference between the media guys who show up every day and the people who drop by once in a while. The everyday guys—the beat writers—they matter. You take care of those guys. If you have a bad game, you stand by your locker and wear it: you answer all their questions. If I have a good game I might talk to the beat writers, but still avoid the columnists. It was easy: all I had to do was say, "I gotta go; I'll catch you tomorrow at three."

The columnists have such a short attention span, they never come back. The everyday guys are different, you talk to them because they're just doing their job—good game, bad game, 0 for 4, 4 for 4—they have to show up and ask you questions. As professional athletes, we *get* that those guys are just doing their job. If a reporter writes about the good stuff as well as the bad, he gets more credit. Maybe you were 0 for 4 but moved the winning run over in a 2–2 game. If a reporter notices that, it's pretty cool.

The columnists, the guys who are here once in a while, stir up some shit, and leave? Hey, I'll catch you tomorrow. Those guys never stay on one subject long enough to show up the next day. The columnists are in the clubhouse maybe once a month. When one of them walks in, there's a buzz around the clubhouse: we know who they are. They come in once in a while, write some big thing, and get fans stirred up. They have no idea what's going on, but their job is to stir controversy. Columnists just aren't around that much. I can't speak for every columnist, but some of these guys might be there six times all summer. Yet they still go out and pose as experts.

The same goes for most of the sports-talk radio guys. If something is said about you? You hear about it. Even if we don't read it or hear it ourselves, someone will tell us. We know who the columnists and the radio guys are and what they've been saying. I get it: their job is to talk negative.

To be fair, I can't say *all* columnists and radio guys are awful. Hell, I love Howard Stern so much I won't rent a car unless it has Sirius XM radio (I've got to listen to the King of All Media). And some of the ex-athletes who are on these shows are pretty good. Let's just say 90 percent of these radio guys don't know what they're talking about, but won't stop talking.

They cover all kinds of sports and act like an expert in every one of them. They know nothing. You listen to some of the sports-talk radio guys and they sound like eight-year-old girls talking about baseball. Guys who have never worn a jockstrap are discussing whether Jose Reyes should have stolen a base in the ninth inning. They don't know what they're talking about. If you listen to them, it might be entertaining, but it probably won't be informative.

That's another reason I'm doing this book: people live and die off of what these guys say, and they're just not around the game, they don't know what they're talking about. They're just trying to make a name for themselves.

After my first five or six years in the big leagues, I didn't read the paper anymore. Why get caught up in all that? But for the first five years of my career, I spoke my mind: I'd tell the media that if ownership would spend some money, maybe we'd win. I'd say half the people in the stadium never put on a jockstrap, how the hell can they boo Al Martin? I was in my early twenties, being totally honest—and getting *hammered* for it. I never cared what people thought, but when you start getting batteries thrown at you in your home ballpark, maybe it's time to shut up.

For the first five years—win or lose—everybody would come to my locker. They knew I was going to say something quotable. I was great for the newspaper, but when fans start following you home at night, when they're smashing the windows in your car, maybe enough's enough.

My brother suggested I change my approach, and I figured I'd try something different: nothing but clichés. "Hey, the pitcher had a great game night, I sucked tonight, my bad, tomorrow's a new day, we worked both sides of the plate, we tried to keep the ball down, that's baseball, that's a good win for us, that's a tough loss for us, and we'll go get 'em tomorrow."

I did that every night and the media quit coming around so much.

In most cases, ballplayers don't think the media is worth the effort. Most media guys don't want to put in the time to really understand what's going on during a baseball game. Afterward, they've got five minutes and need a quote. Professional athletes have their guards up, and you're going to have to prove we can trust you before we're open with you. The columnists, a lot of the radio guys? They hardly ever show up, and they know shit about, number one, baseball, and number two, the team they're covering.

But they still go talk and write and people listen. Everybody wants negativity. If you're a columnist or sports-talk radio guy, most of the time your job is to stir controversy, most of the time your job is to be a dick. Not all of it, but I'd say 75 percent of what these guys say is bullshit.

The beat writers know what's going on. Those guys are with the team every day: road, home, spring training—wherever. You develop a relationship with those guys. You figure out the ones you can trust, the ones who put the effort in to understand what's going on. Players are willing to talk openly, but you've got to trust the guy you're talking to. You might share some inside information just so the guy understands what's happening, but you've got to trust him to use it in the right way. He needs to put it in his own words or confirm what you're telling him with someone else. Sometimes all you do is stop the guy from writing something that's untrue.

But if the writer throws a player under the bus, tells everybody where he got the inside information? That guy is done—100 percent. Nobody will tell that writer anything after that. The guys who do it right, the guys who show up every day, do the grind with you, gain your trust—the beat writers—those are the guys you should read and listen to.

Some unwritten rules

Baseball has all kinds of unwritten rules, some for players, some for the media, and some for visitors to the field. If you ever get a chance to go on the field or into a big league clubhouse, here are some of the unwritten rules visitors should know:

Batting practice: If you're allowed on the field during batting practice, they'll probably keep you on the dirt that separates the playing field from the stands and the dugouts. Even if you stay on the dirt, you should not go beyond first or third base. Visitors and the media should stay around the dugouts; the territory beyond the bases is for the players. Players who don't want to deal with the media or fans can escape to the outfield. Another reason not to go beyond the bases is safety: the batting cage wraps around the hitter so the only balls that leave the cage are going forward. But get beyond first or third base, and you're now in an area where you can get smoked by a line drive.

You don't think it happens intentionally?

If I saw a reporter wandering down the line, you don't think I'd send a little wake-up call his way? A media guy says something bad about me the night before and now he's wandering down the third-base line? I'd hook one his way. I never hit a media guy, but I scared a few.

If we're taking batting practice and you're dumb enough to walk into the line of fire, you probably haven't been on a baseball field very often. Sometimes you see a columnist down the line who wants to talk to the trainer or the general manager. The trainer and the GM know what's going on; they'll keep facing the field and let the columnist turn his back on the hitters. Of course if I'm a rookie, I'm not hitting anything near my GM—I might get my ass sent down.

If the other team was doing stretches down the line, I'd send one that way, too. Hell, I'd do it to our own pitchers. Don't be wandering around a baseball field with your head up your ass. It's the big leagues—pay attention.

It's also a bad idea to approach the batting cage while we're hitting. It may look like fun, but players taking batting practice are working. They'll take their hacks, step out, have a conference with the batting coach, and then think about the adjustments they need to make. You may see them talking to teammates or coaches, but it's usually a bad time for a conversation with anyone else. One of my biggest peeves was a media guy wanting to talk to me during BP.

People forget that this is our job, and that bothers me. A guy I knew from grade school shows up at a game and wants to talk? I don't have *time* to talk. I'm doing what I have to do to get ready for a game. Kids are different—you always take time for the kids—if you *have* time. But if you don't, parents get mad. All the public sees is how much money we make and that we play a game for a living. But this is not Little League, it's not high school ball, it's not college ball; this is our job. It's how we take care of our families. Do we get paid a lot of money? Absolutely—and I'll be the first one to say it's way too much, but I'm not going to say no. If you want to pay me that much money to play baseball, I'm not going to turn it down.

We have a duty to the public and I get that. I did the FanFests, I signed when I could, but once you get into your pregame routine, you need to stick to it. It's the only way to be prepared for a ball game.

Our equipment: Do not touch our stuff.

Whether it's in the clubhouse or the dugout, you should never touch a player's equipment. Guys are touchy about their gloves and bats. These are the tools we use to make a living. Players bring their gloves and BP bats down to the dugout and leave them there while they go stretch or do something else. I've never seen it—and that's good because if I did, I might be in jail—but I've been told visitors to the dugout sometimes can't resist picking up some of our equipment when we're not around. That's why I'd put a big glob of pine tar on the handle of my BP bats. If you pick one up, it takes forever to get the pine tar off your hands. You've got to scrub and scrub to get that stuff off.

Most players won't bring their gamer—the bat they'll use in a game—and leave that lying around during BP. They're more likely to deliver their game bat straight to the bat rack. You protect your gamer, nobody touches that. If the wrong person touched my game bat, I'm not using it anymore. I'm 6 for 6 with that bat and somebody touches it? I'm shoving it up his ass. Don't touch my shit, and I'm talking anybody. I'm talking *teammates.*

If I walked into the locker room and found a reporter or clubhouse visitor by my locker and they had my glove on—especially my gamer—I'd probably knock him out. That's me; but to be honest with you, 99.9 percent of all ballplayers feel the same way. If somebody was in my locker, I don't know if I'd start that game because I'd be in jail; that's *my* shit. Don't touch my stuff. If I *hand* you my glove and say, "Hey, what do you think?"—that's cool, but don't put your hand in it without asking, and even then I'd probably tell you not to put your hand in all the way.

Even ballplayers don't touch each other's stuff without an invitation. That's *my* locker: I've got my cell phone, my keys, pictures of my kids in there. I've never seen anyone in my locker, which is good; because that's *fighting* shit. My game equipment was either in my locker or down on the field with me. In baseball, so much is considered public; players are protective of the little areas that are just for us—the training room, our lockers, and our equipment.

If my son—who I love more than anything else in the world—came in and grabbed my game glove, there's a pretty good chance I'd say, "Dude, put it down."

The clubhouse: If you visit the clubhouse, remember you're visiting; this is *our* home for six months. Sometimes the clubhouse TVs are playing a random sporting event or a television show just to pass the time. Usually the clubhouse TVs are playing video of opposing hitters and pitchers. It's not that a visitor can't look at the TV, but don't *overly* watch it. If a media guy's been in the clubhouse watching TV for twenty minutes and hasn't asked a question? I'll tell him to get the hell out of the clubhouse. If all he's going to do is watch TV, he should watch it somewhere else: "Dude, you done watching *Jeopardy!*? Then leave." Beat writers get a little more leeway. They're in the clubhouse every day. You develop a relationship with them that you don't have with everyone else.

Visitors also don't sit down without an invitation. The chairs in the clubhouse are for the players. If you sit in one of them, you're probably sitting in a player's chair, and he shouldn't have to ask *you* to get up so he can sit in *his* chair. If a player invites you to sit down, that's different.

Do not linger. If you have business in the clubhouse, fine. Do it—then leave. Players are dressing and undressing, playing cards, and talking with their teammates. The clubhouse is one of the few places at a ballpark where a player can find a little privacy. Even then, media and front-office people are in and out all the time. If the clubhouse becomes too crowded with outsiders, a player might retreat to the trainer's room or the dining room. No media or visitors are allowed in those areas.

The first time I was ever in another team's locker room, it was the Pittsburgh Penguins'. It was when they had Jaromir Jagr and Mario Lemieux. They invited us to come over and skate with them, but I couldn't skate. It was me, Al Martin, and Keith Osik. I always wanted to play hockey because I always wanted to be a goon—I'd be great, but not being able to skate was a slight problem. I grew up in San Diego, I'd skated twice in my life, and this was the second time. I wear a size-12 shoe, but they gave me size-14 skates. I was wobbling around the ice, and the Penguins thought it was funny to send slap shots whizzing past my head. But we got even: we invited the hockey players to batting practice. Professional hockey players are great athletes, but some of them couldn't hit the ball out of the infield—on *turf*. That's like hitting a ball on cement. It's hard to take a full swing and not hit a ball ninety feet.

When you walk into another team's locker room, it's uncomfortable. I've been in the Kings' locker room, the Lakers'—other sports—it's always uncomfortable. That's their home. Even for a guy in the big leagues, it's uncomfortable; it's supposed to be. The locker room is a professional athlete's home for six months.

Do your business and get out.

Superstitions

Baseball players are screwed up. We're so superstitious, it's annoying. If we're going good, we'll eat the same food every day, drive the same way to the ballpark, do the same things at the same times; we'll even put on our uniforms the same way every day.

You might have twenty-five pairs of spikes—we're given everything—but still wear the same pair of spikes every day. You might wear the same socks every day or the same pants. I had my game pants and my practice pants. They were exactly the same, but I had to keep them separate. It's whatever you're wearing when you have success. Whatever you're wearing or eating or doing; if you're having success, you do it *every* day.

The same thing happens in the on-deck circle. Watch guys; they'll use the same routine every time. They'll put the same number of weights—batting doughnuts—on their bat for their warm-up swings. They'll put them on in the same order. If they don't get a hit, next time they might put them on in a different order.

I was as bad as anybody else. I'd keep the same routine until I sucked, but if you're 0 for 26, you do something different every time you're in the on-deck circle. You've got to find something to break the pattern. You straighten your socks: right leg, then left. If I still sucked, I'd go the other way: left leg, then right. If I still didn't get a hit, I'd change the number of batting doughnuts I put on my bat.

Tobacco was another thing you could try. If I put a dip in and went 4 for 4, I'd keep the same dip in my mouth the entire game; I'd just keep adding to it. If I got a hit, a walk, or got hit by a pitch, I'd keep the dip in. If I made an out, I'd take the dip out and try a chew. If I got a hit, if I went 3 for 3—same thing, I'd keep the chew in. If neither type of tobacco was working, I might try gum. Maybe one brand of gum is better than another; try anything. Try a different bat—yours isn't working, use someone else's. Try someone else's helmet, yours is no good. When you're 0 for 26, you're completely desperate.

When you're 0 for 26, you end up trying twenty-six different routines. Maybe you try a different toe hole in the box, maybe you screw around with your pants. If you wear them low—down to your shoe tops—pull them up around your knees; which I hate. In my mind, that's a college thing. If someone saw me playing with my pants pulled up around my knees, I was probably sucking at the time.

You get desperate; when you're 0 for 26, there are a lot of different postgame alcoholic beverages you can try.

The same thing applied to defense. I didn't wear batting gloves at the plate, but I'd wear one on my glove hand when I caught. As a catcher I'd sweat so much, the glove would get soaking wet. I had about 162 different batting gloves to choose from, but if a pitcher had a good game the night before, I had to wear the same glove, even if it was still wet the next day. It sucked. The thing's soaking wet with sweat, but if the pitcher went seven innings the night before, I'd still have to use it. You can't change what's working.

Baseball superstitions? It's a bunch of grown men acting like stupid kids.

Leadership

Fans might wonder why an organization brings in a guy who's at the end of his career, but teams are looking for a guy who's been there, done that. That's why the Royals brought me over in 2010: they were looking for guy who could bring some attitude to the team. When you're a veteran, part of the job is helping young players along. A young player might not run a ball out, or something like that; the veteran is there to teach the young guys to play the game the right way.

Sure, a coach could tell a young guy to run a ball out, but it's different when it comes from a guy who has ten years in the league—without a doubt. A respect factor is involved. It's one thing to get to the big leagues; it's another thing to stay. Staying here? Being here ten years? It's hard. You did something right.

Either that or your team sucks and they've got nobody else.

However you do it—have a long career—young guys respect that, they want to know how to pull that off. Older guys helped me along when I was a young player. The one advantage I had was being the son of a former major leaguer; I grew up around baseball. My dad—Fred Kendall—played twelve years in the big leagues. *That* generation? They played the game when it *was* a game. My dad made more as a coach than he did as a player. During the off-season he had to work construction jobs.

Guys today make enough money that all they have to do in the off-season is work out and get ready for the next season. Because of guys like my dad—guys who went through the strikes—today's players don't have to work construction in the off-season. Players today have no idea what the players who went before them had to go through. The players today don't care enough about what the players like my dad did for them.

Guys like my dad made those huge salaries possible.

Today's prima-donna players have all the talent in the world, but have an attitude like the game owes them something. People forget that a lot of big league players are still kids: they're twenty-one, twenty-two, twenty-three years old. They still need to be taught to do stuff the right way—on and off the field. They need to be taught to act like professionals. Take the clubhouse. The laundry bin's right there, but a young guy will still take his sweaty jock off and drop it on the floor. A veteran will tell him to pick it up and put it in the laundry bin—don't make someone else do it.

Young guys need to be taught about behaving in a professional manner, along with playing the game right way. Pros do not launch their batting helmet every time they strike out. Being a professional includes every little thing you can possibly imagine—the way you play, the way you act, the things you say, tipping the clubhouse attendants. Teaching young guys how to be big league ballplayers is what veteran ballplayers do. It comes full circle: if the kids are lucky enough to stay around a while, then it will be their turn to teach someone else.

Veterans don't just teach young players to pick up their own jockstraps; it's hard to win without that veteran presence—absolutely, 100 percent. Go back and look at World Series champions: you'll find that veteran presence somewhere on those teams. There's always some older guy helping the young players through the rough spots, teaching them how to deal with different situations.

Veterans might tell younger players when they need to stand up for themselves. The older guys are dropping knees and throwing inside; it's a battle for territory out there. The young guys need to be taught how to respond. Nowadays guys come up playing for their numbers, not being taught to play the game the right way. Everybody's trying to get to the next level. They're not moving runners over in a 3–3 high school game, they're trying to put numbers on the board so they can get that scholarship or get noticed by a scout. It's the coaches' fault—I'm not saying all of them—but a lot of them don't teach these kids how to play the right way.

These kids are coddled, they're babied, they're brought along through the system, arrive in the big leagues, and then some veteran has to show them the ropes. "Hey, that guy just dropped a knee on you. If you don't retaliate, he'll do it again. Knock him on his ass next time." The veterans will try to protect the kids as much as possible, but at some point, the kid has to stand up for himself.

You get in a fight in baseball? You might kick somebody's ass, you might get the shit kicked out of *you,* but it just takes that one time to show you'll fight back. You get drilled at the plate and you think something was wrong with that? Go to the mound. You do that and word gets around that this kid will fight back.

Veterans also come in handy when you want to know something about the other team. The veteran's been around; he's seen everybody—especially if he's played in both leagues. That also helps during interleague play. The veteran can tell the other guys how much this pitcher's fastball sinks or cuts. The veteran might know what the pitcher likes to throw in certain situations.

You need more than one veteran; teams are made up of twenty-five guys, but we're segregated. It's hard for a pitcher to be a leader for the position players; he's not dealing with the same issues. It's just as hard for a position player to be a leader for the pitchers. Same with the bull pen; they need their own leader down there. The bull-pen guys aren't even *seen* during a game. Every night they're off by themselves.

Starting pitchers need to be in the dugout when they're not pitching. Position players grind it out 162 games a year. Grind it out, grind it out, grind it out—then you go up to the clubhouse to look at video and you see some starting pitcher with the night off, sitting there eating candy or an ice-cream sandwich? You get pissed. You're hot, you just took an 0-fer, and a pitcher walks by eating an ice-cream bar? You don't like seeing that stuff. We're all on the same team, but a rookie sees a pitcher eating a bag of chips while the rookie's killing himself? He gets the ass. A pitcher's out there 30 times a year, I'm out there 150 times a year, busting my ass trying to make this team better. What the hell are you doing eating a bag of chips?

A veteran player can stop that shit, he can clean it up.

Brawls

I've charged the mound a couple times, and I've been asked if I had a game plan: What was I planning to do once I got there?

Easy—kick the shit out of somebody.

But what if there's a fight and you didn't start it? What then? If there's a fight and you don't come out of the dugout, you might as well pack your bags and head back to Triple A: you're done. If you're not the one fighting, you pull your guys out of the pile. Everybody tries to act so tough, but when a fight starts, suddenly a lot of guys don't look that tough. If you're not the one at the middle of the brawl, throwing punches, you just try to protect your teammates. You see a lot of cheap shots in baseball fights: guys running up and punching or kicking someone who's defenseless. If you see that, if you see someone whaling on your teammate's head?

You knock them the [bleep] out. That's *it*.

Arguments

The umpire makes a call, a player disagrees, and an argument starts. The manager comes out of the dugout to stand up for his player. The next thing you'll see is a coach pulling the player away from the argument; the manager can afford to get kicked out of the game—the bench coach can replace him—but you might not be able to replace a player, especially if he's a star.

By the way, if a coach can pull a player away from an argument, the player's not that serious about arguing—it's an act. At times you lose it and go off on an umpire, but if you get thrown out of a game and keep walking to the dugout? You're making a mistake. You're already getting fined; get back out there and get your money's worth.

Making a name for yourself

If you get a chance, you can make a name for yourself; you can show that you won't back down. You get hit by a pitch and you think it's personal? Go to the mound. Someone drops a knee on you while you're sliding into a base? Come up swinging.

People are so impressed with big league ballplayers, and they should be—these guys are something special. But they're not all tough guys; some of them are mentally weak. I'm not saying you should just fight, fight, fight—but I *am* saying there's a time and a place for everything. You've got to stand up for yourself or your teammates. If a teammate won't stand up for himself, somebody better do it for him: that's what a team is all about. It's not like you're going to jail: it's *free*. You might get fined, but where else can you get in a fight and not get arrested? You might get suspended, you might get fined, but you're making at least $500,000.

All teams need some attitude.

A hitter gets drilled and stands there yelling at my pitcher? As a catcher, I'm not going to let you talk to my pitcher like that. I'll knock you on your ass. I don't care whether I like the pitcher or not, he's my teammate. The pitcher may not even know you, but he's thinking, *Oh my God, this guy just stood up for me.*

There's your team chemistry.

I'm not saying fighting is good—actually I'm saying it's *great*—if it's done at the right time. You can't embarrass the game or your team. If you're hit by a curveball and everybody knows it wasn't intentional, you don't go to the mound. You've got to know when fighting is called for. You don't walk around looking for a fight, but you stand up for yourself when the time comes. If done in the proper way, fighting gives your team an us-against-the-world mentality.

Blowouts

After six or seven innings, if you're up by 5 runs or more—maybe 6 runs or more—you shut the running game down. You don't steal, you don't hit-and-run, you don't bunt, and you don't go first to third. You play station-to-station baseball. You play the game ninety feet at a time. If you don't—if you continue to run up the score—somebody's going to get drilled.

But—as I keep saying—it depends on the situation. If you're playing at Coors Field, you can be up by 6 in the eighth inning and still lose in a blink of an eye. If you're playing in a smaller ballpark where you can score a bunch of runs quickly? You might keep on going; it depends on the park.

But if it's 10–0 in the eighth inning and a guy hits a gapper, stretches a single into a double, slides into second on a bang-bang play? Other guys won't forget that. They think, *All right, I'll remember that.* What goes around comes around, especially in baseball.

Moneyball

Great movie, but it never mentioned that the A's had three of the best starting pitchers in all of baseball that year: Barry Zito was 23-5 with a 2.75 ERA, Mark Mulder was 19-7 with a 3.47 ERA, and Tim Hudson was 15-9 with a 2.98 ERA. Their closer, Billy Koch, was 11-4, with a 3.27 ERA and 44 saves.

I respect Billy Beane, his philosophy is great: you get on base, you score—absolutely, that's common sense. But *pitching* is the name of the game. The most important person on the field is your pitcher. No knock against Billy Beane—hell, he had Brad Pitt playing him—that's pretty damn cool. Billy's done amazing stuff for baseball, but you get players who walk and you *don't* have Zito, Mulder, and Hudson on the hill?

There's no Brad Pitt playing Billy Beane.

Bull Durham got it right

I was playing with the A's and we had a young guy from the Dominican Republic on the mound. Our pitching coach was Curt Young and he called time and came out to the mound. Me, Eric Chávez, Mark Ellis, and I think maybe it was Nick Swisher, joined the conference. Curt wanted to tell the kid pitching to do an inside move—pick up his front foot and spin around for a pickoff at second base—but Curt didn't speak Spanish and the kid didn't speak English.

So Curt said to Eric: "Tell him to do an inside move on the first pitch."

Eric: "Dude, do an inside move on the first pitch."

Curt: "No, in Spanish."

Eric: "What? Just 'cause my name is Chávez you think I speak Spanish? Dude, I'm from San Diego. I grew up surfing."

So now *I* tried to tell the kid to do an inside move in half-assed Spanglish: "Premeiro pitcho," and then I made a twisting motion with my hand. The kid nodded yes, he understood—and then threw a fastball right down the middle.

We all broke up laughing.

Ballplayers are movie junkies. We kill a lot of time in hotels, watching movies. Ron Shelton—the guy who wrote *Bull Durham*—got that shit right because he played some minor league ball with the Baltimore Orioles. He knew how crazy things can get out there. Ron became an acquaintance of mine because our kids went to school together. At the time I didn't know him, but he was at a school party and came up to me to congratulate me on having a great career.

After he walked off, I asked someone who the hell that was.

"That's Ron Shelton."

"Who the hell's Ron Shelton?"

I found out he made all those movies: *Bull Durham, White Men Can't Jump, Tin Cup.* The next day there was another school event and I asked him how he got into that. He said he knew he wasn't going to make it in baseball and got into making films. In the minors, all you *do* is watch movies; for Ron, that came in handy.

Playing in pain

The training room is the one sacred place at a ballpark: no media allowed. The media guys can come in the clubhouse, but not the training room. But as a player, if you're always in the training room, you're an idiot—I got that from my dad's era. How bad are you hurting? Unless you have a broken bone or a torn ligament, don't go in the training room. You don't let anyone know that anything's wrong.

Now you've got twenty-one-year-old kids getting massages on their legs. You're twenty-one years old: you don't *need* a massage. You're twenty-one and you're getting a massage on your legs? You got a little twinge? It's the trainer's job to let the manager know that. You know what? You're twenty-one years old, you *don't* have a twinge. If you're twenty-one, twenty-two, twenty-three years old and you're always in the training room? Bottom line: you're soft.

When I pulled my hamstring that time Terry Mulholland tried to pick me off first base, I hid the injury. I couldn't let the trainers see that my leg was black-and-blue from my ass to my calf—hell, no. I've gotta play.

Nowadays guys foul a ball off their foot and they've got to walk it off. You see a guy foul a ball off his foot and he's got to walk around awhile? That guy's going to make an out. His mind's not right. You see a guy foul a ball off his foot and he jumps right back in there? He's going to hit something hard. Eight times out of ten he's going to get a hit. You do *not* show them pain.

Pain is what you make it.

There's a difference between being in pain and being injured. The only time I felt 100 percent was on Opening Day. You're playing every day, and if you get banged up, there's no time to recover—you have to go back out there. There are injuries like my shoulder—I couldn't lift my throwing arm—that's an injury. You tear a ligament or break a bone, fine. Otherwise, your job is to go out for six months and play. I know guys who played with 103-degree fevers, puking in between innings—they didn't think they had a choice. Now guys sit there with thermometers underneath their tongues and ask people what their temperature is. Broken bones, torn ligaments:

you can't play, you're done. You're hurting? You have discomfort? Your hamstring's tender?

Take a couple Advil.

When I blew out my shoulder, I played injured for the next two months—I was blown out. Injured is something's busted: you can't physically do it. Pain is when nothing's broken, but it's painful to keep going. Guys today get a twinge in their hammie and they go on the DL.

Guys today can't tolerate shit.

Hey, you're getting paid at least $500,000 a year. If your teammates see you play in pain, it sends them a message. Playing in pain is part of being a team leader. Some people can handle pain and some people can't. If they can't, they're constantly on the DL.

You know what else sucks about sitting down? It's that whole Wally Pipp thing. The new guy comes in, gets three hits here, three hits there? That's always in the back of your mind—but in my case, I just loved to play. I loved being out there for my teammates because I knew I could do something to help my team win. If I *didn't* think I could do something to help my team win, I wouldn't go out there.

I remember shooting the shit with a star player when we were sitting in a hot tub. He was saying that his hamstring was bothering him. I told him, "Hey, we're in a pennant race in late August, we're not thirty games out of first place—*you play*. You know why? You make a difference on this team. You change the game, you change the lineup, you change the way the other manager handles his bull pen. You change everything. Nobody knows you're hurt except the trainers. If you hit a gapper? Don't go to third, stay at second; be smart about it. You're getting paid a shitload of money to be out there every day. If you're not out there, it changes the game."

A star player can stand on deck and get the guy at the plate better pitches to hit. The other team doesn't know he's hurt; that stuff is all kept secret. A star player has a presence.

Trevor Hoffman couldn't throw much more than 85 miles an hour when I caught him in Milwaukee. But you know what? You hear that music they play when he comes out of the pen—"Hells Bells"—going bong, bong, bong? You get *chills* up your spine. You hear that sound when he comes in the game and you *know* you're in for some shit. This dude's arm was like my arm at the end of my career—but I tell you what: he still had a presence.

And presence is a huge thing in baseball.

Cheating

Everybody is trying to get an advantage. It's not against the rules to bounce a baseball when the catcher throws to second base between innings; if the umpire isn't paying attention and doesn't take the ball out of play, is that cheating? You tell us what the rules are and we want to know where the line is: What's the rule mean? What can I do or not do?

You've got a runner on second base relaying the catcher's signs to the hitter—is that cheating? What if a beer vendor in center field is doing the same thing? If it's okay for a runner to relay signs, how about a team's having someone in the stands to pass the signs along to the hitter? In my opinion, the game's hard enough as it is. As a hitter, you shouldn't be looking into the stands when the pitcher's winding up—but I know people who swear it happens. I've heard all kinds of stuff about other organizations: when certain cameras have a red light on, it's a fastball; no red light, it's off-speed. The Blue Jays were accused of stealing signs from the stands; when the Twins were in the Metrodome, they were accused of manipulating the air-conditioning to help their hitters; and the Rockies have been accused of messing with the baseballs. Against certain teams, I've been asked to use multiple signs even without a runner on second base.

People get paranoid. I'm not saying teams don't steal signs, I'm sure they do. If I knew for a fact—100 percent—that a beer vendor was relaying signs to the hitters, I'd send a bench player up there with a fungo bat and tell him to take the guy's knees out—and get me a Bud Light while he was at it.

But it's just not a black-and-white situation: everybody's pushing it—everybody's looking for an advantage.

For example

I've never been on a team that was stealing signs from the stands, but every team has a TV close to the dugout. We can go down there and look at the signs from the catcher with a runner on second base. It takes you three or four pitches to figure it out. Someone will send you down there to check the signs.

"Hey, Bob, what are they using with a runner on second?"

"Uuuh—let me see—second sign."

TV also allows hitters to check out the pitcher's motion: Does he do something different when he throws his slider? Does he change his position on the rubber when he goes to his changeup? Having a TV right there allows the players access to information that changes the game. Guys have an at bat and go right downstairs and watch it immediately—you can learn a lot from that.

If a guy bounced a pitch, I'd get the ball right back to him just in case the umpire missed it. It's not *my* job to take that ball out of play, and now my guy's got a scuffed ball out on the mound. I didn't break a rule; is that cheating?

But I tell you what—a TV outside the dugout is better than a scuffed baseball.

The grind

For a long time in my career, if I didn't get two hits, it was a bad day. You get older, you've scuffled a bit; if you get a walk, it's a day-saver. You're happy because now you'll go 0 for 3 instead of 0 for 4.

If you somehow go 1 for 4, that's cool. It's just the way it is when you get older.

Baseball is such a grind. It's not that all the other sports aren't tough—basketball, football, hockey—but they don't play *every* day. They beat their bodies up, too, but they don't have the same schedule. They don't travel the way we travel: 162 games a year? We beat our bodies up. It's the best of the best, and if you're not good enough, you're gone.

Spring training sucks—it's too long. Nobody likes it. But the second the first pitch is thrown in the big leagues? Now you're a robot: for the next six months, you're playing baseball. It doesn't matter if you're hurt or not hurt; you're on a schedule. You're into your routine; you know what you have to do to be ready.

The guys who want to come out of a game because they felt a twinge in their calf? Someone on their team will tell them to man up, to get their ass out on the field. If you get a twinge in your calf and decide you want out of the game, you're letting everybody else down. And if you're in a pennant race, it changes everything: this one game might be the difference in your season. And some guys might suddenly feel a twinge if they're 0 for 24 against the pitcher going that night.

If you can't physically do it—if you're incapable—okay. Injured is one thing; less than 100 percent is another. If you're hurting, if you're tired, if you're worn down—get your ass back on the field. If you start sitting down because you're hurting, you'll be sitting all the time. You've got four months off to rest your body; you go full bore until then.

And remember, the other team is hurting, too.

10

THE END

I HAD fun in my career; sometimes I was great, sometimes I was bad—but I had fun *all* the time. I had a blast. I did things the right way: when I was on a baseball field, I gave it everything I had. But no matter how hard you try, sometimes you still suck—you're absolutely awful. Other times you have great games. No matter how you played, if you can look yourself in the mirror before you go to bed at night and know that you gave it everything you had, you have zero regrets.

That's why I tried to come back that one last time: if I hadn't tried, I wouldn't be able to say I gave it everything I had. When you're a catcher and you can't throw a ball to second base, that's it—you're done. You gave it your all and it's time to shut it down.

Now that I'm not playing, I watch more games on TV. Baseball looks so *easy* on television, but it's *so* hard—never forget that. The guys who play big league baseball are the best of the best, but they're still human, they still make mistakes. I played with a lot of good players and learned a lot of baseball over the years; I hope I was able to pass along some of that information to you. But, remember, I've only covered a fraction of what happens every night at a big league ballpark. This book is just one guy's opinion about how the game should be played.

I hope this book helps you enjoy the game a little bit more, the game we all love, the greatest game ever invented: baseball.

One last thing

I saved this for last because it's the most important thing in the entire book and I want you to remember what I'm telling you. When you're at a ball game, keep your eye on the batter. Pay attention to every pitch, *especially* if you have kids with you. Foul balls are coming in *hot*. If a guy throws 90, a foul ball can come into the stands at 93. People treat ball games like they're one big party. They don't understand how hard the ball is coming off the bat.

Fans can be closer to home plate than the third baseman. He's wearing a baseball glove, and he's one of the best third basemen in the world; *you're* holding a beer and a cell phone and your kid is in harm's way. Take the seat closer to home plate; put yourself between the action and your kid. I see people on cell phones, head down, paying no attention to what's happening on the field. Players just wince when we see that: those people are asking for it. Whenever possible, we put *our* families behind the screen at home plate; that should give you a clue.

I've seen little kids with life-threatening injuries because their parents weren't watching *every* pitch. I don't ever want to see another kid hurt. I'm a parent; I'm raising two kids on my own, Kuyper and Karoline, and I love them more than anything else in this world. I can't imagine how it would feel to see one of them seriously injured.

I've given you a lot of things to look for when you go to the ballpark, but nothing's more important than looking out for that kid sitting next to you.

THE SIGNS

TEAMS USE signs that they want to keep secret, but they also use signs that are universal: all teams use some version of them. There might be variations, but what follows are some of the universal signs you might see at the ballpark.

THE CATCHER'S SIGNS

- If the catcher holds up a finger and spins it in a rolling motion, he's asking the pitcher to mix it up: to vary the time he's holding the ball in the set position.
- The catcher might also use the same sign to tell everybody he's switching to the alternate set of signs they've decided on before the game started; he thinks the runner at second base has figured out the first set.
- If the catcher shakes his head while giving the sign to the pitcher, he's asking the pitcher to shake *his* head. The catcher wants the hitter to think the pitcher is rejecting the pitch the catcher has called. If it's an obvious fastball situation, the catcher might signal fastball and ask the pitcher to pretend to shake off—refuse to throw—that fastball. This is done to put some doubt in the hitter's mind as to what pitch is being thrown.

- If the catcher taps his shoulder, he's telling the pitcher that *his* front shoulder is flying open, which can make the pitch off target.
- If the catcher makes an underhand throwing motion, he's asking the pitcher to throw the next pitch from a lower arm angle.
- If the catcher makes an upward motion with the hand, he's asking the pitcher to throw the next pitch above the strike zone.
- If the catcher uses both hands to make a downward motion, he's asking the pitcher to slow down and relax. The catcher thinks the pitcher is overexcited.
- If the catcher points to his eyes and then the runner, he's telling the pitcher to keep an eye on the base runner; he might be stealing.
- If the catcher points his glove at the pitcher after the pitcher does not get a call, the catcher is telling the pitcher that he just made a good pitch, even though it was called a ball.
- If the catcher slides his hand down his thigh, he's asking the pitcher to deliver the next pitch out of the slide step.
- If the catcher flips his thumb as if he were flipping a coin, he's asking the pitcher to attempt a pickoff at first base.

Pitches:

- If the catcher puts down one finger, that's a fastball.
- If the catcher puts down one finger and swirls it, that's a sinking fastball.
- If the catcher puts down two fingers, that's a curveball.
- If a catcher puts down three fingers, that's a slider.
- If the catcher puts down four fingers, that's a changeup or a splitter. Most pitchers don't have both.

The signs could vary depending on the pitcher. If a guy didn't have a slider, three might be something else, like a cutter.

Other signs a catcher might use:

- If the catcher holds his glove or bare hand out to the side during a pitcher's warm-up, he's telling the second baseman warm-ups are over and the ball is about to be thrown his way.
- If the catcher makes a bunting motion, he's warning the infielders that the hitter may be bunting.

THE PITCHER'S SIGNS

Before each inning and each time a new pitcher comes into a game, the pitcher is allowed eight warm-up pitches. The pitcher uses these signals to tell the catcher what pitch he intends to throw:

- *Fastball:* The pitcher will flip his glove toward the catcher with the palm down.
- *Curve:* The pitcher will flip his glove toward the catcher with the palm up.
- *Changeup:* The pitcher will point his glove at the catcher, palm down, then pull the glove straight back.
- *Splitter/forkball:* The pitcher will make a downward motion of the glove.
- *Slider:* The pitcher will make a sweeping horizontal motion with his glove.
- *Sinker:* The pitcher will make a downward diagonal motion, this time with his bare hand, while holding the ball.

Some other universal signs you might see a pitcher use:

- If the pitcher makes a motion over either shoulder during warm-ups, he's telling the catcher this is his last warm-up pitch and the catcher should throw the ball down to second base.
- If the pitcher swipes his uniform right before delivering a pitch, he is probably adding and subtracting. When a pitcher wants to change the sign a catcher gave him, he'll swipe his uniform in a predeter-

mined place to add or subtract. If the catcher gave the pitcher two fingers for a curve, adding one would get the pitcher to a slider (three fingers); subtracting one would get the pitcher to a fastball (one finger).

- If the pitcher holds a baseball up and shakes it, he's signaling the umpire that he wants a new baseball.
- When the double play is in order, if the pitcher makes the "horns" sign—thumb and pinkie extended—and waggles it, he's indicating which middle infielder he'll be looking for if the ball is hit to him and he wants to start a double play.
- If the pitcher does not want to throw the pitch the catcher has called, he'll shake his head—unless the catcher shook *his* head while giving the pitcher the sign. In that case, the catcher told the pitcher to shake him off. If the situation makes the percentage pitch obvious, shaking off gives the hitter something to think about. Slight doubt might allow the pitcher to get away with throwing the obvious pitch.
- If the pitcher nods his head, he's agreeing to the pitch.
- If the pitcher wants the catcher to roll through the signs again, he'll hold up a finger and make a rolling motion.

THE MANAGER'S SIGNS

- If the manager holds up his hand and taps his fingers against his thumb, he's telling the catcher to go to the mound and talk to the pitcher.
- If the manager holds up four fingers, he wants the batter intentionally walked.

THE INFIELD SIGNS

- Middle infielders feint toward second base to get a runner to shorten his lead. If the middle infielder decides to go all the way to the bag—a real pickoff attempt—the most common sign is showing the pitcher an open glove. Some players may have their own sign: a wink, adjusting the cup—anything that the infielder and the pitcher have agreed on will work.

- If the first baseman crosses his wrists, he's telling the pitcher that he will be playing behind the runner. The first baseman will not be holding the runner at first, and the pitcher should not attempt a pickoff. First basemen play behind the runner late in games, when the run doesn't matter, to increase their range.
- With a runner on first base the middle infielders will signal each other to coordinate who is covering second base if the runner takes off. They'll shield their mouths from the rest of the infield with their gloves and use *me-you:* if an infielder shows an open mouth, that's *you* (the shape your mouth makes when saying the word *you*), and if the infielder shows a closed mouth, that's *me* (the shape your mouth makes when saying the word *me*).

THE HITTER/BASE-RUNNER SIGNS

- If the hitter or runner holds up a finger and rolls it, he's asking the third-base coach to roll through the signs again.
- Be aware that common actions—adjusting the batting helmet, touching the belt buckle, touching the end of a bat—can also be used as signs.

THE OUTFIELD AND INFIELD COACHES' SIGNS

You'll see the outfield and infield coaches on the top step of the dugout as each new hitter comes to the plate. The coaches are there to reposition the defense. A coach might develop some of his own signs, but some commonly used signs are:

- *Straight up:* The outfield coach will make an up-and-down motion directly in front of his body. That means he wants the outfielders in their usual positions, no adjustment to either side. The outfield coach finds positioning landmarks in the background—a sign, a scoreboard, anything—so he can tell that an outfielder is playing straight up whenever he stands in front of it. That means the outfield coach has to stand in the same spot every time when moving the outfielders. He also has to remember which landmark indicates straight up in every ballpark his team visits on the road.

- *In/back/over:* Coaches use a variety of signs to move players. Some coaches hold up towels to get the outfielders' attention and just wave defenders to move in, back, or over until they're in the right spot. In Kansas City, infield coach Eddie Rodriguez just stares at a player and then leans his head in the desired direction. The infielder moves until Eddie straightens his head: that means the infielder is in the right spot. Whatever method coaches use, you'll see them reposition players as each hitter comes to the plate. They might reposition players as the count changes; some hitters tend to pull the ball more when they're ahead in the count, and some players go the other way when they're behind in the count.
- *Hit the cutoff man:* If an outfield coach—or anyone else—taps the top of his head, the message is to keep the batter at first base should he get a hit. The outfield does this by hitting the cutoff man, not throwing the ball to third base or home to get another runner. You'll see this sign with a runner on base. The sign reminds the outfielders that the lead runner isn't important. They don't want the trail runner to advance into scoring position on a long throw.
- *No doubles:* The outfield coach will put a hand behind his head. This sign is used late in a game when the batter represents an important run. It's a reminder that the batter should be held, at worst, to a single. The outfielders should play deep, near the warning track. Any ball over an outfielder's head should be a home run. The outfielders should not attempt a diving catch unless they have no choice. No doubles means the team can survive a single, but an extra-base hit represents a problem.

THIRD-BASE COACH'S SIGNS

Once again, certain coaches develop unique signs, but some signs you might see a third-base coach use with base runners are:

- If the coach puts his right hand under his left arm, he's reminding a runner on second base to make sure a ground ball gets through the infield before he comes over to third. This sign will only be used if no force is on.
- If the coach flicks the fingers of both hands away from his body, he's telling the runners to freeze on a line drive.
- If the coach points to the catcher, makes a throwing motion, and then points to a base, he's reminding the runner that the catcher likes to pick off runners.
- If the coach uses his hand to imitate the arc of a fly ball, then points at the bag, he's telling the runner to tag on a deep fly ball.
- If the coach points to his eyes, then spins a finger in the air, he's telling the runner to look around and be aware of defensive positioning.
- With more than one runner on base, if the coach point to eyes, then points to the lead runner, he's reminding the trail runner to make sure the runner in front of him advances before coming to the next base. This sign is used more often when the lead runner is slow; the coach is reminding the trail runner not to run up the back of the lead runner.
- If the coach mimics the motion of a breaking pitch, then points down at the ground, he's telling the runner that this is a breaking-ball count; to be aware of a ball in the dirt.

This is not a complete list of signs used to communicate on a baseball field. Teams and coaches may develop their own set of signs to communicate in a particular situation; the variety and number of signs is endless. But you will see many of these signs used every night on a big league ball field.

Now you know what they're saying.

GLOSSARY

AB: An at bat.

Adding and subtracting: This can mean adding or subtracting a few miles an hour to the speed of pitches to keep a hitter off-balance; it can also mean the sign system a pitcher uses to change the pitch the catcher called. If the catcher flashes curveball (two fingers), the pitcher can subtract one with a sign and get to a fastball (one finger). If the pitcher wanted to get to a slider (three fingers), he could add one. Pitchers often add or subtract with swipes of their uniform with their glove. Pants might be subtract, jersey might be add.

Airmail: Overthrowing the intended target. When an outfielder overthrows the cutoff man, he's *airmailed* the throw.

Air someone out: Telling someone off. If you criticize someone or give him a piece of your mind, you've *aired him out*.

Armor: A hitter's elbow pad or shin guard.

Back end of the bull pen: Usually the reliever who pitches the eighth inning (the setup man) and the reliever who pitches the ninth (the closer). The best relievers are in the *back end of the pen.*

Bag: A base.

Bailing out on the double play: Getting out of the way of the runner coming into second base and making no attempt to complete the double play.

Bang-bang play: A close play.

Banged up: Injured.

Banging the glove: A pitcher whose pitches consistently hit the catcher's mitt, is *banging the glove.*

Barking: Complaining loudly.

Barrel: The thick end of a baseball bat.

Bastard pitch: A pitch with a lot of movement that usually dives out of the strike zone. The bastard pitch is generally thrown when the pitcher is ahead in the count and has two strikes on the hitter. A hitter who strikes out on a slider in the dirt just saw a *bastard pitch.*

Bat head: The same thing as the barrel: the thick end of a baseball bat.

Battery: The pitcher and the catcher combined are referred to as the *battery.*

Batting doughnut: A circular batting weight used when the hitter is on deck to increase the weight of his bat during his warm-up swings.

Battle: A hitter with two strikes who protects the strike zone by fouling off close pitches is *battling.* It usually refers to a long at bat.

Beanball: A pitch intentionally thrown at a hitter's head.

Big boys: Power hitters.

Bitter: Upset or angry.

Bleeder: A weakly hit flare that lands just beyond the infield is a *bleeder.*

Blown up: A catcher that gets flattened by a runner, a hitter that got jammed with an inside pitch, a player that got criticized in the press—all have been *blown up.*

Body up: Fielding a ball with your body directly behind the glove, done with the intention of letting the ball hit you—if necessary—to keep the ball in front of you. (I never used this term, but Chris Getz does; it's a Getzism.)

Bopper: A power hitter.

Borderline pitch: A pitch that catches the border of the plate.

Both sides of the ball: Offense and defense. Players said to be good on *both sides of the ball* are good at the plate and in the field.

BP: Batting practice.

Bunching the gap: There are two gaps in the outfield: left-center and right-center. When the center fielder and a corner outfielder play closer together than usual, they're *bunching the gap.*

Burned: A relief pitcher who's been used and is unavailable has been *burned.* If an outfielder is playing shallow and someone hits the ball over his head, he has also been *burned.*

Burying a pitch: Bouncing a pitch in the dirt.

Calling it both ways: An umpire who is consistent with his strike zone for both teams is *calling it both ways.*

Calling time: Asking an umpire for a halt in play.

Cannon: A good throwing arm.

Carom: A ball that ricochets off a wall.

Cement mixer: A hanging slider. Good sliders are thrown with a tight rotation and the seams will form a red dot on the ball, visible to the hitter. Bad sliders have a looser rotation and the seams look like a *cement mixer.*

Changeup: A pitch thrown so it appears to be a fastball, but is significantly slower. (As far as I'm concerned, Trevor Hoffman threw the best changeup in the history of baseball.)

Chase pitch: A pitch that starts in the strike zone and then moves out of the zone is a *chase pitch.* The pitcher wants the hitter to chase the pitch out of the zone. *Chase pitch, bastard pitch,* and *out pitch* are interchangeable terms.

Cheating: A hitter who makes an adjustment to hit a particular pitch is *cheating* on that pitch. If the hitter starts his swing earlier to hit a fastball, he's *cheating* on the fastball. An infielder who adjusts his position might be *cheating* up the middle to get to a ground ball. This kind of cheating has nothing to do with breaking a rule.

Chew: A wad of chewing tobacco. Chew is leaf tobacco and kept in the cheek.

Choking up: A hitter who holds a bat well above the knob is *choking up.*

Chopper: A high-bouncing grounder.

Clean it up: To improve or fix something.

Climbing the ladder: A pitcher who throws a series of pitches at the top of the strike zone, each higher than the last, is *climbing the ladder.*

Closed stance: A batting stance that has the front foot closer to home plate than the back foot is a *closed stance.*

Closer: The relief pitcher who generally pitches the last inning of a ball game when his team has a lead.

Cock fastball: A hittable fastball, crotch high.

Coming after or at a hitter: A pitcher who's throwing fastballs and being aggressive about throwing strikes is *coming after the hitter.*

Cover a pitch: If a hitter strides toward the outside corner of the plate and hits a down-and-away pitch, he *covered the pitch.*

Crooked number: Anything above a 0 or a 1.

Crossed up: When the pitcher throws a different pitch from what the catcher was expecting, the catcher was *crossed up.*

Crush: To do well. In baseball, you can crush a pitch, a base runner, or a buffet table. Someone who had a big meal might say he *crushed* it.

Cup of coffee: A short stay in the big leagues.

Cup shot: A ball that hits a player in the crotch.

Cutoff man: The infielder who relays a throw from the outfield.

Cutter: A fastball held off center so it *cuts,* or moves laterally. A cutter thrown by a left-handed pitcher will have lateral movement in on a right-handed hitter. A cutter is halfway between a fastball and a slider.

Daylight play: A pickoff play at second base.

Day-saver: Anything good that happens when you're having a bad game on the offensive side of the ball. If you're 0 for 4 and you hit a single, that's a *day-saver.*

Dead-pull hitter: A hitter who tries to pull the ball all the time.

Dealing: A pitcher who is throwing well is *dealing.*

Deke: A decoy, a move made to send a false signal to the opposing team.

Dialed in: Having success. A hitter who is mentally locked in is also *dialed in.* A guy who gets two or three hits a game is *dialed in.*

Dial it up: A pitcher who increases his velocity has *dialed it up.*

Dig in: When a hitter comes to the plate, he *digs in*. The hitter makes a hole in the ground for his back foot. He then uses the hole to push off as he swings.

Dig-Me Tribe: Players who love themselves. Members of the Dig Me Tribe invite the fans to *dig* them and their stylish demeanor or dress.

Dip: Ground tobacco kept between a player's lip and gum. (I prefer Kodiak—if you guys see this, I could use some free dip.)

Dish: Home plate.

Diving: A hitter that moves toward the outside corner of the plate during his swing is said to be *diving.*

Doctoring the ball: Doing something to a baseball that adds movement to a pitch. Cutting, scuffing, and adding pine tar are examples of *doctoring a baseball.*

Drifting: Moving lazily to a fly ball, often resulting in a poor fielding position when the ball arrives.

Drilled: When a hitter gets hit by a pitch, he got *drilled.*

Dropping a knee: Blocking a runner's path to a base by dropping one knee to the ground.

Dropping down: Throwing a ball from a lower arm angle.

Duck fart: A bloop base hit. It's similar to a *bleeder.* It's not impressive, but it's a knock.

Eating the ball: When an infielder picks up a grounder, but decides he has no chance to get an out and decides not to attempt a throw, he's *eating the ball. Eating the ball* is interchangeable with *putting it in your pocket.*

Eyewash: Bullshit—something done merely because it looks good. Unnecessary practice to impress observers is *eyewash.*

Fake ambulance: If a player is down on the ground, then hops right back up, the trainer who came out to check on him is a *fake ambulance.* If you're lying on the ground in a major league baseball game, you *better* come out of the game. The trainer is the ambulance, but he becomes a *fake ambulance* when guys who are soft—guys who put on an act about being hurt—stay in the game.

Falling off the mound: When a pitcher has an exaggerated follow-through that leaves him in a poor fielding position, he's *falling off the mound.* Right-handers fall off the mound to the first-base side, left-handers fall off the mound to the third-base side. So if a hitter wants to bunt for a hit off a right-hander who falls off the mound, the bunt will probably go to the third-base side.

Finding the seams: When players field a ball, if they have time, they rotate it in their hands so their fingers are across the wide part of the seams. This action is called *finding the seams.*

Firm: Hard. A pitch with good velocity is *firm.*

First movement: Stealing second base on the *first movement* a left-handed pitcher makes from the set position. Going on first movement is a gamble, done when a base stealer can't read the pitcher's pickoff move.

Flare: A poorly hit fly ball that lands just beyond the infield is a *flare*. Interchangeable with *bleeder* or *duck fart*.

Flashing signs: Giving signs.

Fly: A fast runner can *fly*.

Flying true: A thrown ball that moves forward in a straight line without lateral movement is *flying true*.

Four-seamer: A straight fastball.

Framing: There's no such thing.

Free swinger: A hitter who swings at everything. Vladimir Guerrero was a *free swinger*.

Fungo: A *fungo* bat is a longer, thinner bat used to hit fly balls and grounders to ballplayers during practice. The balls hit are also called *fungoes*.

Gamer: Equipment that a player uses during a game. A player might have several gloves, but the one he uses in games is his *gamer*. A *gamer* can also be a player who's especially reliable.

Gapper: A ball hit into either the right- or left-center gap; the spaces between the center fielder and the right and left fielders.

Gassed: A tired player is *gassed.*

Gear up: A hitter who changes the timing of his swing in order to hit a fastball is *gearing up* for that pitch.

Getaway day: The day a ball club travels.

Getting big: Overswinging.

Giddy: Excited.

Giddyup: Velocity. A fastball in the upper 90s had some *giddyup* on it.

GM: General manager.

Going bad: Playing poorly.

Going good: Playing well.

Golden child: A prospect, one of the can't-miss guys.

Got the ass: Getting mad about something.

Green light: Permission to do something. A base runner who can steal on his own has the *green light.*

Grooved fastball: A fastball in the middle of the plate.

Hack: A hitter's swing.

Hammered: A pitch that was hit hard was *hammered.* You can also get hammered by the media, a base runner, and, in some cases, alcohol.

Hammie: Hamstring.

Hanging: A left-handed pitcher who can pick up his front foot, stay balanced in that position, and wait to see what the runner at first does is *hanging* the foot.

Headhunter: A pitcher who intentionally throws at a batter's head.

Higher than high: A pitch above the strike zone.

Hole in a swing: If a hitter has a certain spot in the strike zone he doesn't handle well—say down and away—he has a *hole in his swing.*

Horse: A good ballplayer. A stud.

Horseshit: Something negative is *horseshit.* If an umpire makes a bad call, the call was *horseshit.*

Hot: Fast. A 95-mile-an-hour fastball is coming in *hot.* Also a hitter who's getting two hits a night.

Hot zone: The part of the strike zone a hitter hits well.

Huffing and puffing: An exaggerated show of anger or being exhausted.

In-between hop: When a baseball bounces just before it's caught, that's a *short hop.* When a ball bounces well before it's caught, that's a *long hop. In-between hops* are balls that bounce too far away to be smothered and too close to allow the fielder to easily adjust.

In front: A hitter who contacts the ball *out in front* of home plate will pull the ball. A pitcher who throws a breaking ball and gets a hitter to swing too soon has the hitter *out in front.*

Inside move: When the pitcher lifts his front foot as if to deliver the ball to home plate and pivots to attempt a pickoff at second base, he's done an *inside move.*

Inside-out swing: A hitter whose swing is designed to hit the inside half of the ball has an *inside-out swing.*

Insurance run: If you're up by one run and you score another, you've just scored an *insurance run.*

Jacked up: Injured or messed up.

Juicing the readings: Increasing the velocity readings on a radar gun.

Knock: A base hit.

Laser beam: A hard-hit ball.

Late time: A hitter who asks the umpire for a time-out just as the pitcher begins his windup has called for *late time.*

Lay off: A hitter who doesn't swing at a pitch has *laid off* that pitch.

Lay one down: A hitter who bunts has just *laid one down.*

Lay out: To dive for a ball.

Lead runner: When multiple runners are on base, the runner closest to scoring is the *lead runner.*

Let it go: A hitter, taking a big swing, has just *let it go.*

Lights out: A pitcher who's throwing particularly well is throwing *lights out.*

Loading a ball up: Putting a substance on a ball about to be pitched to affect its flight.

Loading up: A hitter who takes a big swing.

Lock a hitter up: Freezing the hitter. A hitter who gets fooled by a breaking pitch and is unable to swing the bat as a result was *locked up.*

Locked in: Focused.

Matchup numbers: The statistics produced by individual encounters are *matchup numbers.*

Matchups: Hitter-versus-pitcher combinations are *matchups.*

Mix and match: After the starting pitcher leaves and before the game gets to the back end of the pen, the manager will have to *mix and match* his relievers against the other team's hitters. The managers are looking for good *matchups.*

Mix it up: Varying how long the ball is held in the set position or throwing a variety of pitches.

MLB: Major League Baseball.

Movement: Pitches have three characteristics: velocity, location, and movement. Movement is how much the pitch deviates from its original line of travel.

Nasty: A *nasty* pitch is one with a lot of movement, a tough pitch to hit.

Nibbling: Trying to pitch on the edges of the strike zone.

Ninety feet: The distance between bases.

No doubles: An outfield defense. The outfielders back up far enough to prevent any ball from being hit over their head, unless it's hit out of the park.

Nut-cuttin' time: A pressure situation.

0-fer: A hitless game. If the batter was 0 for 4, he took an *0-fer.*

On a pitch: A hitter who has a pitch timed is *on it.*

One-way lead: The runner's not going anywhere, he's taking a lead with every intention of going back to the base. Usually done to see the pitcher's pickoff move.

On the black: Home plate has a black border. A pitch that was at the edge of the strike zone was *on the black.*

Open stance: A batting stance in which the front foot is farther away from home plate than the back foot.

Opposite field: The field opposite the side of the plate a hitter stands on: right field for a right-hander, left field for a left-hander.

Out pitch: A pitch the pitcher likes to use once he gets to two strikes. Interchangeable with a *chase* or *bastard pitch.*

Pad your stats: To do something that doesn't help the team, but increases your statistical totals.

Peeking in: A base runner who is trying to see the catcher's signs is *peeking in.*

Phenom: Short for *phenomenon.* A rookie player having a great season is a *phenom.*

Pick it: A player with good hands, adept at catching the ball, can really *pick it.*

Pimp a home run: To show off after hitting a home run: a dramatic pause, a big bat flip, or a slow trip around the bases.

Pitchout: A pitch thrown out of the zone, up and away from the hitter.

Pivot man: In a 6-4-3 double play (shortstop to the second baseman to the first baseman) the player in the middle of the double play—the second baseman—was the *pivot man.*

Playing behind the ball: Getting behind the spot where a ball will be caught in order to make the catch while moving forward is *playing behind the ball.*

Playing behind the runner: When the first baseman does not hold the runner on first and backs up to increase his range, he's *playing behind the runner.*

Playing the ball off to the side: Fielding the ball without getting your body behind the glove.

Plugging the gap: Hitting a ball deep into the gap between two outfielders.

Prima-donna player: A player with high regard for himself.

Primary lead: The initial lead a runner takes when leading off a base.

Pull: To hit the ball to the same side of the field that the batter stands on when he's at the plate—left field for a right-hander, right field for a left-hander.

Pulling the trigger: Deciding to swing.

Pump fake: Pretending to throw the ball, but not letting go of it.

Purpose pitch: A pitch thrown to set up the next pitch.

Put-away pitch: Also an *out pitch* or a *bastard pitch.* A *put-away pitch* is something tough to hit that the pitcher throws once he has two strikes.

Putting it in your pocket: Fielding the ball, but not attempting a throw. *Putting it in your pocket* is interchangeable with *eating the ball.*

Quad: Quadriceps, a muscle at the front of the thigh.

Rah-rah: Amateurish cheerleading.

Reader: A left-handed pitcher who can lift his front foot up, read the base runner's intentions, then decide whether to throw the ball to first base or home plate, is a *reader.*

Rollover ground ball: A weak ground ball to the pull side of the field.

Rotation: The five starting pitchers. The top of the rotation is the team's best starting pitcher, also called a number one. The bottom of the rotation is rarely as good as the top of the rotation and would include the team's fifth starter.

Route: The path a defender takes to get to a batted ball.

Run: Lateral movement on a pitch.

Sac: A sacrifice bunt or fly ball.

Scuffling: Struggling.

Secondary lead: The runner takes his primary lead before the pitcher throws the pitch. The runner takes his *secondary lead*—a couple of shuffle steps—after the pitch is thrown.

Selling the call: Something a player does to sway an umpire. An infielder who tags a runner and then shows the umpire that he's still holding the ball is *selling the call.*

Sell out: A hitter who is convinced he's getting a particular pitch might take an approach that will allow him to hit only the particular pitch he's anticipating. The hitter is *selling out.*

Setting up: A catcher who moves into position to receive a pitch is *setting up.*

Setup man: The relief pitcher who *sets up* the closer by pitching the previous inning.

Setup pitch: A pitch designed to *set up* the following pitch.

Shaking off: A pitcher who wants to refuse the pitch the catcher has called shakes his head no.

Shit: A pitcher's stuff. A pitcher who is throwing well has good *shit.*

Shit-can: If you eliminate something—a slider that isn't working—you've *shit-canned* it.

Shitload: A lot of something. If a pitcher doesn't walk anybody, he's throwing a *shitload* of strikes.

Shortening the swing: A hitter who is cutting down the motion of his swing, to be quicker, is *shortening his swing.* Usually done with two strikes.

Short hop: A ball that hits right in front of a fielder; a *long hop* hits farther away and is easier to catch.

Showing the plate: A catcher who does not entirely block home plate is *showing the plate* to the runner.

Shutdown inning: A scoreless half inning after your team scored in the previous half inning.

Sick hands: Good hands.

Sinker: A two-seam fastball designed to move downward.

Sinker baller: A pitcher who specializes in throwing sinking fastballs, which result in ground balls.

Sitting on a pitch: A hitter, guessing that he'll get a particular pitch, is *sitting on that pitch.* In a 2-0 count the hitter might *sit fastball.*

Situational lefty: A left-handed reliever used primarily to face left-handed hitters.

Slide-step: When a pitcher barely lifts his front foot off the ground and then strides toward the plate, he's *slide-stepping.* It's done to get the ball to the catcher more quickly so he has a better chance of throwing out a base stealer.

Smoked: Anything that got hit hard was *smoked.*

Snapping: Losing it, a temper tantrum.

Spike: A pitch that's bounced has been *spiked.*

Spikes: Baseball shoes with metal spikes on the bottom.

Spikes-up: Sliding into a base with the feet high and the shoes' spikes aimed up, usually done with the intention of hurting an infielder.

Split-finger: Also known as a *splitter.* The pitcher jams the ball back between his first two fingers, splitting the fingers apart. This makes the ball dive down.

Squaring around: A hitter who turns to face the pitcher in order to bunt is *squaring around.*

Squeeze play: A play in which the hitter bunts while a runner on third base tries to score.

Squeezing: An umpire who isn't calling borderline pitches strikes is *squeezing* the pitcher and the zone.

Staring in: A runner at second base who is trying to steal signs so he can alert the hitter what pitch is coming is *staring in* to home plate.

Station-to-station: Conservative baserunning, advancing one base at a time.

Stud: A talented player.

Stuff: The physical characteristics of a pitch: velocity and movement. A pitcher throwing well has good *stuff.*

Sweet hands: Good hands.

Table setters: The players who set the table for the studs. A player who gets on base so someone else can drive him in is a *table setter.*

Tack-on run: A run scored after you've already taken the lead.

Take a pitch: When a batter does not swing at a pitch, he *took* the pitch. When the third-base coach flashes the *take* sign, he's telling the hitter to keep the bat on his shoulder.

Take-out slide: Knocking down an infielder with a hard slide.

Team stretch: Right before batting practice, the entire team stretches and does light calisthenics.

The thing: The inability to make a routine throw, the yips. A catcher who can't throw the ball back to the pitcher has *the thing.*

Throw someone under the bus: If you blame somebody or inform on him, you've *thrown him under the bus.*

Tipping a pitch: Letting the hitter know what pitch is about to be thrown is *tipping a pitch.*

Tip your cap: Giving credit. If the pitcher gets you out with a good pitch, you *tip your cap.*

Tired act: A guy who behaves like a jackass has a *tired act.* Usually a member of the Dig-Me Tribe.

Toe hole: The hole a hitter digs in the batter's box for his back foot.

Trail runners: When multiple runners are on base, the runners behind the lead runner.

Two-seamer: A fastball with lateral or sinking movement.

Warm-ups: The eight pitches allowed a pitcher at the start of an inning or whenever a new pitcher comes in the game.

Warning track: The dirt track between the grass and the wall.

Waste pitch: Throwing a pitch with no intention of hitting the strike zone, often done to see if the hitter will chase the pitch out of the zone. Interchangeable with *setup pitch.*

Wearing one: Getting hit by a pitch. Also used to take responsibility: if a player says something was his fault, he's *wearing* it.

Whack: Swing a bat.

Whacked: A pitch or pitcher who got hit hard.

Working around a hitter: A pitcher who intentionally throws pitches close to the strike zone, but not in the zone, is working around the hitter.

ACKNOWLEDGMENTS

I'd like to thank all the people that made this book possible. At the top of the list—my mom and dad. My dad was my first baseball idol. I remember thinking he was the coolest dad ever for being a Big Leaguer, and I wanted to follow in his footsteps. And my mom? I would never have had a career in baseball if it weren't for her. She played baseball with me, my brother, and my sister every day, while my dad was working one of his two or three off-season jobs; it's what he had to do to pay the bills.

I want to also thank my mimi and papa; my nana and my sister, Kathy; Max and Jordy, Caden, Kiera, and Keri: I love you all.

To my big bro Mike: You always said you were my biggest fan. I want you and the world to know I'm actually *your* biggest fan. You have always been a rock for me, just a phone call away for anything and everything. I love you, man.

To Kuyper, Karoline, Ethan, and Cole: you are my four favorite knuckleheads. And thanks to Tricia—you are my best friend. To Jeff Becker, Jeff Marsh, Laura Stone, Sharon Stark, and Peter Lauzan: thank you for making me believe there are still good people in this world.

I also want to thank all the true fans of baseball. You keep the game alive by watching, going, playing, coaching, and supporting . . . even teaching it to your kids so that they can also learn to love it. But remember this: in youth sports, I see so many parents who push, push, push their kids, trying to live vicariously through them. If you take anything away from this book, it's this: please do not push them too hard. Let them be kids and have fun.

And for all those fans who thought I was an asshole, you were right; but, I still respect you for loving the game.

And thank you, Lee Judge—one of the few people in baseball media who truly looks out for the players and the game. I'm proud to call that dude my friend.

Finally, I would like to thank the game of baseball. This was written from my perspective; behind a mask, behind home plate. I hope this book gives you a little more insight into the greatest game ever. And thanks to all the players who played this game long before I ever came along. Those are the guys who played for the love of the game and not love of the paycheck. They worked off-season jobs so they could support their families. They held strong and endured multiple strikes. They paved the way so today's athletes could make shitloads of money by getting paid to do what every little boy dreams of doing.

And to the players who don't appreciate that: go fuck yourselves.

—Jason Kendall

Well, if we're going to start listing the people who ought to go fuck themselves, we're going to run out of room. For now I'll confine myself to the people who deserve my gratitude and thanks. I'll start with Mike Fannin, editor of the *Kansas City Star*, for saving my career and giving me the opportunity of a lifetime. Thanks to Nicole Poell, for her editing and friendship. I'd also like to say thanks to our agent, Todd Shuster, for patiently walking us through the process; to our editor, Michael Homler, for his faith in us—and for being a cool guy to hang out with at a ballgame—and a big thank-you goes out to the makers of Bud Light; Jason and I couldn't have done it without you.

I also need to say thanks to every ballplayer, coach, manager, and front office guy who took the time to share their knowledge and insight. Russ Morman, Tim Bogar, Jerry Dipoto, Clint Hurdle, Doug Sisson, John Gibbons, Rusty Kuntz, Eddie Rodriguez, Jeff Montgomery, Kevin Seitzer, Greg Pryor, and George Brett are just the start of a very long list of guys who helped me out along the way.

And my thanks to Jason Kendall: one of the funniest, most loyal, outrageous guys I know. It was great to make a book, it was better to make a friend.

Finally, thank you to my wife, Mary, and kids, Matthew, Michael, and Paul. This wouldn't have been possible without your patience and understanding.

—Lee Judge

KENDALL
18